INVENTING
JEWISH RITUAL

INVENTING
JEWISH RITUAL

Vanessa L. Ochs

Foreword by Riv-Ellen Prell

2007 • 5767
The Jewish Publication Society
Philadelphia

JPS is a nonprofit educational association and the oldest and foremost publisher of Judaica in English in North America. The mission of JPS is to enhance Jewish culture by promoting the dissemination of religious and secular works, in the United States and abroad, to all individuals and institutions interested in past and contemporary Jewish life.

The Jewish Publication Society
2100 Arch Street
Philadelphia, PA 19103
www.jewishpub.org

Composition and design by Sandy Freeman

Manufactured in the United States of America

07 08 09 10 11 12 13   10 9 8 7 6 5 4 3 2 1

ISBN 13: 978-0-8276-0834-4
ISBN 10: 0-8276-0834-9

Library of Congress Cataloging-in-Publication Data

Ochs, Vanessa L.
    Inventing Jewish ritual / Vanessa L. Ochs.—1st ed.
        p. cm.
    Includes index.
    ISBN-13: 978–0–8276–0834–4 (alk. paper)
    1. Judaism—Customs and practices. 2. Jews—United States—Social life and customs. I. Title.

BM700.O29 2007
296.4—dc22

                                                    2006032662

JPS books are available at discounts for bulk purchases for reading groups, special sales, and fundraising purposes. Custom editions, including personalized covers, can be created in larger quantities for special needs. For more information, please contact us at marketing@jewishpub.org or at this address: 2100 Arch Street, Philadelphia, PA.

CONTENTS

Acknowledgments IX

Foreword XI

INTRODUCTION • Becoming a Ritual Innovator 1

CHAPTER 1 • Democracy, Open Access, and Jewish Feminism 39

CHAPTER 2 • The Narrative Approach 57

CHAPTER 3 • Material Culture: New Rituals and Ritual Objects 87

CHAPTER 4 • Stretched by Innovation 112

CHAPTER 5 • Change: Resisting and Acclimating 138

CHAPTER 6 • Case Study 1: Miriam's Tambourine 166

CHAPTER 7 • Case Study 2: The Holocaust Torah 187

CHAPTER 8 • Case Study 3: The Wedding Booklet 214

EPILOGUE • Inheriting Invented Traditions 250

APPENDIX • Record, Take It Down, Collect 258

Index 271

For Susan Grandis Goldstein

ACKNOWLEDGMENTS

I have been working on this book for over a decade now, and the obvious is indeed true: many of the Jewish rituals that were brand-new and provocative when I first began are so familiar, especially to young people growing up with them, that they already feel traditional. The book was the idea of Ellen Frankel, editor-in-chief of The Jewish Publication Society (JPS), and I am grateful to her for giving me the honor of working on such a project. More so, I thank her for infinite patience and encouragement, literary and spiritual. Rena Potok, senior acquisitions editor at JPS, stewarded the manuscript through to its current form, along with Karen Schnitker; Ali Galustan and Jesse Davie-Kessler assisted me along the way. Finally, I acknowledge the early guidance of wonderful teachers who challenged me to think more freshly about ritual: Dorothy Austin, Heather Murray Elkins, Leedom Lefferts, Jodie Shapiro, and Leigh Schmidt. For the blessing of her foreword and her friendship too, I thank Riv-Ellen Prell.

Because this book has been in process for so long, parts of it have seen the light of day in various forms in books and journals. To all those editors who offered insight, I extend my gratitude. In chronological order, I note these publications.

"What Makes a Jewish Home Jewish?" *Electronic Journal for the Study of Religion and Material Culture* (Spring 1999) and *Crosscurrents* (Winter 1999/2000), 491–510.

"Miriam's Object Lesson: A Study of Objects Emerging in the New Rituals of Jewish Women." PhD diss., Drew University, October 2000.

"The Contemporary Haggadah" and "Rituals of Mourning." In *Religious Practices in America,* edited by Colleen McDannell. Princeton: Princeton University Press, 2001, 53–66, 284–296.

"Setting a Cup for Miriam." In *The Women's Passover Companion: Women's Reflections on the Festival of Freedom,* edited by Sharon Cohen Anisfeld, Tara Mohr, and Catherine Spector. Woodstock, VT: Jewish Lights, 2003, 59–64.

"Women and Ritual Artifacts." In *Women of the Wall: Claiming Sacred Ground at Judaism's Holy Site,* edited by Phyllis Chesler and Rivka Haut. Woodstock, VT: Jewish Lights, 2003, 310–334.

"Waiting for the Messiah, a Tambourine in Her Hand." *Nashim* 9 (Spring 2005).

"Miriam's Object Lesson: Ritualizing the Presence of Miriam." In *Women Remaking Judaism,* edited by Riv-Ellen Prell. Detroit: Wayne State University Press, 2007.

FOREWORD

J ews are known as the "People of the Book" because Judaism is most
often viewed as a religion based on texts. At the same time, Judaism
is a religion of practices and rituals. Candle lighting for Shabbat
(the Sabbath) and holidays, blessings over wine and bread, affixing a
mezuzah to a doorpost, the Passover seder—these and more constitute
part of the core of Jewish life. What is the relationship between texts
and rituals? The answers reveal how complex and varied Judaism really
is. Continuity does not mean a lack of variation. Ritual practices vary
widely among Jews from different parts of the world and in different
historical periods. Jews not only have maintained standard practices,
but also have created new rituals along the way, though their origins and
inventions may be forgotten. Ritual innovations are particularly bold in
the present in the United States, and they are being integrated currently
into Jewish life in the United States, Israel, and other countries.

Generation after generation, Jews have maintained these ritual
practices. And yet, if we look closely, we see that the details of ritual
practice vary widely among Jews from different parts of the world, and

in different times in history. We see, too, that taking a great leap forward, modern American Judaism has developed some of the most unique interpretations of standard practices, and even has invented new rituals, which are now imprinting themselves on the current history of the people.

Consider the variances in the ritual of *Shabbat* or holiday candle lighting: the blessing may be the same, but the number of candles lit, the positions in which they are placed, the gestures made with the blessings, and who participates all look remarkably different from one culture to another.

While Jewish texts and a body of Jewish laws may provide the script for ritual actions, the lived experience of Jewish practice lies in the drama of it, the actual performances that engage actors in culturally rich and distinctive ways of shaping their lives according to a sacred calendar. The performances may be as varied as the small gesture of lighting candles or the far grander process of how one confesses and repents. The point is the same: a textually and ritually based tradition can vary dramatically as it is lived and practiced under different cultural and social conditions.

In recent years, cultural anthropologists have developed an interest in studying Judaism and Jewish ritual.[1] They are especially intent on exploring the myriad ways in which rituals have been performed in different times and cultures. The small cadre of anthropologists studying Jews and Judaism includes scholars interested in American Jews, and not just those closed off from the larger world like the Lubavitch or Satmar Hasidim. Studying ritual in modern and postmodern societies like the United States is complicated by the range of religious possibilities one encounters in the process. The challenge is no longer to determine how people live their lives according to fixed texts that are diligently applied to everyday life; now, scholars must decide what to make of proliferating texts, invented blessings, new rituals, and bold and unapologetic innovations. Is there any authority in place, any limit on change? Who has the right to make these changes, and what are the conditions that create them? Why do some stick? Is it all Jewish?

Vanessa Ochs invites her readers into this complex world in her wonderful book, *Inventing Jewish Ritual*. The journey takes many turns as she looks backward and forward to analyze what ritual change really means, how it took place in the past as documented in classical Rabbinic texts, and what innovation is about today for Jews. She offers new roads to travel, walking along with us as she examines the sources of recent ritual innovations and how they have developed both in liberal Jewish denominations and in those that avowedly reject change.

In her role as guide, Ochs even provides a new map for what constitutes Jewish ritual activity, including the use of objects such as musical instruments and vessels, and booklets that provide guides to weddings, as well as ceremonies for Torahs "saved" from European communities decimated by Nazi aggression.[2] What a wonderful guide she proves to be! Vanessa Ochs widens our vocabulary for Jewish ritual, sharpens our ability to interpret it, and multiplies what we count as the stages upon which Jewish life unfolds. She accomplishes this work by doing what anthropologists do best: carefully analyzing the contexts in which rituals emerge and are practiced, and patiently unfolding their stories. She examines what happened, how variations emerged, and how innovators and audiences have reflected on their experiences.

Through her careful unpacking, we not only share a journey, but along the way, also stop at critical junctures to look at the various cultural stagings that she analyzes. We are in the audience watching events unfold. We are behind the scenes viewing rehearsals and then attending multiple performances—often to experience the power of ritual as convincing and authoritative, even though we have been aware of the innovations and inventions all along. Readers are even invited to become participants, to read the pages of various ritual scripts not only with the curiosity of a spectator, but also with an eye toward finding the tools to become what Ochs terms ritual visionaries, or ritual innovators.

The journey yields many rewards among which readers will select. What intrigues me as an anthropologist is that Vanessa Ochs makes ritual a critical medium through which to understand the complex dimensions of American Judaism. Her book reveals American Judaism to be a dynamic cultural process, open to change, that is the source of personal and communal meaning. Innovation is as likely to occur in the course of individual life-cycle events, an avowedly personal dimension of experience, as it is to shape and frame historical experience and memory. These new rituals certainly challenge ideas about normative authority, but the surprise is that these contestations occur both in the realm of Orthodoxy, with Hasidic rituals related to messianism, and in liberal Judaism, where women make the biblical Miriam a more central figure in the seder. If personal meaning is sought in ritual language and material objects, then traditional frameworks also exercise their power (if not always their veto) over many of these innovations.

In short, *Inventing Jewish Ritual* offers us an accounting of 21st-century American Judaism, where it is now, and some of the directions it might yet take. Rather than drawing on demographic research, which by necessity dominates so much of the discussion of contemporary Jewish life, ritual innovation provides a powerful case study to appreciate and to analyze the lives of American Jews.

Riv-Ellen Prell

NOTES:

1. A number of anthropologists were studying contemporary Jewish life outside of Israel in the 1970s and 1980s, including Jonathan Boyarin, Harvey Goldberg, Samuel Heilman, Jack Kugelmass, Barbara Myerhoff, Riv-Ellen Prell, and Chava Weissler. Whereas scholarship focused specifically on ritual often had been inspired by anthropological theory, it was written by scholars trained in classical Judaism or Jewish history. Harvey Goldberg has been critical in providing a bridge between anthropology and text. His 1987 collection, *Judaism from Within and Without*, brought ethnographic studies and textual studies together for the first time. He more fully developed these ideas in his 2003 book, *Jewish Passages: Cycles of Jewish Life*.

2. Ochs's focus on material objects—what some scholars term material culture—is, as she notes, an important new frontier in the study of religion.

BECOMING A
RITUAL INNOVATOR

I became, over years of thinking about new Jewish rituals, a ritual innovator myself. Study, practice, and needs of the moment catapulted me into this; and with the passage of time, I embraced the role with confidence—pride and pleasure even. I came to affirm wholeheartedly that Judaism is a dynamic, evolving tradition, one continuously sculpted by its loving practitioners. Jews keep Judaism alive through inventing new rituals—moving, fulfilling, and authentically Jewish rituals. More of us, I discovered, are poised to craft and embrace new Jewish rituals than we may realize.

My early steps in Jewish ritual innovation were tentative, private, and set in my home community. There was a ritual for a teenager getting her driver's license, a healing service for a neighbor, a ceremony to help a friend bring closure to a breakup. I did not see myself in the league of Jewish ritual innovators whom I regarded as visionaries. These were people who turned the ancient holiday of Rosh Hodesh into a monthly occasion for Jewish feminist consciousness raising. They established ceremonies for the adult bar and bat mitzvah, composed alternative *haggadot,* and created an entire Jewish healing movement. In new prayers, they were invoking God differently. For "Blessed are you, Lord our God, King of the Universe," visionary poet Marcia Falk substituted liturgical compositions that preempted patriarchal, transcendent God language: "Let us bless the wellspring of life ...." They were musicians who brought moving chants into *Shabbat* (Sabbath) prayers and invited us to get up out of the pews and to dance. They were artists who wove radiantly colored prayer shawls and crownlike *kippot* for women, or designed cups and tambourines calling to mind the Prophetess Miriam.

Did the visionaries think of themselves in that light? Possibly not. Take Rabbi Sandy Eisenberg Sasso, the first woman ordained from the Reconstructionist Rabbinical College and the first to serve a Conservative congregation, who played an important role in creating a ceremony to celebrate the birth of a Jewish baby girl. She saw herself as a responsible Jew taking logical, ordinary steps totally in keeping with the spirit of ancient tradition. Rabbi Sasso recalls sitting in the living room of a friend with fellow rabbinical students as they held one of the first Jewish ceremonies to mark the entry of a baby girl into the covenant:

> *It should be nothing out of the ordinary, but it is. It is 1970 and such a ceremony has never been done before. We don't think of ourselves as making history, but as making holy a moment that has long yearned for sanctification. What is more amazing than our living room experiment is that some thirty years later covenantal ceremonies for daughters are being enacted in living rooms and synagogues across the country.*[1]

Coming of age shortly after Rabbi Sasso and her cohort, I did not have to champion the transformation of Judaism through new ritual. As a result of a process set in motion in communities across America when I was still in high school, that case had already been forcefully made. I could go about making new rituals without fanfare and without drawing much attention. I needed only follow the lead of those who came before me—people like Penina Adelman, Arlene Agus, Rebecca

Alpert, E. M. Broner, Phyllis Chesler, Rachel Cowan, Debbie Fried-man, Rivka Haut, Judith Plaskow, Zalman Schachter Shalomi and the founders of the Havurah movement—just to mention those who influ-enced me most.

My community came to count on me for direction in creating new Jewish rituals; even members of my own family.

The Interactive Mezuzah

"Can you make a ritual for the Jewish, Christian, and Muslim gradu-ate students who helped me move all my books into my new office at school?" asked my husband, Peter, a professor of modern Jewish thought. I had created a similar ritual for the family when we first moved to Charlottesville to teach at the University of Virginia (UVA), by embellishing the familiar Jewish ceremony for a housewarming. The idea was to hang our mezuzah in such a way that it could be meaningful, even to people who were not Jewish.

"Bring objects from your traditions that might bring blessings to our new home," I wrote our new colleagues in the religious studies department, inviting them to a Jewish housewarming. Because our teaching careers have pulled us outside the orbits of big city Jewish life, we try to open up our Jewish ceremonies so we can share them with the friends who make up our community. Otherwise, they would just be witnesses to our curious Jewish ways and we would not know their support.[2]

They came, bringing salt, bread, coal, black-eyed peas, garden-grown sage for smudging, and prayer beads of all sorts. I gave their children *gragers* (noisemakers) I had saved from Purims past. "Make noise," I instructed, "and frighten away any evil spirits and 'cooties'!" I offered a blessing for our house and another for our new friends. I allowed these words to spill from my heart, a practice I gleaned not from Judaism—but from Protestant friends adept at offering spontaneous prayer at the table or at the hospital bedside. Our guests shared their own housewarming traditions, from faith or family culture, and they blessed our home. To this day, when I do my thorough Passover dusting, I rediscover prayer beads that were tucked into the corners of bookshelves.

Finally, Peter hung our mezuzah, a farewell gift from the friends back in New Jersey. We explained how the mezuzah marked our home as a sacred space, distinctively Jewish. Everyone filed by and gave the nail a little symbolic tap (that was Peter's idea), and then we broke bread together. Ours was clearly a Jewish household, one held up now by many blessings.

Thus inspired, I came up with a plan for Peter's office ritual, and agreed to "officiate," although, as there were but five of us, that word seems too formal. I facilitated. As before, it would be a Jewish ritual open to people of different traditions.

This is what happened: First, Daniel, a Jewish graduate student, hung a mezuzah on the doorway of Peter's office, saying the traditional blessings. He and Peter explained to the others what a mezuzah was, and why it was an important ritual object for many Jews, even those who do not think of themselves as "religious," as it denotes pride in one's Jewish identity and a wish for divine protection. They explained how the text of the mezuzah emphasizes the centrality of study and teaching. I then invited everyone to write their own blessings for their continuing study of sacred texts—Torah, New Testament, and Koran— that would take place here in this office. They rolled their blessings up into tiny scrolls and placed them into a brown envelope that one student had attached to the wall, just below the mezuzah.

During the year, as their studies progressed, they could, I explained, add new blessings to the envelope. I called it an "interactive mezuzah," or in Hebrew, a *mezuzah nosefet*, an additional mezuzah."[3] Like the conventional mezuzah, it could serve to remind Peter and his students of their intentions as they went in and out of the office. Unlike the traditional mezuzah, which contains two passages from Deuteronomy (6:4–9 and 11:13–21) inscribed on parchment, the "interactive mezuzah" holds the words of one's own heart. It is not an alternative to the traditional mezuzah, but an elaboration and extension of its powers and purposes.

I offered this blessing:

> *This is the tent of Abraham,*
> *a place of shelter and welcome, home to the children of Abraham.*

Erecting this tent, we sanctify this space,
and dedicate this as a house of sacred learning.
May all who study in this tent be blessed with reason and wisdom,
and may the learning we share create pathways of peace.[4]

We concluded by eating—Charlottesville's famous Bodo's bagels, of course. The ritual felt right. Granted, the efficacy of any ritual, old or new, cannot really be measured, and certainly the person who has orchestrated the ritual, with a certain vanity at stake, is hardly the person to judge. But I sensed good feeling in the room, and I think that is something you can know. The ritual acknowledged both change and transformation, uprooting and now stasis: an empty space in Halsey Hall was now marked as a home for scriptural study, and the sense of community the students already had created amongst themselves as young scholars of religion was affirmed.

Encouraged by the success of the ritual in Peter's office, I made a similar "interactive mezuzah" for my own office at home using a little Lucite box. Soon after, I extended the ritual further: When I was invited to give a sermon at the first Friday night *Shabbat* service of that academic year at UVA's Hillel, I distributed tiny envelopes that could be used as interactive *mezuzot* to every student who had come. On the envelopes I printed these words: "May you be blessed when you come in; May you be blessed when you go out."

The Jewish Ritual Toolbox

In creating new Jewish rituals, inspiration comes from what could be called a "Jewish ritual toolbox." It holds three compartments:

1. One compartment holds texts. Biblical passages, teachings of the sages, folktales, and prayer liturgies are the primary documents, but there are also Jewish and Hebrew poems and songs. The texts can be quoted whole, but they can also be reworded, given new emphases, or be transformed altogether to reflect contemporary sensibilities and situations. The traditional style of the text might

be used as a framework for a new creation. Legal documents, such as the wedding contract and the writ of divorce, are also in this compartment, and they provide frameworks for adaptation.

2. A second compartment holds familiar and resonant Jewish ritual actions and objects. Among the actions are blessing, praying, singing, lighting candles, memorializing, sitting low to the ground in mourning, tearing one's clothes in grief, smashing a glass, standing under a canopy, smelling spices, holding one's fingers up to a flame, dipping bread in honey, and building temporary dwellings. Among the objects are the Torah scroll, the ark, the prayer book, candles, wine, challah, spices, matzot, red ribbons, prayer shawls, a palm branch, the ritual bath, the wedding canopy, and the ram's horn.

    Turning to this rich vocabulary, the innovator seeks actions and objects that can symbolically connect the new ritual to the past and do its necessary work in the present. Sources of inspiration are manifold, and include Jewish practices that have historically been observed by one gender alone, practices whose observance has been limited mostly to one denomination or to a community of Jews of a different culture, and practices of the past that have fallen from the repertoire. When the new ritual is performed, the borrowings from within Jewish culture are usually highlighted. They make the ritual feel as if it is already "ours," and genuinely Jewish, even if we have never heard of it before. Turning to ways of the past evokes certainty, security, and imagined community. By contrast, the rich inspiration and symbolism that come from the rituals of other faith traditions or from the rituals of secular culture are slipped in more discreetly and their sources tend to go unspoken.

3. A third compartment holds enduring, core Jewish understandings about the presence of God, the merit of ancestors, the obligation to lead a sanctified life, the blessing of the land of Israel, the significance of preserving Jewish memory through study, and all the ethical obligations held toward fellow Jews and all of humankind. A commitment to such core understandings is the compass that guides all Jewish innovation.[5]

In a spirit that is prayerful, and sometimes mirthful as well, the elements of the "ritual toolbox" inspire me and become part of a new ritual I am creating. When it is appropriate to examine the new practice in the light of Jewish law, *halakhah*, I—a liberal, traditional Jew—will do so. I will look at precedents, study legal considerations, converse with rabbinic colleagues, and ultimately make a judgment that I believe is appropriate for my community. Were I an Orthodox Jew, that process would be more deliberate still.

Orthodox Jews Also Innovate New Rituals

How would an Orthodox sensibility guide one's innovations? Beverly Gribetz and Ed Greenstein, both modern Orthodox educators, demonstrate one approach. For their wedding ceremony, they wanted to give the bride and other women they wished to honor the opportunity to play more active roles. They described how, after a lengthy process of study and rabbinic consultation, they were able to do this by introducing multiple innovations. They wrote:

> We knew we were doing something different, but we were also confident and reassured that everything we were doing was within halakhah. Halakhah *is much broader than traditional practice, which tends to preserve things as they are. Our process of study and application only confirmed that* halakhah *provides for developing traditions in directions that speak ever more meaningfully to the heart and mind of the Jew.*[6]

The Red Thread Ritual

At critical moments in my life there have been times, often occasioned by crises, when I failed to uncover existing Jewish rituals that met my needs. At such times, it felt as if Judaism was not there for me. Since I've had the courage and more resources to innovate Jewish rituals, this no longer happens. One ritual in particular stands out as a transitional moment in my development as an innovator, one

I performed with my New Jersey community in the late 1990s. I had gotten a late-night call from Susan, a friend from my women's Rosh Hodesh group. Our group had been gathering for a few years by then to celebrate the new moon, which for Jewish feminists has become a well-established new ritual for coming together, studying both Judaism and feminism, and understanding how they intersect. We had also taken to celebrating and mourning the events in our lives together. Susan now told me that a young woman I shall call Eva, whom many of us knew from the neighborhood and synagogue, had been rushed to the hospital with a virus, mysterious and terrifying.

"What can I do?" I asked.

Relatives were already caring for Eva's young children, Susan explained. "We need to have a healing service for Eva's family and our friends."

Susan was right: we needed to do something right away. The private prayers of our own hearts were insufficient. We could not wait until *Shabbat* morning Torah services, when our cantor invited people to come up to whisper the names of the sick people they were praying for, so that he could, on their behalf, offer a collective *Mi Shebeirach* healing prayer: "May the Holy One mercifully restore them to health, vigor, granting them a healing of the body and a healing of the soul, together with all others who are ill."

Neither Susan nor I had yet been to a healing service, but we had read about the ones in New York City organized by the National Center for Jewish Healing.

We planned to have the service at Paula's house the very next night. Susan would make the calls. Because she was so confident I could create and lead a service, I agreed. I was willing to accept that the trust of my community could designate me as a spiritual leader or ritual expert, someone who could fashion the right ritual for the occasion.

I assembled a photocopied handout of prayers, psalms, and songs selected from mailings I had gotten from the National Center for Jewish Healing. Even with a text to pass around, I hesitated. I had led prayers before, but I was not a rabbi. People would be coming to this service with hearts as heavy as my own. Would I know what to do with all of our wishes and emotions? Could the first freestanding Jewish healing service we had ever been to feel right?

At Paula's house, we learned that Eva's condition had become even graver.

Stunned, we sat in a circle. The traditional prayers, even though some were new to us, gave us language to express our anguish. *"El na refa na lah"* (God, please heal her), we prayed, the same words Moses had said for his ailing sister, Miriam. It did not feel as if we were innovating. The elements were traditional; could there be a more ancient and instinctual impulse than our coming together to cry out for help?

Despite the eloquence of the texts and the soothing sound of women's voices blending together, I felt overwhelmed by terror. Surely the others did too.

Earlier that evening, before leaving my house for Paula's, I had spied a spool of red thread in my sewing box. I brought it along, not quite knowing why.

Now I knew. We needed something tangible to help us feel less alone. Our anxiety was mostly for Eva, but it was for us, too. All of us, mothers of young children, knew that something like this could happen to anyone. How vulnerable we were; we yearned for a tangible sign of hope.

Jewish Women and Red Thread

The tradition of Jewish women performing rituals with a red thread has biblical sources. In Genesis, a midwife ties a red thread around the hand of one of Tamar's twin sons, Zerah, thinking he will be the firstborn.[7] In the book of Joshua, a red thread (legend says it was the very same one) is also used by a woman called Rahav, so the Israelite spies to whom she had once been hospitable would later be able to recognize her house and, out of gratitude, protect it.[8]

Rabbi Geela-Rayzel Raphael points to the special connection between Jewish women and red thread:

Although it is centuries later, we are still binding the sign of a scarlet cord. Red thread is still used ritually by women today at Rachel's tomb in Israel, where the red thread is wound around the tomb seven times. It is used to encircle the belly of a pregnant woman to protect a pregnancy.... This is the symbol ... of our power in situations that may seem beyond our control, and of God's continuous "weaving of the threads" of our lives.[9]

From my mother and grandmother, I have learned about Jewish women using red thread as a sign of protection. When there was a family wedding or bar mitzvah and we were all dressed up in new clothes, my mother always bit off a piece of red thread with her teeth and, just as we were leaving the house, she tucked it into our collars, and said, "Tfu tfu tfu!" For her, our wearing red was a sign of keeping away the Evil Eye—that is, all sources of danger, especially those caused by jealousy. When the Kabbalah Center, popularized by the Hollywood set, created a trend of wearing a red string around one's wrist (theirs costs $26, which had better make it a potent deflector of evil), they were coasting on a well-established practice.

I passed the spool of red thread to the woman on my right. As the thread traveled around the circle from woman to woman, I asked my friends to imagine that we were weaving an emotional and prayerful web that connected us all to Eva, to each other, and to God. I said:

"This red thread symbolizes God's care; it symbolizes God's continuous weaving of the threads of our lives. This red thread is a prayer, a wish for protection when we feel so very vulnerable. This red thread is a sign that a web of caring connects us. With this red thread as a reminder, we can attempt to go back into our lives aware that we are not altogether alone."

"Protect Eva," we prayed. "Protect us all."

Bound by the circle of thread we held aloft, what were we supposed to do now? An idea sprang out of the holy tradition of Jewish women, or that was at least how it felt at the time. Other makers of ritual have used similar locutions to express a source of divine inspiration that appears to emerge from outside the self like an ancestral inheritance, bestowed at a propitious moment. Surely, the memory of my mother breaking off red thread with her teeth and attaching it to us had been triggered. I suggested we each break off a piece of the red thread that held us together, and find ways to attach our own red thread to ourselves—around a wrist or ankle, onto a ring or bracelet. Reminded by our red threads, we could remain aware that none of us was altogether alone in our prayers for Eva. The wish for her protection and for ours could stay with us even as we returned to our own homes. We helped each other make the knots.

Over the next weeks, we gathered again for other healing services for Eva at Paula's house. We prayed, sang, and listened to updates. If the practice of holding a Jewish healing service in a private home seemed unfamiliar or off-putting to anyone at first, by now this was just what we women did. It had become, in the briefest time, our tradition. Each time we told stories of how the pieces of red thread were still somehow holding us together. Telling these stories became part of the tradition, too.

Eva survived, the illness taking a terrible toll. We visited her, usually in small groups. Months passed, and long after our red threads had slipped off or shredded away, the memory of their once having woven us together in hope continued to strengthen us.[10]

Inventing Judaism?

When I first become aware of Jewish ritual innovation, and long before I become a ritual innovator myself, I wondered: was religious innovation even permissible, a good idea, let alone a cause for celebration?

I was born in the '50s, at a time when a haggadah[11] was a haggadah. We used the free *haggadot* distributed by the makers of Maxwell House coffee as Grandpa, sitting at the head of the table, led the seder with one break for a single, glorious participatory moment: the child (me, for a good many years) asking the four questions. Artists such as Ben Shahn might have illuminated their own *haggadot* in the tradition of artists of the past, many commissioned by wealthy families, but we would never have imagined making a homemade haggadah of our own, one reflecting our family or our values.

Homemade *Haggadot*

Since their appearance in the 1970s, homemade *haggadot* have reflected contemporary concerns, among them: feminism, egalitarianism, ecumenicism, liberation, the plight of Soviet Jewry, Holocaust memoralization, peace, and race relations. In the '90s, ecology and gender issues (of late, transgender awareness and bisexuality) became focuses as well. The haggadah might be created to match the needs of a special interest group (say, for an interfaith community seder), or to accommodate the attention span of young children or adults who are only marginally interested. Some of the *haggadot* originally made for private use have since been commercially published. One of the earliest was a 1977 version of *The Woman's Haggadah* created by Esther Broner with Nomi Nimrod: it was first published in *Ms.* magazine. Even after dozens of alternative haggadot were published, families continued to "cut and paste" their own versions, using desktop publishing programs, "open source" seder materials in Hebrew and English, and templates they could easily locate on the Internet.[12]

In my family, you lived and performed Judaism—you did not invent it. If you knew of no Jewish response to some event in your life, say a high school graduation or a 50th birthday party, you responded with your "secular hat" on, doing what other Americans might do. Maybe you added a little Jewish touch: you raised a glass and toasted, "*L'chaim!*" If yours was an observant home, the food was, by default, kosher, and the men wore yarmulkes.

If there was a Jewish response available but it did not speak to you—say going to the *mikveh* (ritual bath) before your wedding, or sitting on low stools for a week as a sign of mourning during the week of shivah—either you went through the motions because it was expected of you and you saw no way out, or you chose not to participate in the action, either making clear your refusal or concealing your rebellion with silence.

As I have suggested, I did not become a ritual innovator overnight. I had to learn to honor good faith efforts made to celebrate and transmit Judaism. I needed to recognize that even clumsy or misguided efforts held redemptive possibility—if only for the innovator. Less successful ritual practices would fade away. Even the innovations that were misguided, even crude or tasteless, would not destroy "the whole thing." Successful practices might catch on, grow in popular acceptance, and become legitimized and promoted by rabbis. But neither the endurance of a new ritual nor rabbinic approval defined its success. A meaningful ritual might be created by just one person drawing upon Jewish tradition. Even just once.

Being "Really" Jewish

My earliest response to ritual innovation, conditioned by growing up in the home of my grandparents in Paterson, New Jersey, was reticence. My Russian-born grandparents were Orthodox, though we never spoke of the Judaism they practiced by specifying a denomination. We simply said they were "religious," meaning they were traditional. Calling them "religious" was not meant to designate the nature of their practice, but to say that as far as Judaism was concerned, they were "the real thing." This was long before Jews used the word "pluralism" to suggest that one could respect, affirm, or even acknowledge different ways people practiced Judaism.

I was sent to a yeshivah and my world was narrowly constrained. The only people who ever came visiting were religious relatives; my uncles' friends Lazar and Joel from yeshivah; and the people who came over after shul (their little synagogue) for sponge cake, herring, tidbits of toothpicked gefilte fish, and schnapps poured into tiny shot glasses.

I assumed there were three kinds of people in America: religious Jews like my grandparents, a few nonreligious or "once-a-year Yom Kippur" Jews like the neighbors to our right (whom I felt so sorry for, as their house did not blossom, each Friday, with the smells of chicken soup and brisket), and a few Catholics (which I thought was the word for religious Christians) like the neighbor to our left. When JFK ran for president and people said it was unusual as he was Catholic, I thought they meant that presidential candidates were usually Jewish. Perhaps many of the past presidents had been Jewish too—with first names like Abraham or Samuel, and with last names like Eisenhower or Roosevelt, they could have been members of the shul.

In this world, any Jewish practice that I wasn't used to seemed spiritually illegitimate and aesthetically offensive. It was clear and simple: what we did and how we did it was correct in the eyes of God and the community. We were not making choices or adapting. Any way other than ours was pitiable, weird, ignorant, an embarrassment, and a desecration.

My mother once mentioned that there was a Reform synagogue downtown. I knew the word "reform" in one context alone—reform school—so I already had some concerns. (I must have seen a prison movie that frightened me, as I also resisted reading the books in the public library marked "Juvenile" as I feared it might mark me as a juvenile delinquent.) My mother said you could not believe what went on among the Reform: women and men sat together in pews and prayed in English. My grandmother said "Shah!" to quiet her, either because my mother did not know what she was talking about or because she did, and such information was too explosive for a curious child like me to hear.

Given this buildup, in junior high school, as others explored sex and drugs, I sneaked into this Reform synagogue on Yom Kippur, dared by the "once-a-year" girl from next door. My grandmother was right in shielding me: I was startled by what I saw; more startled still to see that my mother, who tended toward exaggeration, had been correct.

Yet I was also very much a child of the New York World's Fair, ready to cruise merrily and confidently toward the future's promise of modernity. Picture phones, meals at the push of a button, and flying cars seemed best of all, but I would have been satisfied with a color television, as *Walt Disney's Wonderful World of Color* was less wonderful on our black-and-white set with its hard-to-adjust rabbit ears antenna. Still, I held fast to a conservative view of religious practice.

Private Orthodoxies

Such a conservative response characterizes not only people of Orthodox backgrounds. Consider a student of mine who grew up in a classical Reform temple: she was shocked when she went to Hillel for the first time and discovered that the Reform service there lacked a full professional choir, an organ, and a rabbi in a black robe. It felt illegitimate to her, not like real Judaism. She didn't know what to make of the shabby sofas pushed together in a circle or the student leader strumming a guitar who encouraged the group to "get into" the singing. Consider too my colleague, fairly estranged from Judaism, who says that the very thought of religious innovation makes him cringe: "I am not observant at all, but when I do Judaism, I want to do it right." What does he mean by "right"? I ask. His eyes twinkle, but he means what he says: "Whatever they did in my parents' synagogue on Long Island 40 years ago." My student and colleague may be historically naïve, but they have reason to feel that the practices familiar to them express *the* right way of expressing Judaism, right since the beginning of time.

Today I practice being Jewish much the same way my grandparents did. The pink sponge is for meat dishes and the blue one is for milk. We get ready for Passover and hunt for *hametz* with feather and candle. I mimic their Yiddish-English vocabulary for Jewish practice, calling my Sabbath preparations "making *Shabbos*." I can imagine my grandparents sitting on a heavenly porch: "Look how nicely she keeps the tradition," they say, blessing me doubly for keeping their sacred practices and for passing them on to my daughters.

I also practice being Jewish in ways that would confuse, upset, or simply elude them. By studying and teaching Talmud. By being a member of the *beit din*, the local rabbinic court that presides over conversions. By setting the Passover table with my growing collection of Miriam's cups and feminist, egalitarian, and social justice *haggadot*. By reading aloud the names of children who perished in the Holocaust at an annual vigil. By performing healing ceremonies. Transformations, innovations—who would have imagined?

Angel Cards

These and others are practices I perform. Some I have passed on to my daughters and students. Now, just as often, the young people invite me to join them in their new rituals. Reflection upon *Shabbat* angel cards was one of the first.

The practice of using Jewish angel cards[13] began in the late 1980s. One version of the ritual goes like this: at the *Shabbat* dinner table, after singing *Shalom Aleichem* (the song welcoming the angels of peace who visit the homes of those who celebrate *Shabbat* and bring blessings), each person picks an illustrated *Shabbat* angel card and reflects on the positive "angelic" character trait written on it, such as "openness," "insight," "perspective," or "healing." People are invited to share how the trait relates to the past week or how they might incorporate the trait into the coming week. It might concern hopes, say, about starting a new job or a new relationship; or it might occasion a prayer for peace in the Middle East

In the mid-'90s, after we had heard about the practice from both friends in Philadelphia and a young rabbi in New York, my older daughter, Julie, helped her sister, Elizabeth, design a handmade deck of Jewish angel cards, copying and distributing them to the guests who came to celebrate Elizabeth's bat mitzvah. Now our *Shabbat* angel cards make a regular appearance at our Friday night *Shabbat* table. While our friends are protective of Elizabeth's angel cards, keeping them in special boxes or cloth pouches and calling them "the real thing" or "the original *Shabbat* angel cards," there are now commercially produced Jewish angel cards. I know of one set made by Rabbi Eisenbach-Budner, which she calls *Malachim* (angels or messengers),[14] and the other by well-known Judaica artist Betsy Platkin Teutsch, which she calls *Kavanah Cards*.[15]

Torah Yoga

Of late, Elizabeth has organized Torah Yoga sessions on *Shabbat* mornings in Charlottesville. We first encountered Torah Yoga in 2004 when visiting the Germantown Jewish Centre in Philadelphia where, on certain *Shabbatot,* multiple options for prayer are offered. As an alternative to the *Shabbat* morning worship held in the main sanctuary, Myriam Klotz, a Reconstructionist rabbi, led Torah Yoga. I later learned that in the 1990s, Diane Bloomfield, an Orthodox Jewish yoga instructor who had studied Jewish texts, began to incorporate classic Jewish mystical wisdom and biblical concepts (such as the experience of leaving Egypt or remembering to rest) into yoga instruction.[16] She intuited that when the study of Torah was combined with the physical practice of yoga, they would enhance each other. She and Rabbi Klotz, also a yoga instructor, are among the most well-known teachers adapting yoga to Jewish practice so that people can have a Jewish experience grounded in their own bodies.[17] While a Torah Yoga session looks like a conventional yoga class, it is framed by teachings drawn from Torah and laced with references to prayer practices. More important, links to Hinduism are absent. Instead of chanting "*om*" to begin and conclude the practice, in Torah Yoga one might chant "*hineni*" (here I am) or "shalom."

Now, when Elizabeth and Dorothe—a friend from synagogue who is a yoga teacher as well as a professor in the German department at the University of Virginia—announce that they are inspired to have a "Torah Yoga *Shabbat*," I get out my yoga mat and go. In fact, the sessions are often held in my home, and the participants include college students, faculty, Elizabeth's friends, and my friends from synagogue. Often, I'll take a turn leading the Torah teaching part of the session, which, for us, has come to mean finding a way to link a theme of the week's Torah portion to an awareness of the body.

A Prayer Shawl of One's Own

I could not have explained or justified many of the innovations to my grandparents when they were alive. But I try to do so now in imagined scenarios such as this one, in which they read this e-mail sent by my friend Marcia.

7:05 AM 7/5/2001
subject: tallit for women on Fairway Ave

Are you up for tallit service on the 22nd, Sunday at 8:30
AM? We can meet at my house and walk down to the water.
Wear good shoes, it's a steep hill. I'll get OJ and vodka and we
can mimosa it with bagels and lox afterwards! Let me know
by e-mail or phone.

"A tallit service, there's no such a thing." I hear my grandfather say. "A man goes to shul, puts on his tallis, then he davens (prays). The tallis isn't the point. This is a letter from a woman? A woman wears a tallis and drinks vodka? Like Yentl! You're not going to this, are you?"

I give the short answer, telling him that in the last 20 years, Jewish women seeking equality have begun to wear prayer shawls. They never asked for permission—they seized this right. Even so, it was often not easy for women to begin to wear the *tallitot* they have acquired, and to overcome their inherited prejudices about what women could do in the eyes of the community and God.

"The religious don't do this, honey, only the women's libbers," my grandmother says, speaking, as she did in her later years, for them both.

"Yes, Grandma, even religious women."

"Gotenyu!" she says, not grasping that when I say "religious," I refer not just to Orthodox Jews committed to Jewish observance but also to Reform, Reconstructionist, Conservative, and Renewal Jews who have made regular Jewish practice central to their lives.

I think to add that there is no law forbidding it, and there is, in fact, historical precedent for Jewish women in antiquity wearing a tallit. This information will not help: my grandparents could not imagine that I—or any woman—would ever be in a position to know, let alone debate or teach, Judaism beyond the wisdom of the kitchen.

They counter, "It's just not done," and in their day, they'd have been right.

I stop, having been well trained to spare my grandparents grief. These are the people who famously responded to announcements of good news, like births or weddings, with a long sigh. "Even good news takes a lot out of a person," Grandma would say. So it is that in my imagined conversation, because I cannot bear their shock, I do not let on that I too wear a tallit. As a matter of fact, I have two: the white one my family bought with me one Mother's Day when they knew I needed moral support in going to a Judaica store on the Lower East Side of New York to make my purchase (Web purchases were not yet an option) and the colorful flowery one honoring the biblical Matriarchs that I bought for myself in support of the worship practices of the Women of the Wall. With two *tallitot,* I now had one for the holidays and the other for *Shabbat.*

My friend Marcia had given me two weeks to design a ceremony that would inaugurate the tallit she was given for her birthday. When I remarked that she never wore her new tallit in synagogue, she explained that owning the tallit was not sufficient to begin using it. She needed a ritual so she could actually put it on, preferably one held among her Jewish women friends, so she might overcome a lifelong image of herself as "the Jew who cannot wear a tallit."

I imagine enticing my grandparents to hear more: about how in the 1970s, many Jewish women became attracted to public expressions of being Jewish that had previously been off limits to them: reading Torah, leading services, wearing prayer garb, becoming rabbis and Torah scholars.

Expanding Spiritual Options

Early on, Jewish feminists recognized that appropriating the rituals of Jewish men was but one spiritual option. One of the first women rabbis, Lynn Gottlieb, understood that Jewish feminists might design novel ways to identify themselves with and practice a Judaism that emerges out of women's experiences. She recalls:

> The first meeting of Banot Esh (Sisters of Fire), a group of feminists, is held in the late 1970s.... We initiate the retreat by praying a traditional service. After the prayers, I raise an uncomfortable question: Why are we davening (praying) exactly like the men? How can we explore feminism if we stay within the bounds of traditional liturgy?[18]

When women first bought prayer shawls, the only ones available were made for men and boys. Often enough, these women feared the owners of Judaica stores would be shocked to learn that they were purchasing a tallit for themselves. Because this occasion for spiritual growth might easily turn humiliating, many a woman would go shopping undercover, telling the shopkeeper, "I am buying a tallit for my son's bar mitzvah. He is just my size." Some women found the available *tallitot* simply too big. Some found that the bold black or blue stripes reminded them too much of the prayer garb of their husbands, fathers, and grandfathers—the very garment seemed too quintessentially male, making appropriation less possible.

Around this time, inspired by the Jewish catalogs (to be discussed later), young people at Jewish summer camps and retreats were making their own *tallitot* out of colorful fabrics (batik and tiedyed were characteristic of the time), and were attaching fringes (tzitzit) to them, tying the knots themselves; these were the years when doing macramé as a craft was popular. In this period, distinctive women's *tallitot* were born. Structurally similar to men's, with fringes at the four corners and an *atarah,* a neckpiece, they were better cut for a woman's body. Some were later cut poncho-style, convenient for a woman holding a baby. Women were beginning to design and make their own *tallitot* or create them in collaboration with weavers, fiber artists, and painters of silk. They also transformed heirloom scarves, lace shawls, or the embroidered tablecloths of beloved ancestors into sacred garments. The Judaica industry took note, and soon women's and girls' *tallitot* were being commercially manufactured and sold in shops, synagogue gift stores, Web sites, and at markets set up at Jewish retreats and conventions. If the owners of Judaica stores had personal reservations about women wearing *tallitot,* they suppressed them.

Making a ritual of selecting one's own tallit became an important milestone for a bat mitzvah girl along her path of preparation for the ceremony. Often grandparents got involved, and as they participated in the selection, they were creating a new link between one generation and another—ironically through a ritual object brand-new to all. Boys too learned not to be passive recipients of a tallit purchased for them; they also searched for the "right" tallit, one that expressed their personality or some major theme of their life (yes, and here I confess I cringe—even the colors of their favorite sports teams). Many adults, preparing for the new ritual of adult bar or bat mitzvah—a daunting but widely popular initiation rite allowing Jewish adults to feel religiously enfranchised—give weight and deliberation to their own search for the "right" tallit.

In some families, purchasing a tallit would become linked to a "heritage pilgrimage" taken to Israel, Eastern Europe, the Lower East Side, or Ellis Island, a discovery of the family's Jewish roots calculated to precede the bar or bat mitzvah. At the synagogue, on the Friday evening before a bat or bar mitzvah, the parents would be invited to stand before the congregation. They would explain the meaning belonging to the particular tallit they had selected and the feelings of connection and continuity it evoked. Aware of their place in an intergenerational chain of transmission that had survived displacements, they would drape the tallit on their child's shoulders.

I spared my grandparents these details of contemporary ritual innovation, which they would have found about as engaging as the details of the priestly sacrifices in Leviticus. Still, I reminded myself, Torah is not in heaven alone, not with my grandparents, and not even with God. When we proceed to innovate Jewish rituals with the best intentions: love, respect, learning, integrity, and responsibility for Jewish communities, Torah is here, with us. The Torah was with Marcia and us, her woman friends, as we walked down to the water. On the banks of the Rivanna, Marcia, braced by the stories her friends told of their own important first times, wrapped her tallit around her shoulders. We prayed together with her for the blessing of this first time and for the courage needed to wrap herself in holiness; and yes, we raised cups of Mimosa, saying, "L'chaim!"

The Birth of a Jewish Baby Girl

Becoming this enthusiastic about the new rituals has been a process.

In the mid-1970s, when the lived implications of the women's movement for Judaism were starting to register, I was invited by friends to a ceremony to mark the birth of their Jewish baby girl.

Scheduled when the baby was about a month old, it took place in the
social hall of a Conservative synagogue in Westchester, New York.
The parents called it "a baby-naming ceremony for our daughter," as
the term *simchat bat* (rejoicing in the birth of a daughter) was not yet
commonly used. As we began, the new parents handed out collated
sets of pages, the script for what would be said and done. They had
based it on ceremonies they had been to or read about. Clearly designated were ritual actions that would be performed and parts the rabbi,
parents, grandparents, and invited guests would recite. The father was
a rabbinical student, and the mother worked in Jewish education,
which meant both were adept at reading Hebrew and chanting the
prayers. Accordingly, their comfort performing Jewish rituals showed,
and their aspiration to have a Jewish practice for this new situation
seemed legitimate.

The ceremony was touching, though I had to admit: it is harder to
be moved by a practice that surprises you at each step than by a familiar practice that evokes dozens of memories and strums a lifetime of
patterned responses. Following their script, the new parents washed
their daughter's feet and wrapped her in the tallit that had been their
wedding *huppah* (canopy). Then they passed her from one grandpar-
ent to another—even a great-grandmother!—and each welcomed her
into the covenant and struggled through tears to give her their blessings. We smiled when her older brother, a toddler, patted her head.
There were the grandparents' tears, the sweet baby, and an intense
awareness of life being a fragile, precious gift, one that called for Jewish blessings of thanksgiving.[19]

Here, Jews were treating the birth of a girl as a joyous public celebration and not as a nonevent or, worse, a disappointment. In this
setting, I had my first concrete inkling that Judaism could be repaired
and reframed to include women. Here, I glimpsed the possibility of
greater enfranchisement for Jewish women, greater active participation, even for myself.

With all this positive feeling percolating, I had some concerns that
gave me pause. Was there not an intrusion of gender politics, using
the birth of a daughter to make a point? Was it appropriate to present
a Jewish ritual as a vehicle for achieving one's ethical agenda? While
this ritual was not physically intrusive like a son's circumcision—the

baby girl's body was neither marked nor changed—still I wondered: "Is this permitted?" (What did I imagine to be the source of permission granting? I had yet to investigate this.)

I had attended the ritual circumcision (called a *bris* or *brit*) for this couple's son two years earlier. That ceremony certainly made multiple points: points about honoring ancestors and points about keeping a pact with traditional practices, not to mention points about the continued importance of the male, the male body, and the "member that makes you a member" in Jewish culture. Why had those points expressed by the circumcision not seemed heavy-handed? Was it because the brother's ceremony was a rehearsal of cultural beliefs and practices that most attendees, myself included, took for granted, even if they were beginning to call out for sober analysis? I believe so. It was as if we were witnessing facts of nature, which is, of course, what persuasive, established ritual leads us to believe.

Simchat Bat

A ceremony for welcoming a baby girl is now generally called a *simchat bat*, or naming ceremony, in America. In Israel, depending on one's community, the ceremony has various names: *tekes huledet habat* (ceremony for the birth of a daughter), *tekes simchat ha-bat* (celebration of rejoicing for a daughter), *mesibat ha-bat* (party for a daughter), *seudat hodaya* (thanksgiving banquet), *brita* or *brit ha-bat* (a daughter's *brit*); or *zeved habit* (celebration of the gift of a daughter), which is a the traditional Sephardic ceremony. Before there were festive ceremonies for daughters, the baby's father or grandfather was called to the Torah during a morning Torah service, whereupon a prayer for the mother's heath and a formulaic blessing stating the baby's name were recited. Quite often, the mother and the baby were not present, and if they were, they played no active role. This began to change in 1973, when "On the Birth of a Daughter," by Daniel and Myra Leifer, was first published in the journal *Response*. The text was widely circulated, reprinted, and expanded upon, at first among Jews of the liberal denominations, and eventually among Orthodox Jews.

Wasn't it permissible to perform a new ritual because it seemed politically and ethically correct? I asked myself. Was that not the whole point of the Jewish directive, "Justice, justice, you shall pursue?" If Jewish life compels one to work toward social justice, should that impulse and its outcomes not be felt in ritual settings, as well as in political and social ones? Being a pious Jew has entailed following inherited practices, but it has also meant being compelled by ethical considerations to alter traditional practices and to innovate new ones.

I must not give the impression that by the end of the *simchat bat*, as I kissed our friends good-bye, my concerns were resolved. I may have been part of a generation that rebelled against the establishment and the dull acceptance of cookie-cutter religiosity, but I also yearned to be a nice Jewish girl, which meant compliance with social norms. I needed time, but not much, for when my own daughters were born just a few years later, I knew we would have *simchat bat* ceremonies to welcome them, even if our out-of-town relatives would not feel obligated to come, as they would have for a son's *bris.*

New Ways to Pray

In the late 1980s, I was teaching a class on women and Talmud at the summer institute of the National Havurah Committee. This was a weeklong retreat for Jews dedicated to Jewish learning, egalitarianism, and community building to come together for study and prayer. Many of the participants belonged to *havurot* (the plural of *havurah*, meaning fellowship) back in their hometowns.

Havurah

A *havurah* is an informal Jewish fellowship group that usually meets weekly or monthly, often in private homes, though sometimes they are held within synagogues. Members gather for prayer services, Jewish study, and life-cycle celebrations. Characteristically, a *havurah* is egalitarian and members share in its leadership and direction. Members of the Havurah of

South Florida describe the motivation underlying their community: "We form a *havurah* because something is lacking in our Jewish lives. Perhaps we lack intensity in Jewish study, or Jewish prayer, or Jewish celebration, or Jewish community, or Jewish social action. If our desire to fill the void is great enough, we become willing to expend some energy to find others who have a similar desire, and a *havurah* is formed. The *havurah* determines for itself how often it will meet, how many members it will have, what its programs will be."[20]

I had come with an open mind: egalitarian, informal *havurah*-style worship was not new to me. When I was 17 and in college, in the early '70s, I walked down the street from my dorm at Tufts University most *Shabbat* mornings to pray at the yellow house in Somerville, Massachusetts, home of the first residential *havurah* Havurat Shalom. There, *havurah* members, their wives (at that point, membership had not yet been extended to women), and like-minded friends in the community, mostly graduate student age, sat hippie-style on pillows on the floor before an ark covered with curtains of macramé.[21] They chanted and swayed with their eyes closed, embracing a style that bridged Hasidism, Woodstock, and Jewish summer camp. There was passion and warmth. What an antidote it was to regular synagogue life, where congregants watched the rabbi and cantor perform onstage from the synagogue pews. Most of the core group were liberal Jews with strong Jewish learning, seeking fresh, countercultural ways of being Jewish. Some had roots in Camp Ramah, the camp of the Conservative movement that had shaped my own religious sensibilities. A few were on the most liberal fringe of Orthodoxy, and there might also have been some traditional Orthodox Jews for whom this represented a daring departure.

At this summer institute, I attended the *Shabbat* morning service. We were led in a guided meditation by a woman rabbi in flowing white clothes; a small hand drum was slung over her shoulder. She was a rabbi of the Jewish Renewal movement, an alliance of rabbis and communities of Jews bringing creativity, joy, and healing to their spiritual practices.[22] This was my first exposure to Jewish Renewal. I had heard that Jewish Renewal was experiential and New Age in its focus, and, from what I observed, this seemed accurate.

I closed my eyes, in part to concentrate, and in part to shut out some of the worshippers whose exuberance made me feel, by comparison, stiff and suburban. The prayers that followed were sweet and refreshing, and I caught on easily to the *nigunim*[23] (simple wordless melodies) and chants. I was glad to reconnect with the languid and repetitive prayer style, with all the "ya da da dai dais" and "ya ba ba bai bas" that I had encountered over a decade earlier at Havurat Shalom. With my eyes closed, I was becoming happily lost in prayer, something rarely possible for me in the pews of the Conservative synagogue in New Jersey where we were living then. There, the cantor sang, and on cue, the rest of us droned along. Familiar and comforting it was, but it did not raise my spirits.

Because I was used to praying without instrumental accompaniment, it felt strange to hear the rabbi's hand drum. But the drumbeat did keep us together and focused. The beat resounded in my body, and I was praying differently, with my whole self. In synagogue, I had sometimes experienced belonging, a connection to all Jews, or at least to the Jews in that room. Here was a different experience: transcendence. My eyes welled up, as I could hardly contain the surge of feeling.

The rabbi instructed us to chant each word of the *Shema* prayer ("Hear O Israel, the Lord our God, the Lord is one") on a single long breath.

Breathing the *Shema*

Rabbi Rami Shapiro's published direction for breathing the *Shema* reminds me of the one I heard that day:

> *Sit comfortably; breathe naturally; close your eyes. When you have settled down a bit, slowly and silently recite the* Shema *in sync with your breathing. Start on the in-breath and end on the out-breath: Breathe in* Shema, *breathe out* Yisrael, *breathe in* Adonai, *breathe out* Eloheinu. *Continue in this way so that the final word of the* Shema

(Echad) *is recited on the out-breath. Pay special attention to this final out-breath, extending it a bit as a means of melting into the One from Whom all breath comes and to Whom all breath returns. At the conclusion of each recitation sit silently; breathe; and allow a deep stillness to quiet both your body and your mind. If and when your mind wanders, return to your recitation. Do this for 30 minutes every day. In time the silence between recitations will lengthen until, with the grace of God, you will finally melt into the ineffable presence of* Adonai Echad: *the nondual reality of God.*[24]

This practice has caught on, and one hears the *Shema* chanted in this way not just in Jewish Renewal circles, but also in liberal congregations, large and small. This, however, was my first time. Fancying myself as being open to new Jewish practices, I was dismayed to feel my body stiffen. The breathy innovation reminded me of people praying in ashrams or meditation centers. This is the *Shema*, the central prayer of Judaism! We're supposed to do it the "right" way, the way it's done by Jews all around the world.

I looked to the other rabbis among us. Their eyes were closed and they were chanting the *Shema* in this breathy way with great feeling and *kavanah*, intentionality. If they, ordained by the conventional seminaries, were saying the *Shema* like this, perhaps I could do it too. So I tried. I discovered that my breath was indeed a powerful untapped instrument of prayer. (I have since learned that there is a long tradition of Jewish prayer practices that integrate breathing into worship and meditation. But even had that not been the case, even if Jews had only learned about using the breath as a spiritual practice from their recent experiences as seekers in Eastern religions, then we had acquired a valuable spiritual teaching.) I remembered hearing that the melody of the *Shema* prayer sung in most synagogues, what many think of as the "right" way to sing the *Shema*, was originally a German drinking song. (I later learned this was a stretch of the imagination, but with roots in fact: 19th-century Reform Jews were inspired by Lutheran hymns in their compositions of liturgical music, and the ecclesial music surely drew from Germanic folk motifs.[25]) I remembered too that this was not the only version of the *Shema* melody I had ever heard in my travels.

I breathed, "*Shema.*" I breathed, "*Yisrael,*" relaxing into the practice.

Surviving Initial Discomfort

Witnessing ritual works-in-progress in those earlier days, I noticed the rough transitions, the awkwardness of improvisation, the difficulty of being moved by a practice that came with no memory of having done it before. When an innovation felt especially uncomfortable to me, the feeling was visceral, almost like disgust, something I couldn't always think away. I was irritated when an innovation took place without my being given fair warning or the chance to step out.

But I discovered that I could modulate my response to innovations. I could remind myself that my unfamiliarity was not sufficient to disqualify the potential blessings of a new practice. We have all learned to overcome multiple gut responses to unfamiliarity. Who isn't terrified on the first day of school? But still we press forward and walk into the classroom. I noticed that ritual practices clearly borrowed from other cultures made me feel especially uncomfortable. I realized I could either choose to resist the practices (huffing to myself: "Jews don't use burning sage or talking sticks" or "we don't take calming breaths") or I could give them a chance. In time, I could consider the plausibility of their fit and evaluate their spiritual power in light of any ruptures they might impose. I could train myself to notice my hesitancy in the face of a new ritual and contemplate it. Then I could let go: I could watch, wait, and perhaps, eventually, accept.

Will It Endure? Is It Authentic?

About new practice, I once worried about its long-term endurance: would it last? That is not, I learned, such a weighty matter. I once worried about authenticity. But what did "authenticity" even mean? I was not so naïve as to think that the rituals most people considered as "authentically Jewish" originated from some mythic beginning of Jewish time. I had never embraced the Rabbinic legends claiming that long ago, Abraham prayed wearing tefillin, and Sarah, in her tent, lit *Shabbat* candles. Ritual practices, I knew, could acquire the feeling of being natural. For me, a natural ritual was one that *seemed* to be so old and distant from the here and now that it felt timeless; this is what made the ritual have the patina of venerability: full of power and resonance, it demanded to be preserved. The authenticity of a ritual was a feeling cultivated over time, through repeated practice, and sustained by enough cherished memories to guarantee predictability and when necessary, flexibility. I noticed too that gifted ritualists—those who facilitated traditional rituals and those who coined new ones—had techniques that allowed them to veil or disguise the novelties and innovations of new ritual. I saw that a new ritual had a better chance to pass muster and gain acceptance when overt links to major Jewish themes, ritual objects, and the Hebrew language were highlighted. The more the new ritual felt continuous with the past, the more plausible it might seem. I saw too that a ritual was more apt to succeed when the leader prepared participants in advance for what was to come—getting their permission, involving them in bringing necessary materials, even asking them to rehearse a part they would play.

The 1980s progressed, and I was progressing too in my openness to new Jewish rituals. Most of the rituals reflected the movement toward greater egalitarianism. Others reflected the impulse to have heartfelt Jewish ritual responses to life's joyous and traumatic moments, those previously unmarked (at least in the communities I circulated in) and, hence, unrecognized by Judaism. Such impulses for new ritual struck increasingly sympathetic chords within me.

Friends, especially those knowing my interest in Jewish feminism, sent me mimeographed, and then Xeroxed, scripts for various new rituals concerning women, saying, "This is your kind of thing." I studied these compilations of directions for who does what, who stands where, and who recites words in Hebrew or English, all culled from ancient and contemporary texts. I still felt hesitant. I attributed this resistance to various flaws within the new rituals themselves. Perhaps they did not resonate Jewishly for me. They did not evoke a complex of images, thoughts, gestures, and memories that linked me to other Jews and to a sacred story that defined, energized, and organized us. John Z. Smith put it well: "The creation of a new ritual site is always an intriguing process. For, from the standpoint of ritual, novelty may result in a functional gain, but just as often, in an ideological loss. If the former allows the freedom to innovate, the latter may result in a lack of resonance." Borrowing the terminology of linguistics, Smith suggests that novelty in ritual can result in "impoverishing associative relations."[26]

Looking back, abundant Jewish resonance was there all along. I just needed more time to open myself to it. I needed to study more, not just in Judaism, but also in anthropology.

The Lessons of Anthropology

When I trained to become an anthropologist of religion, my hesitancy toward ritual innovation finally dissolved. I no longer asked, "Is this new ritual really Jewish?" but instead asked, "What new rituals are Jews actually practicing?"

The first question, essentially, "What ought a Jew do?" leads to limited answers. One finds oneself defining Jewish ritual according to formal, textbook criteria: holiday rituals, life-cycle rituals (that is, birth through death), rituals of prayer and study. But what about the Jew who spontaneously innovates a ritual in Jewish language on a mountaintop to mark a private milestone? What about the Jew who completes chemotherapy and wishes to immerse in the *mikveh*? If there is no formal box you can drop such practices into, does that mean they are not Jewish rituals after all, but aberrations? That did not seem acceptable. Hence, I tried to define Jewish rituals more expansively by thinking about what rituals Jews actually did, as opposed to what they were said to be doing. I began to widen my lens, focusing on the work that any ritual performs:

Rituals establish new communities and sustain existing ones;

- They give us things to do and ways of being that help us to give sense and order to life;
- They carry us through changes and crises in life that might otherwise be unendurable;

- They coordinate our expectations of what we think is going to happen and how we are supposed to react;

- They create boundaries and necessary separations;

- They create bonds and links between people that can transcend time and space;

- They allow us to recognize, experience, and be sustained through life's great joys and sorrows, and all the hard-to-categorize emotions in between;

- They allow us to remember, to mark time, to synchronize our psyches with natural cycles;

- They confirm a sacred presence in the world, and move us to live in ways that are more moral and more righteous.

I came to determine that when a new Jewish ritual fulfills any of these functions, then it is working effectively, even if there are those who may feel uncomfortable with it.

I learned to relinquish the belief that for Jews, the only rituals that really "count" are the ones commanded in the Torah. There is no denying that a source in the Torah, both written and oral, continues to be a compelling source of precedent. But it is acknowledged that nowhere in the Torah does God command Moses to tell the Children of Israel to cover their heads with yarmulkes. There is no commandment in the Torah to have separate dishes for milk and meat. All this I knew, but it easily slipped from my mind.

I would also stop looking backward for signs of an authentic Judaism in an enchanted shtetl. There has never been a totally separate and endogamous community that knows only Jewish culture, beliefs, texts, and traditional observance. Along with nostalgic Judaism, I let go of its familiar icons, for they have been replaced. The carp swimming in the bathtub has been replaced by the kosher sushi restaurant. The matchmaker has given way to speed dating and Jewish Internet dating. The Reform rabbi, once austere in his black robe and respectfully bareheaded, now wears a *kippah* and tallit to match her elegant suit. The *mechitzah* of the Orthodox synagogue that gave women a narrow, dark side passage for prayer has been replaced, in some congregations, by a divider that goes down the middle, halving the congregation equally.[27] Instead, I began to acquire a more nuanced understanding of nostalgia's place in religion. Nostalgia can be a powerfully motivating force in one's religious life, if it leads us to experience loyalty and connection.[28] Certainly, for most liberal Jews, it is not duty, fear, or being commanded by God, but the promise of feeling loyalty and connection, that motivates practice. Of course, nostalgia can be deadening, if it is experienced as a grumpy weddedness to "how things used to be" but never really were, and if it renders anything new as suspect.

Leigh Schmidt, professor of religion at Princeton University, taught me to see that Jews were "making" Judaism and were being expressively Jewish when they sent New Year cards, shopped and cooked for Passover, and searched obsessively for the right dress for the bat mitzvah girl and her mother. I had never thought that going to Hallmark to buy Jewish New Year cards, to the Grand Union for my Passover foods, or to Macy's for a special dress counted as Jewish rituals, but they did. The "real" Jewish ritual was not just the big public moment when the family sat down at the seder or when the shofar was blown in synagogue. The rituals of Judaism encompass all those preparatory acts that come before the main event: inviting guests, the shopping, the trying on, and the kneading and chopping. Likewise, the rituals include the events that come after: cleaning up, writing down memories, and assembling photographs in an album.

I could see then how individuals and communities are continually shaping rituals. Rituals—which I will define as conventional or patterned ways of doing things that have shared and often multiple meanings—have always been the products of a time, a place, available physical materials, and appealing practices of other peoples. All rituals are made and remade, all rituals mean different things to different people, and all rituals were once new and are renewed—even the Jewish rituals we may cherish most of all. For example, the square, store-bought matzah we know and love was once handmade, "round, irregular or oval shaped." Also according to historian Jonathan Sarna, when machine-made matzot were first introduced, some rabbis proclaimed that they were a "dangerous instrument of modernity leading inevitably to assimilation, reform, and apostasy," and would uproot the Torah.[29] Given the iconic nature not just of the store-bought matzah, but the matzah box itself, it is hard to imagine how threateningly novel this practice was in the recent past.

Moreover, when we perform ancient rituals in this place, and in this time, they are no longer the same rituals they once were. With changes in performers, in context, in personal and world history, we could almost go so far as to say that every ritual act is a debut, an innovation. This *Shabbat* meal, this Passover seder, this wedding: each is a first.

Studying the origins of Jewish rituals inevitably has a "demagicalizing" effect. Our discomfort with new Jewish rituals of our lifetimes may dissipate when we learn that many rituals that we consider quintessentially Jewish, such as the *huppah*, trace their origins to the church. When we learn that the rabbis of the Middle Ages failed to suppress the popular folk practice of breaking a glass at a wedding (thought, by Jews and non-Jews alike, to ward off evil spirits), can we tell the contemporary bride and groom who *both* want to break glasses as an expression of egalitarianism that doing so will make their wedding less authentically Jewish?[30]

Some fear that studying ritual might diminish their private experience of its sacredness. I understand their concern. Many who perform rituals regularly do so because they "believe in them" or because they could not imagine living in any other way. They tend to assume that the sacred acts they perform—and the precise ways in which they are performed—are not only authentic but also necessary in maintaining order in their lives, and even cosmic order. Dislocations in ritual might lead a practitioner to feel as if "the entire order of the universe would be destroyed."[31] As Claude Levi-Strauss once explained, to the practitioner in the moment of practice, there is little consciousness of the constructed character of ritual.

But I came to see that the opposite is also true: study increases our capacity to experience our rituals as sacred. Granted, analyzing the ritual we practice requires that we work with two mind-sets, one practical and one scholarly. In the practical mind-set, the one most respectful of our religious commitments, we can maintain the notion that a ritual is "really real"—that is, it reflects divine will, keeps a pact with our ancestors, holds ultimate meanings, and guides us wisely through life's fraught passages. If properly performed, the ritual restores and maintains order in the universe. In the scholarly mind-set, we can acknowledge and contemplate the social and historical construction of ritual, seeing our practice along a continuum. The Jewish commitment to scholarship surely extends beyond the pages of Torah, Mishnah, and Talmud to the rituals we practice and hold dear.

Of this I became ultimately convinced: the new Jewish rituals crop-ping up around me were hardly affronts to God. They were not danger-ous Golden Calf-like practices heralding the demise of Judaism, as I knew it.

They were blessings.

Minhag America

All these new American Jewish practices are the handiwork of a gen-eration that has not allowed anxiety about innovation to hamper rit-ual creativity. With verve, this generation has reshaped familiar practices and designed new ones.

This book explores the most recent version of *minhag* America, the Jewish traditions that have emerged in America at the turn of the 21st century. It is based upon 15 years of ethnographic study of new ritual in dozens of contexts, the extensive collection and analysis of new liturgies and ritual objects, as well as my own personal experiences in ritual innovation.[32] While I take delight in describing the new practices, I am more deeply concerned with the question of how we experience the newness of rituals that are unfamiliar to us. I look at how rituals develop, changing our sensibilities along with our practices, expanding the turf of the sacred to include new spiritual opportunities. Extending the definition of what counts as a sacred practice, this book celebrates the range of creative ways that American Jews are living, making, and elaborating Judaism. We will examine Jewish ritual innovation and transmission as a process and encounter a range of new rituals and rit-ual objects, some through glimpses and others in greater depth.

Judaism is precious but not fragile. As a group, Jews have sur-vived, over and over again, exile, destruction, persecution, and near annihilation. As individuals, we have survived our run-ins with Judaism: rabbis who dismissed important questions, Hebrew schools that bored us, families that pressed too hard for our compliance with traditional ways, congregations we thought we could not afford to join, and communities that shunned interfaith relationships. We have survived theological wrestlings and anger at God.

Surely, we can also survive new Jewish rituals. Our hearts might beat thunderously the first time we see a woman tentatively but bravely lifting an opened Torah scroll and holding it overhead. Did hearts not once beat when the men performed this very practice—*hagbah*—for the first time? I do hope they did. Torah survived, Judaism survived, and Jews were sustained. Innovation will continue.

NOTES:

1. Rabbi Sandy Eisenberg Sasso, foreword to *Celebrating Your New Jewish Daughter*, ed. Debra Nussbaum Cohen (Woodstock, VT: Jewish Lights Publishing, 2001), xi.

2. To me, the most moving popular expression of opening up a Jewish ritual so that one's community can take part is the *"Kaddish"* episode of the television series *Northern Exposure*, in which a Jewish doctor serving a small town in Alaska searches high and low for 10 Jews to constitute a minyan so he can say *Kaddish*, only to discover that the people who can best comfort him are his non-Jewish neighbors, who have been present all along.

3. Was this concept of an "interactive mezuzah" something I made up for this occasion? I think so, but I am not sure. Was it a "take" on a ritual I or someone else had made up earlier? It is altogether possible, as I vaguely recollect once passing out Lucite boxes to a Jewish women's group in Virginia.

4. This blessing was inspired by Peter's work with an international organization called The Children of Abraham Institute in which Jews, Muslims, and Christians join together to study Scripture.

5. Mordecai Kaplan, founder of Reconstructionist Judaism, would likely have referred to this entire toolbox as the repository of Jewish practices of the past, which are selectively reconstructed to construct a spiritually compelling Jewish life of the present.

6. "Something Old, Something New," *JOFA Journal* 11, no. 3 (Summer 1999): 6.

7. Gen. 38:27–30. Zerah's brother Perez edges out his brother.

8. Josh. 2:21.

9. "Va-yeshev," in *The Woman's Torah Commentary*, ed. Rabbi Elyse Goldstein (Woodstock, VT: Jewish Lights Publishing, 2000), p. 97–98.

10. An earlier version of this story of the red thread appears in *Take My Hand*, a guidebook about healing and friendship created by Robbie Bravman Marks and the National Education Division of Hadassah.

11. Literally, "the telling." It is the text used at the seder, the festive Passover meal.

12. Vanessa L. Ochs, "The Contemporary Hagaddah," in *Religious Practices in America*, ed. Colleen McDannell (Princeton: Princeton University Press: 2001), 2:53.

13. Jewish angel cards are an adaptation of *The Angel Cards*, a set of 52 illustrated cards developed in 1978 by Joy Drake and Kathy Tyler of the Scottish Findhorn Foundation. Originally part of the game Transformation, the cards depict angelic qualities and have been used as tools for personal growth, insight, problem solving, and personal transformation.

14. *Malachim* cards suggest such traits as: healing, intention, and patience. See http://www.jewishangelcards.org.

15. The instructions for *Kavanah* (meaning intention) *Cards* are as follows: "Draw a *Kavanah Card* when you begin your day. Contemplate its significance, how it is manifest or lacking in your daily life. You could take it along with you, stand it up on your desk, or place it in your wallet and see it during the day." *Kavanah Cards* suggest such themes as balancing, choosing, flexibility, and stillness. *Kavanah Cards*, http://www.kavanahcards.com.

16. Diane Bloomfield, *Torah Yoga: Experiencing Jewish Wisdom through Classic Postures* (San Francisco: Jossey-Bass, 2004).

17. Katie Zezima, "In Yoga Classes, Poses and Prayer," *New York Times*, September 17, 2005. (Zezima, interviewing Rabbi Klotz, learned that "if Rabbi Klotz is teaching about the Jewish principle of people being grounded on Earth but stretching their souls up, she has students stand in mountain pose as a physical expression of that teaching.") Aleph-Bet Yoga is another form of Jewish yoga. Developed by Stephen A. Rapp, it links yoga postures to the shapes of the Hebrew letters.

18. Lynn Gottlieb, *She Who Dwells Within: A Feminist Vision of a Renewed Judaism* (New York: Harper Collins, 1995), 206.

19. The film *Miriam's Daughters Celebrate*, produced in 1986 by Lily Rivlin, documents two feminist rituals, a baby-girl naming ceremony and a women's seder.

20. For information about the National Havurah Committee, see http://www.havurah.org. Click on "What is a havurah?" under "About Us."

21. There is a picture of that room and the macramé-covered ark on p. 7 of *The First Jewish Catalog,* ed. Richard Siegel, Michael Strassfeld, and Sharon Strassfeld (1973; repr., Philadelphia: The Jewish Publication Society, 1999).

22. Many Renewal rabbis have been ordained privately by Rabbi Zalman Schachter-Shalomi, whose own roots were in the outreach-oriented Chabad movement of Hasidism and who founded, in 1962, a religious fellowship that would be called P'nai Or. The organization now representing the Jewish Renewal movement is called Aleph: Alliance for Jewish Renewal. According to its mission statement, "ALEPH supports and grows the worldwide movement for Jewish renewal by organizing and nurturing communities, developing leadership, creating liturgical and scholarly resources, and working for social and environmental justice." Jewish Renewal rabbis (they often call themselves "rebbes") emphasize the inspiration of Hasidism, describing themselves as "neo-Hasidic." See http://www.aleph.org.

23. The *nigun* is a Jewish spiritual melody often sung with universal sounds, rather than words. Initially used among Hasidim to warm up for prayer and also as a prayer in and of itself, the *nigun* was popularized by the singer Rabbi Shlomo Carlebach and found a place in *havurah* worship.

24. Rabbi Rami Shapiro, *To Listen and Love* (Los Angeles: Simply Jewish Foundation, 2001). See http://www.rabbirami.com.

25. Cantor Sam Weiss, *"Ein Keloheinu," Chazzanut Online,* See http://www.chazzanut.com/articles/on-ein-keloheinu.html. First published on Shamash Jewish music e-mail list, 2002.

26. John Z. Smith, *To Take Place: Toward a Theory in Ritual* (Chicago: University of Chicago Press, 1987), 75.

27. In 1997, Richard L. Axelbaum, Ph.D., a professor of mechanical engineering in the School of Engineering and Applied Science at Washington University, applied for a patent for his "one-way" *mechitzah* that allows Orthodox women to observe the prayers and Torah reading taking place on the men's section, but blocks the men's view of women. The innovative design is used at his own synagogue, Young Israel of St. Louis. See Tony Fitzpatrick, "Engineer's Design Finds Many Uses," http://record.wustl.edu/archive/1998/05-07-98/articles/synagogue.html.

28. For different insights into the role of nostalgia in Jewish practice, see Arnold Eisen, *Rethinking Modern Judaism: Ritual, Commandment, Community* (Chicago: University of Chicago Press, 1998), 89.

29. Jonathan D. Sarna, "How Matzah Became Square," sixth annual lecture of the Victor J. Selmanowitz Chair of Jewish History, Touro College, New York, 2005.

30. Joseph Guttman, "Jewish Medieval Marriage Customs in Art: Creativity and Adaptation, " in *The Jewish Family: Metaphor and Memory*, ed. David Kraemer (Oxford: Oxford University Press, 1989).

31. Claude Levi-Strauss, *The Savage Mind* (Chicago: University of Chicago Press, 1966), 10.

32. The appendix offers methological suggestions for readers in their own study of ritual innovation.

DEMOCRACY,
OPEN ACCESS, AND
JEWISH FEMINISM

T wo forces have influenced the abundance of ritual innovation in contemporary Judaism. The first is the spiritual stance shaped by democracy and open access, and the second is the dramatic change brought by Jewish feminism.

Catalog Judaism

Many innovations came about during a period whose spiritual and moral aesthetic are best captured by the Jewish catalogs. *The First Jewish Catalog* was published by The Jewish Publication Society in 1973, and was followed by a second volume in 1976, and a third in 1980.[1] These volumes documented emerging Jewish rituals and promoted the creative spirit that would lead to more. The writers, Sharon and Michael Strassfeld, expressed an initial hope, which has since been achieved:

If this book opens you to an awareness that there are manifold ways of approaching the facets of Judaism, it will have fulfilled an important function. It is up to you, however, to build on these flexibilities and extend them according to your own creativity.[2]

If the catalogs seem quaint or outdated now, they were revolutionary in their time and cultivated a spirit that continues to exist. And they are still used—where else would you turn if you wanted to make your own shofar out of "the horn of a ram, antelope, gazelle, or of a Rocky Mountain goat"?[3]

When the catalogs were first created, as ritual scholars Lori Lefkovitz and Rona Shapiro observe, "a generation of middle-class Americans [was] in rebellion against empty religious conventions and in search of meaning and self-expression."[4] Democracy and open access were the two keywords behind the catalogs, capturing their spiritual aesthetic. A similar aesthetic characterized the mood of the secular hands-on, do-it-yourself books of that period, the best known being the series of *Whole Earth Catalog*s and the guide to women's health, *Our Bodies, Our Selves,* originally published by the Boston Women's Health Book Collective in 1970.

All these books, offering a plethora of accessible tools to those who embraced counterculturalism, communicated an ideology born out of the movements for peace, civil rights, women's rights, ecology, and consumer rights. You did not have to be an expert or depend upon others to make the world a better place, to be responsible for your own body, or to have a meaningful spiritual life. You, yourself, had the right to challenge inherited traditions and to penetrate formerly mystifying practices. You could—and should—stand up against injustices, challenging paternalistic authorities and venerable institutions. But while you might eschew establishment organizations, you did not have to change the world all by yourself: just as living was communal, projects were cooperative. You, having agency, had the right and responsibility to take control, choose from a broad range of options, and find personal meanings that satisfied you.

American Jews were not the only ones who felt responsible and privileged to navigate the path of their own spiritual journey or

sacred quest. Americans of all faith traditions are expressing a preference for "seeker-oriented spirituality."[5] Few are persuaded to carry
on religious traditions by guilt toward ancestors, the fear of censure
by peers, the loss of religious institutions as a home away from home,
or the threat of punishment in the afterlife. Less willing to be
recruited by God's conventional armies, we sign on as spiritual con-
sumers on the alert for anything and everything that can make life
more worth living. Choosing spirituality[6] over religiosity, we demand
to be touched by diverse experiences that offer us meaning, wisdom,
and paths for inner growth and healing. Sociologist Robert Wuthnow
has described the resurgence of interest in spiritual practices as
engaging "intentionally in activities that deepen ... [one's] relationship
to the sacred."[7] How would the general theme of spiritual quest be
applied to innovation in Judaism in particular? We may find a
response in this comment by Rabbi Arthur Green, a founder of the
Havurah movement and dean of the transdenominational Rabbinical
School of Hebrew College:

> We, diminished both by genocide and assimilation, are a small
> people bearing a great tradition. Most of its heirs do not care
> about this legacy. Some who do love it so much and hold on so
> tightly that they cannot let it move forward into this new and
> universal age that stands before us. And so I would say: If you
> were born a Jew, or if you are drawn to Judaism .... Perhaps what
> the human future needs of you is your reading of, your encounter
> with, this great portion of our shared spiritual legacy.[8]

The Legacy of Catalog Judaism

The legacy of the Jewish catalogs remains strong, and their influence
remains palpable today. Most enduring is a spirit of empowerment
that each individual Jew is presumed to possess.[9] Even if you cannot
draw upon a conventional Jewish education or a history of personal
practice and piety, you may still learn what you need to know to be

Jewish in meaningful ways. With more Jewish texts translated into English than ever before,[10] you can obtain necessary access to valuable resources and navigational tools. The Internet makes available nearly every Judaic resource: Torah, Mishnah, Talmud, midrash, Maimonides' *Guide of the Perplexed*, commentaries on the Torah, responsa, the Zohar, Hasidic texts, Jewish folklore, modern Jewish thinkers, guides to ritual practice, and audio files for cantillation of sacred texts and prayers.

Rather than blaming Jewish tradition for its being hard to penetrate or complaining that synagogues are boring and cold places, you can take responsibility for your own spiritual well-being by shaping Jewish experiences that resonate with your world and your life. You may acknowledge that you are less animated by older religious themes, such as increasing one's devotion to God through acts of penance and purification. Rituals intended to ensure your place in the world to come might be less pressing than those that enhance life right now, especially if they increase joy and mitigate suffering. If you feel that the Judaism with which you are familiar is too rigid or narrow, you may be challenged to open it up and bring in more light. If the Judaism you inherited was insufficiently rigorous and comprehensive, you can establish more intense practices. If the conventional rituals do not adequately celebrate or mark the significant moments of your life, you can take the initiative to make Judaism present for you at those times. In this spirit, it is a sacred undertaking to engage in a critique of pieties of the past, which in turn leads to new devotional practices.[11]

The Jewish catalogs offered concrete alternatives to standing outside of a problematic Judaism, finding a home in a new religion, or dropping out altogether:

> *This is a non-exhaustive selection of materials that offer the possibility for immediate application and integration into one's personal environment. The orientation is to move away from the prefabricated, spoon-fed, nearsighted Judaism into the stream of possibilities for personal responsibility and physical participation .... Many access routes to ritual, celebration, and*

the various facets of life are suggested through the interweaving
of dynamics, laws, intentions, actions, possibilities, etc. You can
plug in wherever you want.[12]

Providing tools and a handy guide to Jewish living, the catalogs inspired people to see themselves as having the agency to dream up new or refreshed rituals. You did not have to be ordained or even "religious" to practice or design and introduce new rituals. You did not have to resolve any theological issues: you could ritualize whether you were sure, unsure, or undecided about God's presence. You did not have to be a member of a congregation or a denomination. If you were seeking company, with the catalog's "blueprints for a *havurah*," you could create your own alternative antiestablishment, antiauthoritarian community for study, celebration, fellowship, and activism.

Unresolved Issues

Despite their belief that a Judaism worth transmitting could be collectively refashioned, there were issues the Jewish catalogs writers could not initially resolve. The best they could do was to point out the problems, suggest resources, and hope for a resolution in the future. (Bear in mind that the catalogs were written before women were ordained as rabbis and cantors in the Conservative movement, and before most Orthodox women had access to advanced study in Torah and Talmud.) One unresolved issue the first catalog struggled with was the problem it called "mutualizing the wedding ceremony." The traditional Jewish wedding, in which the husband essentially pays a "bride price" as in days of old, could be alienating to the couple who saw marriage as a state into which they each entered with equality. In the 1970s, some solutions were proposed. Following the traditional ceremony, for example, the bride might also give the groom a ring or say some additional biblical verses. Despite these gestures, however, the bride continued to lack agency. Revising or dramatically transforming the text of the *ketubah* (marriage contract) was considered with the caveat that such an action was "very tricky and should be approached with great caution,"[13] for an unconventional marriage might not be considered legitimate in the eyes of the Jewish community. For further consultation, the catalog's writers offered the names of three visionary rabbis: Al Axelrod, Larry Kushner, and Everett Gendler, noting that "how far you can go before jeopardizing the validity of the marriage from a Judaic/legal point of view ... is dependent largely on the attitude of your rabbi and your own tolerance for risk."[14]

In fact, it is heartening to see just how many new solutions to Jewish rituals that were problematic during the "catalog years"—particularly from the perspective of gender—have since been addressed and put into place.

Having Choice

New rituals allow more choices than were ever imaginable. In the case of the *ketubah,* the wedding contract given by the groom to the bride, there was once a single text used at most American Jewish weddings, the Aramaic text familiar to Orthodox Jews. Now, when commissioning an original *ketubah* from an artist or purchasing a printed one, a couple can select the text they prefer. Provided the officiant does not object, the *ketubah* one uses need no longer designate the groom's acquisition of the bride. It can express, instead, a couple's mutual commitment to each other, even within an interfaith or same-sex relationship.

The *ketubah* artist Melissa Dinwiddie offers *10* choices for *ketubot:*

1. Orthodox text (traditional Aramaic only).
2. Orthodox with English text (traditional Aramaic with egalitarian English).
3. Conservative with Lieberman clause text (this text, used by the Conservative movement, states that either husband or wife can request a *get*—a Jewish writ of divorce, without which a woman cannot remarry—in the event of a divorce).
4. Conservative with Lieberman clause and English text (Aramaic with

Lieberman clause and egalitarian English. This *ketubah* is innovative in that the Aramaic text is not egalitarian: in acquiring the bride as his wife, the text stipulates that the groom will assume duties and responsibilities; the English text, however, is egalitarian).

5. Egalitarian text (Modern Hebrew and English).
6. Interfaith text (Modern Hebrew and English. This text makes no specific references to Judaism).
7. Equal partners commitment text (Modern Hebrew and English).
8. Anniversary text (Modern Hebrew and English. Given as an anniversary present, or used ceremonially in a new ritual in which a couple reaffirms their vows, typically on a 50th anniversary).
9. Blank (no text).
10. Custom text.

Dinwiddies's interfaith *ketubah* text reads:

On the ___ day of the week, the ___ day of the month of ___ in the year _____, corresponding to _____ in _____, _____, _____ and _____ entered into a mutual covenant as husband and wife, loving and supportive companions in life, and said each to the other: I betroth you to me forever. I betroth you to me in everlasting faithfulness. With trust and devotion, I will be your loving friend as you are mine. Set me as a seal upon your heart, like the seal upon your hand, for love is stronger than death. And I will cherish you, honor you, uphold and sustain you in all truth and sincerity, in times of joy as well as hardship. I will respect you and the divine image within you. May our hearts be united forever in faith and hope. Let our home be built on truth and loving-kindness, rich in wisdom and reverence. May we always keep these words in our hearts as a symbol of our eternal commitment to each other: I am my beloved's and my beloved is mine.

We joyfully enter into this covenant and solemnly accept its obligations. Our promise to each other, in the presence of loving family and friends, is valid and binding.[15]

Jewish Feminism

Jewish feminism has been the second major influence propelling the creation of new Jewish rituals.

Over the last 30 years, Jewish feminists have gained access to advanced study of Torah, and can now read, interpret, and live the Torah in ways that support, sustain, and honor Jewish women. Women have achieved positions of leadership as rabbis, Jewish legal decisors and consultants, professors of Jewish Studies, and leaders of Jewish organizations. With access and position, they have achieved influence. Notably, they have innovated a new body of Jewish rituals being performed here in America and around the world by women as well as men. The many new rituals reclaim, refashion, and revise traditional ways. Felicitously, much has been written describing the birth and growth of American Jewish feminism, its goals and accomplishments since the 1970s, and its current directions, so I need not rehearse that history here.

Jewish Feminist Sourcebooks

Rachel Adler, *Engendering Judaism: An Inclusive Theology and Ethics.*
Judith Baskin, ed., *Jewish Women in Historical Perspective.*
Rachel Biale, *Women and Jewish Law: The Essential Texts, Their History, and Their Relevance for Today.*
Sylvia Barack Fishman, *A Breath of Life: Feminism in the American Jewish Community.*
Ellen Frankel, *The Five Books of Miriam: A Woman's Commentary on the Torah.*
Blu Greenberg, *On Women and Judaism: A View From Tradition.*
Susannah Heschel, ed., *On Being a Jewish Feminist.*
Vanessa Ochs, *Words on Fire: One Woman's Journey into the Sacred.*
Judith Plaskow, *Standing Again at Sinai: Judaism from a Feminist Perspective.*
Riv-Ellen Prell, ed., *Women Remaking Judaism.*

Jewish Feminist Rituals

In creating new rituals, Jewish feminists have alternated between two approaches: adaptation of existing rituals and creation of new ones. In adaptation, the Jewish practices men have traditionally performed are made available for women. (If men wore prayer shawls and yarmulkes, now women would; if 10 men constituted a prayer quorum, now women would be counted too.) Feminists critical of adaptive rituals (sometimes referred to as "add women and stir") have questioned the value of putting their energies into either making women's versions of the already existing, privileged rituals that Jewish men are performing, or fighting for the right to perform those rituals in communities that forbid them to do so. They would ask: Even if all the battles are successfully fought, have Judaism's patriarchal assumptions been challenged? Instead, they have proposed creating "distinctively female alternatives," derived from insights and practices that emerge out of the lives of Jewish women, which will transform Judaism into what Judith Plaskow described as "a religion that women as well as men have a role in shaping."[16]

Years of negotiating between these approaches have compelled feminists to articulate a vision of what a flourishing Jewish women's spirituality might look like. That task is ongoing. For the time being, both paths—adaptation and creation—are still followed.

Jewish feminists continue to ask these core questions that pertain to new ritual: How can we avoid replicating the mind/body split of traditional Judaism and still honor the many experiences particular to women's bodies? What place will the Law have in feminist Jewish practices? Should a patriarchal, transcendent God be replaced in feminist ritual and theology by an immanent spiritual presence? If aspects of the traditional separation of genders benefit women, should they be maintained?

Having created a body of satisfying rituals for women, Jewish feminists are currently asking a new question: how might the fruits of their labors—egalitarianism, acknowledging bodily experiences, marking life's unmarked passages, and attention to healing and inclusiveness—be effectively brought back to the entire community to revise the Judaism that is shared by men and women alike?

Why is Passover (for Jewish Feminists) Different from All Other Holidays?

Passover, more so than any other occasion in Jewish life, has inspired the greatest amount of Jewish feminist ritual innovation. Elizabeth H. Pleck, a historian of American family celebrations, hypothesizes that this is so because for many American Jews, the home-based Passover seder has become the primary occasion for strengthening family ties and expressing pride in Jewish ethnic identity. It is a holiday one can observe without setting foot in synagogue. Second, many are aware that this is a fluid holiday that has evolved over time, from ancient agricultural feast, to historical commemoration of the biblical Exodus, to a more generalized symbol of liberation. Third, its problems for modern women are blatantly evident: unlike other home-based holidays, Passover "was a religious ritual with a written text. The patriarchal words of *haggadot* gave feminists written evidence of unequal regard ...."[17] Finally, many people have deeply entrenched memories of Passover's gender-based division of labor, with women "slaving" in the kitchen and men seated at the table singing about freedom. Given these factors, when new easy-to-follow rituals that critiqued and repaired the practices of the past became available, they were widely adopted.

Characteristics of the New Rituals of Jewish Women

The new women's rituals that have been evolving since the 1970s share certain common characteristics:[18]

1. **Marking the unmarked.** Many women's rituals mark events linked to women's bodily experiences that previously have not evoked formal Jewish responses. They include the onset of menstruation, pregnancy, giving birth, menopause, miscarriage, infertility, hysterectomy, healing after rape and abuse, and completing a course of cancer treatments. Furthermore, the rituals often rec-

ognize the unmarked moments of a woman's social life: becoming a mother, a lover, a divorcée, a widow, or a mourner.

2. **Fostering community.** Often held in all-women groups, the rituals encourage supportive sharing and telling one's own story. This aspect reflects the influence of the consciousness-raising sessions of early secular feminism and has been preserved primarily in Rosh Hodesh groups. Evoking the mood of a support group that has come together, the rituals emphasize the participation of a community of equals, even when the ritual highlights the experience of one woman. They create opportunities for women's bonding across lines that might otherwise be divisive, such as age, economic class, marital status, sexual orientation, and denomination or ideology.[19] They strive to be inclusive, so that even those without Judaic knowledge will feel comfortable.

3. **Allowing for improvisation and personalization.** Most new women's rituals are not meant to change or challenge laws or be legally binding. Thus, they do not have fixed liturgies, specific words that must be said, or a series of actions that must be performed to make the ritual valid. The preference for improvisation, personalization, and choice that the rituals reflect leaves a wide opening for creativity. For example, suggestions for Rosh Hodesh meetings that one might receive from the Hadassah organization or a newer group, "Moving Tradition: It's a Girl Thing" (promoting Rosh Hodesh observance among young girls), are often presented as inspirational templates from which one can pick and choose. Likewise, in Debra Nussbaum Cohen's book of rituals for baby daughters, the reader is given a template for most ceremonies, as well as "hundreds of elements to consider incorporating, in an easy-to-follow menu of options."[20]

4. **Privileging the spirituality of the individual over that of the entire Jewish people.** While the new women's rituals foster the growth and cohesive feelings of communities, they tend to emphasize the psychological and spiritual well-being of individuals within the group. Thus, new rituals typically address questions

of personal meaning rather than concerns about *Klal Yisra'el*, the good of all Jews. In fact, the benchmark of a new ritual's appropriateness is generally the subjective response, "It feels right to me." Because of the emphasis on the individual over the group, it is worth noting that American Jewish feminists have not attempted to create brand-new holidays to be celebrated by all Jewish women or all Jews.

5. **Taking place in less regulated space.** The earliest new women's rituals typically took place in homes or in nature. They were enacted away from institutionalized settings, both physically and metaphysically, so as to avoid being subject to rabbinic, communal, or male jurisdiction. There were feminist seders that moved from one woman's apartment to another each year and then expanded so that they now take place in community centers and catering halls. There are prewedding *mikveh* parties that take place, among women friends, in the ocean, under the moonlight. There are gatherings of Lubavitch Hasidic women in basement recreation rooms for designing and decorating Miriam's tambourines (see chapter 6). Only later, as the new rituals have become more familiar, are they held in synagogues and Jewish community centers.

6. **Being self-explanatory and easy to use.** The new women's rituals are highly user-friendly. To be included as a celebrant, one need only show up, be ready to experience something new, and be willing to temporarily suspend judgment and critique. Effective leaders acknowledge the discomfort one might feel in experiencing a ritual for the first time and assure attendees that however unfamiliar the ritual may be, it is linked to Jewish tradition. When women who are rabbis or ritual experts lead rituals, they often try to minimize their authority by inviting significant group participation—so that they are not experienced as emissaries of God.

The new rituals are performed in gender-neutral or female-friendly English. If a Hebrew verse is spoken, it is often a familiar one, like the *Shehecheyanu* prayer. God language is either degendered or rendered multigendered.

Like traditional rituals that often contain instructions for what to do in the body of the liturgy, and explain why the ritual is done and what its symbolic actions and objects mean (the Passover seder comes readily to mind), the new women's rituals often contain within them instructions, clues for interpretation, and allusions to Jewish history or tradition. If a text is distributed, it will explain everything one needs to know, and Hebrew will be translated and transliterated.

Materials needed for the new ritual are familiar: paper, candles, matches, wine, spices, incense, cups, tambourines, and cloth. One need not travel to Jerusalem or Borough Park or even ponder how to buy those things that are locked inside the glass case of a synagogue gift shop, as they can nearly all be easily found.

7. **Allowing for spontaneity.** The new women's rituals are often flexibly timed. They are created when a situation calls for ritual marking and intensification and are set to fit the emotional needs and schedules of the celebrants. A baby girl's naming ceremony, for instance, rarely takes place on the eighth day of the infant's life or during the first time Torah is read after birth. Instead, it is usually held when the mother has regained her strength after childbirth and when beloved relatives can conveniently arrive. The feminist seder is also flexible: it can take place before Passover or during one of the intermediate days—any time that does not place it in direct competition with family observance.

8. **Promoting a Jewish women's agenda.** As living performances, the new rituals promote a women's agenda within the context of Judaism. That agenda includes respecting women's needs, contributions, and insights. Seeking to address all ritual scenarios in which a woman's status or her agency is in any way diminished under Jewish law, the rituals recognize that if Jewish women have been silenced, belittled, objectified, or demonized in the past, this is no longer acceptable. In some cases, parallel rituals for women have been created as rectifications, and in others, variations on the ritual have been introduced.[21] This maneuvering—often carried out through fresh readings of traditional sources—can be a

formidable project for women who identify as "halakhic Jews," and are reluctant to be viewed as radical or disloyal. But it can be no less daunting for women of other traditions with entrenched practices and assumptions. While Jewish feminists rarely invoke "the will of God" as justification for particular rituals, I believe—and here I speak personally—that to many women, the creation of a Judaism suffused with women's gifts feels divinely sanctioned, even ordained.

The Future Agenda for Jewish Feminist Rituals

Just as the writers of the catalogs once pointed to issues resolvable only in the future, Jewish feminists see beyond the enormous strides they have made in new ritual and look forward to tasks that remain to be done. For instance, the editors of *The Women's Seder Sourcebook* set forth this statement as a call to action to its readers: "It is up to us, as it is up to our daughters, to carry on what Miriam began when she first lifted up her tambourine and invited the women to add their voices to the song of the Jewish people."[22]

Guidebooks

While you will read about many new ritual practices here, this is not really intended as a how-to book. Dozens of guides to new Jewish rituals already exist, typically organized by theme. They include guides to welcoming new baby girls, having a "new" Jewish wedding, navigating a Jewish divorce, holding a women's seder, pregnancy, infertility, celebrating the New Moon, and Jewish meditation. Rabbis, Jewish scholars, and journalists who cover contemporary Judaism are typically the authors of these guidebooks. Often inspired to write because they were once at a loss for the right Jewish ritual, they now provide others with resources they wish they had had. Two groups of readers are addressed: professionals—rabbis, hospital chaplains, synagogues educators, Hillel directors, and ritual leaders—who will use the guides as references; and lay people—individuals seeking Jewish rituals they can perform at particular junctures in their lives. They may find, in addition to rituals, wisdom from the Jewish tradition, as well as comfort and guidance from an author who can claim: "I have been there, and being able to turn to Judaism has made all the difference."

Guidebooks

Penina V. Adelman, *Miriam's Well: Rituals for Jewish Women Around the Year.*

Sharon Cohen Anisfeld, ed., *The Women's Seder Sourcebook: Rituals and Readings for Use at the Passover Seder.*

Susan Berrin, *Celebrating the New Moon: A Rosh Chodesh Anthology.*

Nina Cardin, *Tears of Sorrow, Seeds of Hope: A Jewish Spiritual Companion for Infertility and Pregnancy Loss.*

Debra Nussbaum Cohen, *Celebrating Your New Jewish Daughter: Creating Jewish Ways to Welcome Baby Girls into the Covenant.*

David A. Cooper, *The Handbook of Jewish Meditational Practices.*

Anita Diamant, *The New Jewish Baby Book: Names, Ceremonies & Customs, A Guide for Today's Families.*

Anita Diamant, *The New Jewish Wedding.*

Sandy Falk, Daniel Judson, and Steven A. Rapp, *The Jewish Pregnancy Book: A Resource for the Soul, Body & Mind during Pregnancy, Birth & the First Three Months.*

Nan Fink Geffen, *Discovering Jewish Meditation.*

Gabrielle Kaplan-Mayer, *The Creative Jewish Wedding Book: A Hands-On Guide to New & Old Traditions, Ceremonies & Celebrations.*

Irwin Kula and Vanessa Ochs, eds., *The Book of Jewish Sacred Practices.*

Perry Netter, *Divorce Is a Mitzvah: A Practical Guide to Finding Wholeness and Holiness When Your Marriage Dies.*

Debra Orenstein, ed., *Jewish Women on Life Passages and Personal Milestones.*

Jonathan P. Slater, *Mindful Jewish Living: Compassionate Practice.*

Many of the writers realize their books are educational, even remedial. They imagine that their readers include those whose previous experiences with Judaism may have been limited, unpleasant, or alienating. They write to make amends, to seize the opportunity of the door now opened as a chance for further engagement. They will explicate not only this new ritual and its sources in tradition, but will also try to make the Judaism that has been corrected by the inclusion of new rituals as enticing as possible.

Thus, the guides leave nothing unexplained. They offer clear instructions, providing all Judaic references, never taking a sophisticated level of Judaic knowledge for granted.

Attentive to readers who are anxious or ambivalent about innovation, the authors may clarify how the new rituals either conform to Jewish law or diverge from it, in both cases maintaining the spirit of the law. In so doing, they sanction the suitability of bringing Jewish experience to the situation at hand, especially when it is a new situation, such as a ceremony for a same-sex union. As Deborah Nussbaum Cohen explains in her guide, "We don't feel so much that we are breaking from Jewish tradition as much as we are building upon it, extending it, creating the next chapter of our prayer books."[23]

In their format, the guides often begin by justifying the need for innovation in general and for a specific innovation in particular. They move on to provide information about traditional precedents for their innovations and offer a wide anthology of rituals, some familiar and others recherché. Alongside practices harvested from within Jewish tradition will be resources that they and others have located or created. Endless choices and options are provided for readers who will use the guide as a springboard for their own inventions, and sample ceremonies are provided for those readers who want to follow a scripted ritual. For the reader who has never led a ritual before, the authors may provide a primer, explaining why rituals in general are important and suggesting how to prepare for and perform a ritual (where to hold it, whom to invite, how to prepare the guests—including non-Jews) so that it can be moving. The authors may promise that the process of *building* a ritual, based on the study of Jewish sources, can be as spiritually fulfilling as performing the ritual, especially when it is a collaborative effort. Those who innovate rituals, they suggest, play a role in shaping the Jewish future.

Internet Resources

An Internet search on any individual new Jewish ritual reveals thousands of sources: Google searches for "women's seders" and "Jewish rituals for baby girls" each yielded 500,000 results; and the topic of "New Jewish rituals" yielded no fewer than *two million* results. As a starting point I recommend two trustworthy Web sites available at this time: One, www.Ritualwell.org,[24] provides a comprehensive resource for particular new Jewish rituals and for preparing oneself intellectually and spiritually to innovate. The other, myjewishlearning.com, is a transdenominational educational Web site, rich in content in the areas of holiday and life-cycle rituals.

NOTES:

1. Siegel, Strassfeld, and Strassfeld, *The First Jewish Catalog* (Philadelphia: The Jewish Publication Society, 1973); only the Strassfelds edited *The Second Jewish Catalog: Sources and Resources*, and *The Third Jewish Catalog: Creating Community*.

2. Siegel, Strassfeld, and Strassfeld, *The First Jewish Catalog*, 9.

3. Ibid., 71.

4. Lori Lefkowitz and Rona Shapiro, "The Politics and Aesthetics of Jewish Women's Spirituality," *Nashim* 9 (Spring 2005): 101.

5. Robert Wuthnow, *After Heaven: Spirituality in America since the 1950s* (Berkeley: University of California Press, 1998), 15.

6. Ibid., viii. Wuthnow defines spirituality as "all the beliefs and activities by which individuals attempt to relate their lives to God or to a divine being or some other conception of transcendent reality."

7. Ibid., 169.

8. Arthur Green, "Restoring the Aleph: Judaism for the Contemporary Seeker," *Council for Initiatives in Jewish Education Essay Series* (1996), 25.

9. Surely my Charlottesville congregation is not the only one where each *Shabbat* a different congregant—and not our erudite and eloquent rabbi—will stand before the congregation and offer a *devar Torah*, a "take" on the Torah portion of the week.

10. *The Steinsaltz Edition of the Talmud* (Random House), Judaism's multivolumed compendium of tradition, law, and legend, became available in 1989.

11. This observation is suggested by Barbara Kirshenblatt-Gimblett and Jeffrey Shandler in their essay, "Jews/Media/Religion: Mapping a Field, Building a Resource," *AJS Perspectives* (Spring 2005): 25.

12. Siegel, Strassfeld, and Strassfeld, *The First Jewish Catalog*, 9.

13. Ibid., 164.

14. Ibid., 164. By "risk," they meant that if you were too creative with the text of your *ketubah*, the validity of your marriage might one day be challenged.

15. Melissa Dinwiddie, KetubahWorks, http://www.ketubahworks.com. Reprinted with permission of author.

16. Judith Plaskow, *Standing Again at Sinai*, (San Francisco: Harper San Francisco: 1991), xvi.

17. Elizabeth H. Pleck, *Celebrating the Family: Ethnicity, Consumer Culture, and Family Rituals* (Cambridge: Harvard University Press, 2000), 115.

18. Some of these observations have been inspired by the work of Chava Weissler, *Voices of the Matriarchs* (Boston: Beacon Press, 1998) and Shulamit Magnus, "Reinventing Miriam's Well: Feminist Jewish Ceremonials," in *The Uses of Tradition*, ed. Jack Werthheimer (New York: The Jewish Theological Seminary, 1992).

19. A feature noted by Shulamit Magnus, 344.

20. Debra Nussbaum Cohen, *Celebrating Your New Jewish Daughter: Creating Jewish Ways to Welcome Baby Girls into the Covenant* (Woodstock, VT: Jewish Lights Publishing, 2001), xix.

21. The topic of Orthodox feminists in Israel engaging in these strategies and others is addressed by Irit Koren in "The Bride's Voice: Religious Women Challenge the Wedding Ritual," *Nashim* 10 (Fall 2005).

22. Sharon Cohen Anisfeld, Tara Mohr, and Catherine Spector, eds., *The Women's Seder Sourcebook: Rituals and Readings for Use at the Passover Seder* (Woodstock, VT: Jewish Lights Publishing, 2003), xviii.

23. Nussbaum Cohen, *Celebrating*, 4.

24. Ritualwell.org (http://www.Ritualwell.org) is a project of Kolot: The Center for Jewish Women's and Gender Studies at the Reconstructionist Rabbinical College, and was created by Kolot and Ma'yan: The Jewish Women's Project, a program of the Jewish Community Center in Manhattan.

THE NARRATIVE
APPROACH

A s we try to understand how new Jewish rituals are generated, we will consider them from a variety of angles. We will turn to two approaches as we explore the overarching questions of why we gravitate both toward and away from ritual innovation and how new rituals are incorporated into cultural practice. One approach studies the narratives of new ritual, and the other studies ritual from the perspective of material culture. Narratives will be discussed in this chapter; material culture in chapter 3.

Characteristics of a Narrative of New Ritual

With new rituals come stories. It could be the story of a ritual's beginnings and its development over time. The story might be informally related each time one experiences the ritual, and hence modified with each telling. It could be a more formal narrative: a written document presented as a memoir or scholarly account, one based on personal experiences, interviews, and research. Studying these narratives generated by new rituals can help us better understand their underlying meanings .

We compose such narratives in various ways. We might describe a new ritual's accumulated rules and regulations and comment on distinctions between liturgies or ritual objects for newly created ceremonies (or between various new ritual objects). We might note how this new ritual builds upon or rejects rituals of the past, or how it rehearses major Jewish themes of the past in new forms. In the telling, we might integrate the experiences various people have had as they planned for and performed the new ritual. We might relate the forces that alternately pulled us toward and away from the new ritual. We might speak of our desires, excitement, and entitlement; we might speak of our anxieties about our right to innovate and even our fear of ridicule.

The Poignancy of Narration

Personal narrations of the struggle to balance transformation and tradition often reflect complicated streams of emotions: in the telling, we reveal we feel moved, conflicted, perplexed—sometimes, all at once. We might tell the story to make a point; other times, we discover that the stories we tell reveal multiple, even contradictory points. As an example: One writer applauds two friends—a transgender man and a bisexual woman—for changing the Jewish wedding ceremony to read, "Behold you are sanctified to me with this ring with the traditions of Moses, *Miriam,* and Israel before our God and this community," as they affirm their commitments. The writer tells the couple: "It's beautiful how you have updated our customs in ways meaningful to you both, while preserving the sanctity of their origins." Yet when attending a LGBT (lesbian, gay, bisexual, and transgender) Reform congregation, the same writer finds less peace:

> *I find myself uncomfortable with all the tweaked passages, prayers and melodies of the synagogue's siddur. Admittedly, there are times that I, and several of my friends, are annoyed that the neutralization*

of Hebrew has gone so overboard that the familiar Judaism we were raised with is no longer recognizable. Understandably though, the amended wording is highly significant to many congregants, mostly women, alienated by the original text.[1]

The Pleasure of Reading

Narratives about new ritual can make for fascinating reading, satisfying our curiosity, especially when we believe we are finally learning how the new ritual "really" started—of course, this may not be as straightforward as it seems. Still, we listen with pleasure to the biblical story of the first Passover, or the much more recent first bat mitzvah of Mordecai Kaplan's daughter.

In the coming chapters, I extend the repertoire of ritual narratives with many brief descriptions and three case studies that I will present at greater length, including a story practically unknown outside the Lubavitch Hasidic community: the creation of "Miriam's tambourines," a new ritual that played a potent role for Lubavitch women during the months before and after the death of the Lubavitcher Rebbe.

Formats

Written narratives of new rituals appear in various formats and can serve distinct purposes. Aside from strictly academic studies, they include:

1. **The personal chronicle.** Often published as essays in magazines, in Jewish newspapers, or as chapters of books on contemporary Jewish practice, the narrative that is a personal chronicle starts as a memoir and subsequently becomes a guide for others. In effect, the writer says, "Here is the new Jewish ritual I made, what led up to it, and why I felt it was necessary because the available rituals were neither sufficient nor appropriate. Here are the pertinent sources in Jewish tradition I consulted. Here is how the ritual actu-

ally worked when I performed it, and here are resources and inspirations you can also use if you choose to make the ritual your own."

Frequently, the writer emphasizes the ritual's initial reception—for example, when Julia Andelman circulated a letter describing a megillah reading ritual she and her classmates in rabbinical school instituted (having the congregation repeat aloud verses about Esther in addition to those already repeated about Mordecai), she added this reflection:

I should mention anecdotally that, while there was resistance to the new practice beforehand, it was experienced uniformly positively (as far as I know) once it was actually done, including by those who had been uncomfortable with it initially. It is a very subtle, traditionally resonant, and entirely halakhic way of increasing the celebration of our female biblical role models in our contemporary performance of traditional rituals.

Some writers share their story simply hoping that others might adapt the ritual that they have worked hard to create. Others, impassioned by preserving and promoting Judaism, hope others will be inspired by their story to practice this particular ritual, to study Judaism more deeply, and to embrace a more meaningful Jewish life.

2. **The lifestyle newspaper article.** Appearing in both the Jewish and secular presses, this narrative of new Jewish ritual practices places them in context, notes conflicts and disagreements that have emerged along the way in their establishment, shows geographical and denominational variations, and emphasizes personal touches and creativity. In highlighting the rituals as "news," the story becomes a vehicle for glimpsing a richly textured Judaism as it is being lived now.

Consider one article written by Ira Rifkin for the *Religion News Service*, titled "A Personal Passover Seder: Jews around the Nation Customize Their Ritual Meals with Items of Special Meaning."[2] Rifkin illustrates how many Jews are now personalizing a

3000-year-old tradition, making it fresh, as Rabbi Susan Schnur describes it, "by loving it and making the Seder your own." What are the "individualized extras that make the gathering personally more meaningful," extras, sanctioned by tradition, that draw participants into the story? Rifkin tells us that at Rabbi Schnur's seder, for instance, guests are invited to bring along photographs of individuals who have inspired them in their struggles for physical and spiritual liberation; they can march through the rabbi's bathroom, where "shower and sink on opposite sides of the room have been turned on full force to simulate the parting of the Red Sea; they can eat 'liberated eggs,' produced by free-range chickens." Like the practices or not, glean inspiration to adapt them or not—for Rifkin, this is not the place for debate or discernment. The author's goal here is to document what American Jews are doing.

3. **The educational essay within the context of a Jewish organizational newsletter or Web site.** Just about every Jewish organization has a newsletter or Web site designed to inform recipients, members in good standing or potential members, about the organization's good work, leadership, upcoming events, and the opportunity to make a contribution. The communication is filled with educational materials as well, such as sermons and guides for text study. As part of this educational segment, many of the newsletters now offer essays narrating new rituals that are consistent with the organization's mission and ideology. Often written by rabbis or educators, the narratives not only affirm the existence of the new ritual but assure readers that this is a ritual that is permissible for them to embrace—it is "kosher," so to speak. In fact, it may be implicit that when readers perform the new ritual they have read about, they can also affirm their membership in the organization. For those already performing the ritual, such organizational endorsement is reassuring: while the innovations might deviate from historical convention, the innovators themselves are not deviants. For some, reading a narrative of the new ritual in their organization's official publication may come as a sign of it having been sanctioned and being in keeping with the letter or spirit of Jewish law. These essays tend to offer guidelines, a means

by which the invented ritual outcroppings in their variations might coalesce and become a communal norm.

As an example of this type of narrative, consider this entry in the Summer 2003 newsletter of JOFA, the Jewish Orthodox Feminist Alliance, an organization that draws over 1,000 participants to its annual conference. In a newsletter focusing on weddings, amidst news of the organization and opportunities to make donations, JOFA has chosen to publish an essay by Rabbi Dov Linzer, head of the Orthodox Yeshivat Chovevei Rabbinical School in New York, called *"Ani l'dodi, vi dodi li* (I Am My Beloved's and My Beloved Is Mine): Towards a More Balanced Wedding Ceremony."[3]

Rabbi Linzer chronicles opportunities that exist within *halakhah* for constructing a wedding that is "more balanced between the sexes" and "between tradition and innovation." (If you will recall, this is the very issue that the editors of the catalogs once found so irresolvable.) One might hold a *kallah's tish* (bride's table) before the wedding ceremony proper, in which a bride presides over singing and rejoicing with her female guests while offering them words of Torah. This practice mirrors what the groom does at his *hatan's tish* (groom's table), and would replace the more passive practice of the *kabbalat panim*, in which the bride, sitting on an elaborate chair and flanked by her mother and mother-in-law-to-be, receives her guests. There is the possibility of a ceremony that also parallels the *bedeken* (veiling of the bride) in which the bride is not just herself veiled, but also "veils" her groom, so to speak, with a new tallit or white *kitel* (a ceremonial coat worn by some men on their wedding, on Yom Kippur, and as a shroud). There is also the new circling ritual under the *huppah*. Instead of having only the bride circling the groom seven times, now the bride circles the groom and the groom also circles the bride. Both make circuits, separately or together, that symbolically consecrate the *huppah* as the sacred space of their shared home.

These practices are not only possible and imaginable within *halakhah*, as Rabbi Linzer affirms in his narration. They are actually being done, not just once as a novelty or aberration, but with enough frequency in America and Israel that he can say, based on his experience as a guest and as an officient, that such practices as *huppah* circling are becoming "more common at Modern Orthodox weddings." The practices are being established as *minhag* (a community's custom or practice). If you are a member of JOFA reading this narration, you may be comforted to recognize that others are also struggling with aspects of inherited tradition, sharing your discomforts and sensibilities, and trying out a range of solutions. You may be happy to read, in this same issue, about one groom who admits:

As the day of our wedding drew nearer, I learned that my preoccupations with certain elements of weddings made Esther uncomfortable .... Esther's reasoned dislike of various traditional elements of the ceremony was more persuasive than my sentimental attachments to them .... Regarding the veil, Esther did not want to wear one, but I wanted her to .... In the spirit of compromise, Esther chose to wear a veil that extended slightly below her chin—but only at the bedeken (i.e., not for more than 10 minutes) and not while walking down the aisle. We twinned my veiling of Esther with her dressing me in my kitel ... and those two interventions in each other's wedding garment seemed an appropriately mutual way to reflect the uniqueness of the day.

The Known Compensates for the Unknown

I suspect that some of the keen interest in narratives of new rituals is rooted in our inability to know fully the circumstances and experiences surrounding the conception of ancient rituals. Scholarship tells us that scenarios of ritual adaptation were likely infinitely more complex than one might imagine, and that they remain largely unknowable beyond the hypothetical reconstructions of biblical scholars and archeologists. However rich the resources of Bible and midrash might be, we can never adequately reconstruct the stories of the first Passover seder, the first Day of Atonement, or the first Feast of Booths. Only through "magical thinking" can we be content to take the biblical accounts of these once-new practices at face value, or imagine a narrative such as, "The Lord spoke the instructions for innovation, and the people practiced."

Knowing the story of a new ritual, however, allows us to believe that we can know authoritatively the details of its formation and development. Indeed, we know a great deal more about new rituals than we know about practices presumed to have been initiated in the biblical period. We can trace the appearance of the first decks of *Shabbat* angel cards, the first Miriam's cups, and the first commitment ceremonies between gay partners—to name but a few. And yet, mystery and complexity still surround new ritual, even when the practice seems to have just begun—even if we were there and took photographs. Even if we know the initiators. Even if it was our own idea.

Contemporary Ritual Narratives Can Illuminate Biblical Passages on New Ritual

The contemporary narrative forms we have discussed may help explain a curious phenomenon: When we read in the Torah about new ritual practices that God ordains, we tend to assume that the ancient Israelites immediately and accurately filled God's command. We do not notice that the text itself reveals the fact that inaugurating a new ritual can be a complex and messy process. Many biblical passages concerning ritual are a series of God's spoken directives to Moses concerning practices that are to be performed by the priests or by the people, and they are intended for Moses to relay. We imagine Moses will pass on God's instructions just as he received them. But Moses does not always present the divine plan verbatim. Like anyone who must make a master plan concrete, Moses adds and omits. Moreover, we tend to assume the priests and Israelites performed the new practices correctly the first time, in complete cooperation and obedience, and kept them faithfully the rest of their lives. Such assumptions, I believe, flow from our thirst for precise descriptions of how our ancestors constructed and experienced holiness.

Permitting ourselves to believe that our ancestors dashed from spiritual blueprint to engrained enactment allows us to embrace, for example, the sacred narrative of the holiday of Shavuot and to take literally the edict,

"Na'aseh v'nishma": What God spoke, the people heard. What they heard, they did. What they did, they all sufficiently understood in the same way to perform it correctly the first time. No need for process. No argument. No committees. We imagine they had all the right equipment for novel practices right on hand: anointing oil; sacred donations (burnt offerings, freewill offerings, thanksgiving offerings, meal offerings); libations; unleavened bread; sheaves for the elevation offering; the loud blasting instrument; the booths; the branches of palm trees; leafy branches and willows; the kindling lamps; the 12 loaves (and the recipe); and the frankincense.

Narrations of contemporary ritual can help us read about the biblical rituals with greater accuracy. They demonstrate that a new ritual practice—in biblical times or our own—rarely emerges when a novel edict comes down from on high and is immediately understood, embraced, and enacted by the people. New practices do not come out of the blue—*min hashamayim* (from heaven)—so to speak. Practices being chronicled as new are already in the air; they are "news" that is not really new. Ritual leaders, even those as great as Moses, rarely succeed in imposing totally new practices, top down. Quite often, ritual practices emerge *first* among the folk and then become legislated.

Ritual Stories and Life Stories

Creating narratives of new rituals is as complicated as telling the stories of our lives. There might be a chronology, but there is not always logic and reason behind the unfolding. As we have seen, accidents and misunderstandings matter as much as intentional plans. Behind the construction of any story are complicated motivations for telling it, and they too shape our story. For example, when I told the story of making an "interactive mezuzah," I may have been motivated by the idea of "taking credit" for having a good idea. Perhaps I thought I could do this by emphasizing, in my narration, certain rules that needed to be followed. I may have eliminated from my story all mention of the sources of my idea or speculation about other people having done similar things already. If I had interviewed anyone else who had participated in the "interactive mezuzah" ceremony, I may have discovered that they were not interested in the story of how the ritual began or in the liturgical details of how it was performed. If they were narrating the story, they might have chronicled their own experience, and reflected upon what it felt like to perform the ritual, or how it became part of their spiritual path. They might have focused on the story of how the ritual initially challenged them by its newness and then, over time, felt more meaningful.

One's position in the community and the perspective this position yields also determine how one narrates a new ritual. A rabbi I know leads a congregation of both Reform-leaning and Conservative-leaning members. To serve all their needs, a Reform *Shabbat* service is held on Friday evenings, and a Conservative one is held on Saturday mornings. It is no small task to remain sensitive to each group's sensibilities.

The rabbi tells the story of how he tried to introduce adding the names of the biblical Matriarchs—Sarah, Rebecca, Rachel, and Leah— to the *Amidah* prayer in his congregation's worship services. While the rabbi might well have concentrated on the ethical importance or liturgical issues entailed in adding the Matriarchs, his narration focuses on how the Reform and Conservative members of his diverse congregation reacted differently. As it turns out, he was surprised that this radical change in the liturgy seemed quite acceptable to the Conservative Jews, even though the older version of the *Sim Shalom* prayer book of their movement that the congregation used did not include them. He expected them to be more "conservative" in their attachment to traditional liturgy, raising questions about the permissibility of liturgical addition to so central a prayer.[4] By contrast, the Reform Jews who came to services on Friday nights vocally resisted the addition of the Matriarchs' names. This was not the service with which they were comfortable. Keeping the integrity of their "ancient feeling" and familiar service was more important to them than this ethical nod to feminism, which felt like it could well be a passing fancy. As the rabbi narrates it, the Reform faction of the synagogue was willing to make the change only when the synagogue acquired, for its Friday evening service, the new and updated prayer book of the Reform movement, which included the Matriarchs. At that point, because it seemed inevitable, "engraved in stone," so to speak, and "handed down from on high," the change, which may not have felt acceptable, was nonetheless accepted.

Talmudic Narratives

The Talmud's narratives, just like our own, offer ethnographically convincing evidence that having power plays a complex role not just in negotiating a new ritual but in telling the story of how that ritual came about. (We will, of course, keep in mind that talmudic passages are literary constructions, not ethnographic field notes. What we can draw from them are hints of the cultures they reflect.) In the Babylonian Talmud tractate *Berachot* 19a, we read a teaching of Rabbi Yosef.

Todos of Rome (according to Rashi, he was a prominent Jew, a great scholar, and a respected member of his community) instituted a custom for the Jewish people of Rome. They were to eat a kid that was roasted with its entrails alongside it on Passover night.

Shimon ben Shetach opposed the practice and sent Todos this message: "If you were not Todos, I would excommunicate you for instituting this practice, for you are causing Jews to eat something that resembles the sacrificial offering outside of Jerusalem."

In this passage, we learn that new rituals establish themselves for diverse reasons. (Were we to take this study further, we might ask, "Was there ritual innovation going on in Rabbi Yosef's own time that led him to narrate this story, which took place before his time, in this particular way?") In this case, a motivating factor for Todos of Rome was gaining political power and the capacity to influence people to become habituated to a new practice: eating a roasted kid on the night of Passover in order to remember the Passover sacrifice. Shimon ben Shetach is not at all pleased that Todos has allowed the ritual practice of eating a roasted kid, once permitted only in Jerusalem, to emerge in Rome. If it were anyone other than Todos, he might at least imagine that he could curtail the practice by excommunicating the innovator. But for multiple reasons, ben Shetach is altogether powerless. Todos the innovator has too much going for him: he is prominent, he is a scholar, and he has his community's respect. The establishment of the new ritual is a fait accompli: ben Shetach can register his complaint for the ages, but in his lifetime, he must acknowledge that the new ritual currently stands.

A second talmudic passage, similar to the previous one, narrates how leaders might innovate new rituals in times of crisis. The source is again the Babylonian Talmud, this time tractate *Rosh Hashanah* 29b. This teaching concerning a new shofar-blowing ritual is set after the destruction of the second Temple. In the year in question, Rosh Hashanah was to fall on *Shabbat,* and the recently exiled people were pouring into the city of Yamnia to mark the holiday. The leading scholar of the time, Rabbi Yohannan ben Zakkai, said to the B'nai Batera, a scholarly family of Babylonian descent, "Let us sound the shofar." This was a shocking idea. Outside the walls of Jerusalem, the shofar had never been blown before on Rosh Hashanah when it fell on *Shabbat.* Ben Zakkai must have known how rousing the sound of the shofar could be—and to miss it, this year, would be heartbreaking for an exiled people. How better to ensure continuity, for the B'nai Batera, than to designate another city—Yamnia—to serve, for the purposes of ritual, as the equivalent of Jerusalem?

The B'nai Batera were reasonable people. To ben Zakkai they said, "First, let us discuss it."

"Let us sound the shofar," said ben Zakkai, "and then we shall discuss it."

Because he had more power than the B'nai Batera, there could be no discussion and his decree was apparently followed. Were we to side with ben Zakkai, we might say that this was a time of crisis, with people devastated by loss and dislocation, and at times like these a leader must step forward and take responsibility for making speedy, bold, and unilateral decisions.

After the holiday, the B'nai Batera were prepared to resume the discussion that never really got started. Surely they agreed to the blowing of the shofar on this urgent occasion only because they were certain they could look forward to a proper analysis that would determine the course of the practice in the future.

Ben Zakkai's answer to the B'nai Batera is almost shocking in its presumption and in its realism: "The shofar has now been heard in Yamnia, and we cannot retreat after the act has been performed."

In other words, ben Zakkai says, there is nothing to discuss. The new ritual stands; its precedent will determine future practice.

In this scenario, a new ritual came into being because of a potent decision made in a crisis. Ben Zakkai used his power in two ways: he declared a new ritual permissible and he curtailed the natural discussion that would otherwise have arisen among a community of the learned. But the very performance of the new ritual itself had even more power than ben Zakkai. The shofar had been sounded on *Shabbat*. The ritual had been established, and with that fact on the ground—at least in that era—it stood.[5]

With these insights in mind, we can acknowledge that our ancestors—the leaders and the populace whom we encounter in the Talmud—had the capacity for ritual agency. They were able to revisit their past practices in light of new realities and understandings; they were able to stay connected to formerly dear habits that had come to define their identities while finding ways to institute, justify, and sanctify the practices of their present community. They also had the capacity, through the oral teachings of the Talmud, to transmit a narrative form of their own, sustaining the ever-transforming and still-authentic practices of their time and projecting them into the future. In inheriting the Talmud, which documents our ancestors' conversations and debates concerning practices of Judaism that had been established before their own time, we inherit the possibility of experiencing holiness through evolving ritual.

Establishing a Narrative Chronology

The intense desire to establish a chronology of a new ritual may be illustrated through a digest of e-mail correspondences among a group of young adults who participate in gatherings known as "Jews in the Woods." Note below the challenges of establishing a narrative reconstruction of events, even when the story of a new ritual has unfolded in our own time, within one's circle of friends, or within one's own family.

Importantly, chance and serendipity are elements in new ritual construction, as demonstrated by these e-mails that constitute a narrative. Many know the old joke about the family who ritually cut off the edges of a pot roast[6] generation after generation, only to find that the practice originated because a great-grandmother didn't have a large enough pan; and yet, we may still find it hard to acknowledge that the rituals we cling to may have come about in equally unintentional and roundabout ways.

Case Study: The "e-o" Song of Jews in the Woods

Our story begins in New England in the late 1990s. Students from colleges such as Brown, Dartmouth, Barnard, The Jewish Theological Seminary, Yale, Wesleyan, Vassar, and the Rhode Island School of Design began gathering in New England in the fall for a *Shabbat* retreat *(Shabbaton)* of spirited prayer, study, good eating, intense singing, hiking, and fellowship called Jews in the Woods. Dan Smokeler, then a freshman at Yale, was one of the founders. (Students below the Mason-Dixon line have since created a Southern Jews in the Woods retreat.[7]) Between retreats, many keep their relationships, spirit, and sensitivity to consensus and pluralism alive in cyberspace. Now, the alumni of this group include young rabbis, Jewish educators and community leaders, scholars, and social activists.

The gatherings of Jews in the Woods are, broadly speaking, a new American Jewish ritual. In fact, not only is attending Jews in the Woods a ritual; preparing for it in a mindful, inclusive spirit is its own ritual. For instance, in between gatherings, elaborate, deeply considered plans for how to organize the *Shabbat* gathering are made communally in cyberspace. The group strives as well to be emphatically inclusive of all expressions of Judaism and is obsessively attentive to anyone's experience of being "othered," (that is, made to feel like an outsider), on account of issues such as sexual preference, level of Jewish knowledge, or familiarity with Jewish practice.

Singing, for prayer and delight, is a central and powerful ritual for the Jews in the Woods. Like most young people, they identify strongly with "their" music. In one of their e-mail digests, they attempt to discern how a new, wordless melody (*nigun*) has grown and spread beyond their circle. This new *nigun* is a canon in three parts, which they refer to as: (1)"e-o," (2) "kum kum lei lei," and (3) "bada-dada-da."[8] Initially, they sang the canon with only the first two parts; part three was added later. Over time, it became popular among the Jews in the Woods as a signature piece.

In 2005 Lev Nelson, a graduate of Brown University, began to investigate the history of the "e-o" *nigun*. How did the song spread to the youth of the Reform movement and beyond? he queried. Could he maintain his belief that the *nigun* had its roots in Jews in the Woods? Would he discover that he was wrong and it originated elsewhere? Or would he discover that it was the act of embracing and shaping a new liturgy, rather than inventing it, that made it one's own? Lev writes:

> *I encountered a musical mystery over the summer that I would like your help solving. I was very surprised this summer at camp [Eisner, Reform, in the Berkshires] to hear first kids and then Noam Katz, a songleader-turned-Jewish-rockstar, singing "kum kum lei lei" with the "e-o" and "bada-dada-da" parts all together. I had never heard anybody outside of this/these community/ies sing it before, much less all three parts together, and was under the impression that was our innovation. Adin [his brother] and I are now trying to track down exactly where the nigun in its current three-part configuration started, and how it managed to spread through the NFTY [the youth movement of Reform Jews] camp world. By asking Noam we've traced it to Kutz Camp, which is NFTY's high school leadership camp, and backwards from there possibly to NFTYites at National Convention. Anybody have ideas about how it got there? I think the whole thing is exciting ... and interesting enough to work out the details.*

A former Brown classmate, Zachary Teutsch, responds a few minutes later. Clearly this is a topic that has touched a nerve, but the quick response also reflects the centrality of cybernetic activity among members of this community. Certainly, Zach knows that he played a role in spreading the *nigun* outside Jews in the Woods, having learned two parts of the song at the retreat:

> *I don't know if this is part of the answer but here is the most I have done to teach that beautiful piece of music. Dan Carmeli suggested we teach that set of nigunim during a Shabbaton in Israel. We taught it, with help, to several hundred people (about 325 if I remember correctly) who were part of various Hillel leadership trips last winter. It went over rather well despite our hoarseness. That group of Hillel folks had a lot of Reform folk in it. Perhaps that is part of this ongoing process.*
>
> *I learned the "e-o" / "badadadada" part as a pair from Benj [Kamm, a Brown University student] and possibly EO [Elizabeth Ochs, also a student at Brown] in 2002. I think I first heard the "kum kum lei lei" piece as a companion from Yona, though I had heard it as an independent piece previously. I suspect both Elizabeth and Benj will have more info on the origins of the music.*

A Barnard student, Hannah Krieger-Benson, offers a few more details:

> *Hooray for ethnomusicology.... Anyways, the music in question is two songs. One was taught to me by Elizabeth Ochs (EO!). The other is from a different part of Africa and was taught to me by Shahar. I was the one who first put them together, walking through NYC on Simchat Torah 2003. I was with Shahar, Sarah "bean," Aviva, and Miriam-Simma ... there's the original source and I'm sure the five of us know enough people that could explain the way it has spread.*

Julia Appel of Harvard then adds her voice explaining that, in the summer of 2003, Jews in the Woods who were also active in the Havurah movement first heard parts one and two of the song at the previous summer's National Havurah Institute from Elizabeth Ochs. That fall, they brought the new song with them to the Jews in the Woods retreat.

> *The "e-o" and "bada da da da da" Elizabeth brought back from her trip to South Africa and taught to a bunch of us at a late night singing session at National Havurah Institute the summer of 2003. I believe that's the first time Jews were singing it as a nigun anywhere. From what I remember of Elizabeth's explanation, it was a sports song sung by crowds at soccer games in South Africa that she learned while attending a game.[9] From there it traveled to those in attendance's various communities, most notably Jews in the Woods and Brown Hillel. (I did not even try to introduce it to zmirot [songs sung on the Sabbath] at Harvard Hillel ....) Which is I presume how Zach and the rest of the crew at that Shabbaton in Israel received it. The "kum kum le le" I believe is from the Ethiopian community, but I think Margie Klein can tell us more if I remember correctly?*

Ilan Glazer, who had been working at the Teva Learning Center (a Jewish environmental institute for young people), addresses his peers, titling his letter, "Subject: musical mystery—guilty as charged." I find it interesting that in many of these missives, the writer expresses pride in having been a transmitter, an innovator, or both. Ilan clarifies the mystery of how the song was transmitted from Jews in the Woods to the Kutz camp of the Reform movement, acknowledging his responsibility and also crediting others. (Giving credit is an honored rabbinic practice referred to as *"b'shem omro,"* attributing a teaching to the one who first taught it. Some say that one's care in properly attributing Torah wisdom is rewarded with "a place in the world to come.")

Ilan writes:

> *Hey Fruity Jews,[10] Ok, I did it. Your masked bandit is me. Well, not entirely me. I learned the tripartite "kum kum/e-o/badaum-bada" and some other great tunes at Jews in the Woods Fall*

2003. I immediately taught it to the fabulous staff at the Teva Learning Center where I was working.... It became a major hit at Teva, and we started teaching it to the kids at our Monday evening bonfires, and then singing it during song sessions, and often while out on the trails as well. One of my Teva colleagues is my good friend Chana Rothman, who as of 2004 was one of the head song leaders at Kutz. She brought it there, and called me after teaching it to tell me that it was spreading like wildfire throughout the camp and everyone was singing it. She returned to Kutz this summer and continued to use it. So, I hope that clears it all up for ya. As far as I'm concerned, I hope the tune keeps spreading to more and more camps and youth groups. It's a great tune! Many thanks to Hannah, Elizabeth, and everyone else for putting it all together. Keep those funky tunes coming!

Benj Kamm responds. He grants that it is indeed interesting to gather facts about a central piece of the group's informal liturgy, tracing the way a secular African song became a Jewish *nigun*. It is just as important—more so, perhaps—to see this collaborative and unfolding process as indicative of the spiritual essence that characterizes Jews in the Woods. Benj marvels:

WOW! What a fun musical mystery and solution—and how much it says about how our community functions as a nexus of other Jewish (and non-Jewish spaces). I think this would make a really great story.

Benj, the product of a Jewish day school education, and a long-standing, active member of the Havurah movement since childhood, knows the power of text for Jews and the importance of documentation to forestall the evanescence of memory. He therefore urges his peers to document the "e-o" song, raising a question of a more metaphysical nature to extend the discussion: What can the development of this new ritual reveal about the nature of this nascent Jewish community?

1. *Is there anyone here who'd be excited to talk to a few of the people involved and write up a blurb for our wiki? [The "wiki" is an online knowledge base similar to the Wikipedia open-source encyclopedia, which members of the Jews in the Wood (JITW) community use for organizing events, building community, and storing institutional knowledge and fun stories.]*

2. *Would anyone be interested in writing a (slightly) more formal piece which we could share as an example of what makes JITW, JITW?*

As the e-mail string continues, Alison Levine of Columbia University adds her part:

I also taught the three-part "kum kum" song this summer! I first taught it on my NOLS course [the National Outdoors Leadership School, which teaches wilderness skills] to a group of 9 (not Jewish) college students from all over the country. Who knows where it will go from there? Later in the summer I taught it to a group of ninth graders at Camp Ramah in Canada who loved it and spread it to the rest of the camp. I was also there in Israel and taught it with Zach and Dan on the Shabbaton [Sabbath retreat]. Keep spreading the music and love!

Later in the correspondence, Elizabeth Ochs adds significant clarification. She acknowledges she has enjoyed reading the discussion of the song as it "journeys across borders, campuses, and denominations." She offers her version of the first two parts of the song:

I was in South Africa the summer of 2003 working at an organization called Tikkun, which ran cross-cultural camps for Jewish kids, kids from the townships, etc. The counselors and students from the townships were always singing the most lively and catchy songs. One song had the two-part "e-o," "badada" tune. I asked one of the counselors named Lizeka to teach me this particular song so I could remember it and bring it home. The words (in !Xhosa) were too difficult for me to learn in the short time that I had, but I remembered the tune (of course I probably changed the tune without knowing it once I brought it back). Lizeka told me that this song (with words) is usually sung at sports game events but for the purpose of the camp she and others changed the words to fit the camp-context.... And now we have fit the song into a wordless melody for our context. This dialogue has reminded me that I would like to get back in touch with Lizeka and maybe even learn the song again.

Elizabeth's description helps to explain the original mystery. We now know that the song was a sports song with words, but that a fellow counselor from Cape Town apparently adapted it, giving it new words appropriate for a multicultural, interfaith camp for young people sponsored by the Cape Town Jewish community. While a musicologist might go on to discover the original and adapted words in !Xhosa, the JITW discussants appeared satisfied at last with the facts at hand.

Late in 2005, a new twist, surprising and remarkable, was introduced into the narrative of the "e-o" song. Here was a narrative beyond the imagination of the greatest Jewish fabulists, one involving jumping Maasai warriors and Ethiopian Jews. As difficult as it was to believe, Benj confirmed the authenticity of this narrative.

The story: Leora Abelson, a student at Wesleyan University, spent a semester in Kenya on a study program. During the program, she spent ten days in Tanzania, where, at a workshop with the African Traditional Dance Group, she learned a traditional Tanzanian dance. She and her fellow students were asked to offer a performance of their own for 40 community members who had assembled. She writes:

There are two girls in my program who love to sing as much as I do, so a while ago I taught them the three parts of "kum

kum le le."... We decided to teach it to everyone to perform, and they all learned it and sang it! In the audience was Kesuma, a Maasai warrior who took us to his village the next day for three days of camping. The first night there ... the warriors and young women performed a dance for us, so we thought we ought to perform for them. "Kum kum le le" was the natural choice, plus Kesuma said he loved it. Long story short, we sang it and all the Maasai picked it up immediately and sang along with us, doing their famous jump on every fourth "yo." For the next two days, as we trekked all over this mountain in Maasailand, I could hear people—Maasai and Wazungu (foreigners)—singing it!!! We came back to the center near Arusha and spent the afternoon at an orphanage, where we taught it again. Little kids from the village who came to our performance see us on the road and sing it. I was told once that it's the song (at least the "kum kum le le" part) that Ethiopian Jews sang as they walked to Israel. Does any one have background on that? In any case, it's back in East Africa now.

But in the Fall of 2006, there was another surprise, equally wondrous. A Brown classmate told Elizabeth that the Jewish singer and liturgical composer, Debbie Friedman, a veritable icon for young Jews who had grown up listening to her liturgical compositions, was singing the song and teaching it to others. I contacted Friedman to find out if this was true, and indeed, it was. Young American Jews who believed it was an African song had taught the song to her. But when her African friends heard it, they assured her that they recognized neither the melody nor the words. In jest, Friedman wrote to me, "Personally, I think the song came to us from a shtetl in Pinsk. I have my own thoughts about how the lyrics came to be. If you can let your imagination go ... it is really a scene I have in my mind. Tevya and his three beautiful daughters singing away ... and the cow."

Wherever this song shall travel next, and however its aficionados will give meanings to its unfoldings, a compelling mystery remains, and it should be of great interest to those who worry about how Judaism will be transmitted from one generation to another. Why does singing this particular song resonate so powerfully with young Jews when they gather together? Why has it ignited a fire, so spiritually fulfilling that it has traveled and grown, across Jewish movements, and across continents? (Moreover, why are the young people so eager to establish the narrative of its origins and to document their ownership?) These are precisely the questions Jewish educators ask when they strive to find ways to ignite a passion for Judaism among their students.

One clear answer is that the power of the "e-o" song suggests that young American Jews are yearning to produce and hear a harmony of multiple voices, particularly at a time when neither the State of Israel nor any single concern within American Judaism galvanizes them. When they sing the song within a Jewish context, it allows them to feel Jewish connection. Its international flavor allows them to identify, as well, as citizens of the world. The result: they are simultaneously experiencing distinctiveness and connection.[11]

The Limitations of Narrative

Studying new rituals through narratives has limitations we must keep in mind. In telling the stories of new rituals, it is too easy to imagine that the process develops coherently, with an evolution that can be traced. Even if we are good detectives and we get the facts of the ritual reasonably accurate, it is nearly impossible to pin down the "real" story. Ritual acts have a life of their own. The challenge of constructing a narrative can be confirmed by anyone who has ever read multiple and conflicting versions of the story behind the relatively new ritual of "the orange on a seder plate."[12] I will not attempt to demystify the story of the orange here—that would be impossible; like fairy tales, which are collective efforts that circulate in multiple versions, as Maria Tartar once wrote, it is "reconfigured by each telling to form kaleidoscopic variations with distinctly different effects."[13]

But I will still try to relate the character of the narratives constructed around the orange ritual. By examining this constellation of stories, we will see that narratives share an essential quality of ritual: The act of *telling the story* of a ritual—like a ritual itself—can exist in multiple forms that we continually shape and reshape.

The Story of the Orange

The practice of placing an orange on one's seder plate affirms women's place in the history and observance of Passover; it also affirms women's inclusion as full-fledged liturgical participants, not just in the seder ritual, but in all areas of Judaism. But has the practice itself truly caught on—or has the essential practice become the effort to tell the story of the ritual's origin?

Here is an early telling of the narrative: According to feminist scholar Rabbi Rebecca Alpert, when a Jewish women's group at the University of California at Berkeley once invited the Chabad House *rebbetzin* (rabbi's wife) to speak, they asked her about the place of lesbians in Judaism. The *rebbetzin* responded that lesbianism (compared to male homosexuality) represented but a small transgression, one that was like "eating bread on Passover," that is, something you would try not to do, but if you did so by accident, you would not be considered an outcast. That spring, the group was still troubled by the *rebbetzin's* curious response. They were convinced lesbianism was seen as being "much more problematic and transgressive in a Jewish context."[14] In a ritual response, they placed bread on their seder plate that year as a gesture of solidarity with lesbians. This gesture struck a nerve and spread. By the 1980s, it was included in several lesbian *haggadot.* Groups not comfortable handling bread, forbidden on Passover, just told the story about the *rebbetzin* and the group that initially used bread as a ritual object. An orange soon replaced the ritually problematic bread, and it came to represent the inclusion of gay women as well as gay men in Judaism. (Some have noted that the orange, which originally pointed to lesbians in Judaism, was communally co-opted when its meaning was broadened to lesbians and gays in Judaism, and then to all feminist change in Judaism.)

The story soon changed. In later tellings, it became "a Jewish feminist, who, speaking in Florida, was upbraided by a man who said to her that women rabbis had as much of a role in Judaism as oranges did on a seder plate, or alternatively that women had as much place on the *bimah* as oranges do on the seder plate."[15] (Though feminist scholar Susannah Heschel, daughter of Abraham Joshua Heschel, is often cast in the role of "the feminist" in this tale, she has denied having participated in any such interchange.)[16]

With this new telling in place, a telling that obscured the earlier ones, the orange on the seder plate has come to represent the full participation of women in Judaism. The symbol affirms that women and their wisdom *do* indeed belong at the seder table, no matter how unsettling their involved presence may be to others.

With its ever-changing story of origins, the Passover orange continues to spark discussion on the Internet about how new rituals emerge in Judaism. Such self-consciousness about the development of new rituals characterizes this contemporary period in which lay people feel as entitled to experiment ritually as clergy do. This posting in 1998 on a moderated discussion group of the National Havurah Committee (www.havurah.org) suggests the democratic flavor of such discussions. Here, Justin Lewis, a Jewish storyteller and a rabbi, casts doubts about Alpert's version of the orange story, which leads him to a more generalized reflection about the origins of new rituals. (His posting recalls Benj Kamm's thoughts about what can be learned from a particular group's reflections on the origins of its rituals.)

How ought one, Lewis asks, reflect upon the origins of ritual in the context of a life of spiritual practice? He writes:

> *It is absolutely fascinating to me that a custom that has become well known in the last decade and can't be much older is already shrouded in mystery and having different stories attached to it. We've even heard (maybe this is a strictly Canadian variant) about people putting a lemon on the seder plate. This is a wonderful example of how impossible it is to find the real reason for a Jewish custom, as many of us so often want to do in our learning. After all, to many people "a rabbi said that*

a woman belongs on the bimah ...." is what the custom means. This—after a decade or two—how much more so do customs and meanings change and accumulate over hundreds of years. To me it makes more sense, therefore, to consider what a custom is like experientially, what it feels like to do it, and also which of the many meanings assigned to it ring true to us and what new meanings we can give to it—rather than trying to figure out and focusing on an original meaning, either mythical or historical.

Lewis appears to advise those who are engaged in practicing new ritual that they need not become preoccupied with the origins of that ritual. He reminds us that the narrative of a ritual's origins is a literary artifice that will keep changing to fit the perceived meanings of the ritual as it is being established. The longer a ritual is around, the more capacious its ability to hold multiple meanings. People may take less interest in how it came about, for its origins seem to feel primordial, or at least as old as Sinai. Consider the *karpas* (parsley or other green vegetable) on the seder plate that can represent spring, and when dipped in salt water, can also symbolize the tears of the Israelites, the difference of this night of Passover, and in our time, environmental concerns. That the *karpas* probably originated as an hors d'oeuvre at Greek banquets comes as a curious fact without liturgical or symbolic weight.

What ought to matter to practitioners, Lewis advises, is how they themselves actually feel when they perform the ritual. Such advice is relevant to all who construct narratives of new ritual. Does it feel right, Lewis asks? Can it contain meanings that feel sufficiently linked to the past and meanings that are spiritually moving in the present? (Interestingly, as much as people are fascinated by the story of the orange, the ritual is not catching on widely, and when it does appear, it comes as a visual joke of sorts. Perhaps it hasn't caught on because the orange evokes no sacred Jewish texts or practices, although we could argue that the orange is a reminder of the precept to empathize and care for the stranger, the one who is different).

The Real Beginning

When we notice that the sacred has come to be experienced in distinctly new ways, we may find ourselves driven to reduce the phenomenon to a single story of how an inkling or a yearning became a practice, obscuring the accidental elements and highlighting those that are intentional. As the stories of the orange suggest, however, this is not always possible. Most new rituals have multiple originators and multiple initiations—and as they percolate, various stories of origin often accompany the performance of the ritual. The mishearings generated in the game of "telephone" are a useful image here. One performs a new ritual and hears the story of its origin; when one performs it again, one may choose to tell as its story of origin not the tale one heard before, but the story of one's own "first time"—an interesting story in its own right. Perhaps the details of that first story are unintentionally altered or forgotten. By the time people are present at the third performance of a new ritual, one is hearing stories of multiple first times—all of them, in their own way, true and relevant.

Like the game of telephone, a narrative reconstruction can authorize certain versions of the ritual and exclude others, leading one to an unconscious conclusion that there are right and wrong ways to perform or even think about an emerging ritual. It can lead one to conclude that the story of its affective import—how it meets certain pressing emotional needs of a community—is less important than the scholarly and rabbinical discussions carried out in order for the new ritual to be understood as acceptable within Jewish law. The very terms "evolution" and "development" are problematic in the context of new ritual, suggesting as they do that in time, the new ritual necessarily gets better, becomes more effective, or achieves the form that it was "meant" to have.

Despite the multiple, shifting strands of narrative that explain ritual practice, this same narrative can ironically lead us *away* from acknowledging these qualities of inventedness and fluidity present in most new ritual. Freezing a new ritual in time can privilege beginnings over the subsequent path: one need only imagine the problem of a eulogy for an 80-year-old man that emphasizes only the story of how he was born and omits the story of the rest of his life.

Blind Spots

Just as our interests shape the way we construct our narratives of new ritual, so do our blind spots. For instance, I tend to assume people from all backgrounds should be made to feel welcome in the context of a new Jewish ritual. Thus, in narrating a new ritual, I might fail to chronicle how being attentive to the presence of non-Jews and unaffiliated Jews may have played a significant role in its construction or performance. Additionally, I often assume that egalitarianism is both desirable and possible within Jewish ritual practice. Therefore, while some might narrate the story of a new ritual (e.g., the ceremonial signing of a prenuptial clause that gives Jewish women the legal protections that are absent from the traditional *ketubah*) by emphasizing the efforts to "legitimize it" within Jewish law, I might eliminate or sideline the topic of achieving legitimacy in my narration, choosing instead to highlight the way the ritual's spiritual and ethical aspects were crafted. Of course, blind spots may also be strategic. Those with an agenda at stake may refrain from exploring certain issues in their ritual narratives because it permits them to maximize one set of concerns and minimize others—with the hope that they might figuratively disappear from the discourse.

NOTES:

1. T. J. Michaels and Ali Cannon, "Whose Side Are You On? Transgender at the Western Wall," in *Queer Jews,* ed. David Shneer and Caryn Aviv (New York: Routledge, 2002), 96.

2. April 9, 1997.

3. Dov Linzer, "Towards a More Balanced Wedding Ceremony," *JOFA Journal* 4, no. 2 (Summer 2003).

4. I suspect that many of the Conservative Jews were aware of this change being made in many other congregations and were glad that their rabbi took a formal initiative to introduce it. Perhaps they themselves had consulted rabbinic and scholarly studies about the implications of adding new words to old prayers.

5. In some Reform congregations, when Rosh Hashanah begins on *Shabbat,* the shofar is still sounded, as many worshippers will only be attending services on the first day.

6. When Christians tell the joke, it is a Christmas ham; when Jews tell it, it is a brisket.

7. I have gleaned information about Jews in the Woods primarily from both of my daughters, who have attended their retreats, and from a former student, Abigail Sage Bellows, who has written about Jews in the Woods in her senior research paper for the Jewish Studies Program at the University of Virginia.

8. Elizabeth Ochs shared the digest with me, knowing it might illuminate my studies of new ritual. I read the correspondence with particular delight, for two reasons: First, many of the discussants are the sons and daughters of my peers in the Havurah movement—and I feel proud to see how they are finding fresh ways of their own to make Judaism meaningful for their generation. Second, as the e-mails will reveal, I believe I knew one of the clues they were seeking, which is how the melody first made its way to Jews in the Woods.

9. I have it on good authority that Elizabeth Ochs did not learn the song while she herself was at a soccer game. But she was in South Africa that summer, and heard the song there. She sang it to her parents when we picked her up upon her return to the States. Later that summer, she indeed taught it to her friends at the National Havurah Committee Summer Institute and was surprised it had caught on.

10. The affectionate name some in the group use in referring to each other.

11. Abby Bellows (personal communication, 2005) suggests that in communities that value inclusivity, it is essential to have a number of simple songs on hand for newcomers, not to mention non-Jews, to catch on to quickly (as well as for "regulars" to enjoy) so as to foster a sense of unity and belonging. She also adds a musical observation: In keeping with the form of most traditional African music, the idea is to have some baseline melody (in this case, "e-o"), with variations over it. Some hold to the baseline, while others harmonize and add new parts. There is a balance between mutual appreciation and listening, and each person having the mobility to express their individuality or *kavanah* of the moment. She says, "I see this as a value in much of the music we celebrate: it reflects the balance of consensus and creativity for which we strive." Zach Teutsch (personal communication, July 2006) offers this analysis: "Apparently part of the power of the JITW social network was (perhaps still is) the ability to quickly and effectively deliver music and ideas to key people in diverse and influential young Jewish communities. It seems to be somewhat of a connector-meets-maven role in Gladwell's terms and it's not surprising that that combination has resulted in several tipping points. Many of the folks who come to JITW *shabbatonim*

are early adopters as well as leaders in a very wide variety of denominational communities. It is partly because of that diversity that JITW can facilitate neat things jumping across boundaries. This process of facilitating the learning and sharing of wonderful innovations in music, ritual, and thought from many different communities with varied ideologies is certainly the best aspect of trans-denominationalism."

12. Rebecca T. Alpert, *Like Bread on the Seder Plate: Jewish Lesbians and the Transformation of Tradition* (New York: Columbia University Press, 1997).

13. Maria Tartar, *The Classic Fairy Tales* (New York: W. W. Norton and Company, 1999), ix.

14. Ibid., 2.

15. Ibid., 3. This is the version Rabbi Stuart Kelman of congregation Netivot Shalom offered his congregation in 2001: "An incident that happened in Florida a few years ago. Susanna Heschel, one of our leading theologians, was addressing a group during an adult education series. Her topic, as is often the case, centered on the role of women in ritual, in particular with women as rabbis. Suddenly, a man stood up, and in exasperation shouted out, 'A woman belongs on the *bimah* as much as an orange belongs on a seder plate!!!' Well, our custom today is to place an orange on our seder plate stating very publicly that women do belong on the *bimah!*"

16. Journalist Aleza Goldsmith, writing for *The Jewish Bulletin of San Francisco,* interviewed Susanna Heschel. Below is her quote:

> *What you hear is not what actually happened,"* Heschel recently told a crowd at the Marin Jewish Community Center program on "Women Who Shook the Jewish World." "It's been circulating for a long time and it's become a bit of an urban legend." Here is what actually happened: Heschel was visiting a college in the Northeast where she learned that some of the students had started placing crusts of bread on their seder plates as a way to express the exclusion of women and homosexuals from Judaism. Heschel thought this was great. But since it violated the Passover dietary restrictions, she decided to modify the act, placing an orange on the plate instead of the bread crust to represent both women and homosexuals. "The first year I used a tangerine," the mother of two revealed to the packed room of mostly women and some men. "Everyone at the seder got a section of it and as we ate it. We would spit out the seeds in solidarity with homosexuals—the seeds represented homophobia." Heschel, chair of the Jewish Studies Program at Dartmouth College, said she

was "horrified" at first by the way the story of the orange metamor-
phosed. First, "they took my idea and put it into a man's mouth." Sec-
ond, "they erased the whole idea of the homophobia that needs to be
spit out.

"Orange-on-Seder-Plate Tale Is Flawed, Feminist Says," *The Jewish News*
Weekly, April 5, 2002.

MATERIAL CULTURE: NEW RITUALS AND RITUAL OBJECTS

R eligious objects have great power. Serving as spiritual agents, they produce a sense of religious identity, prompt holy and ethical actions, and forge connections between the individual and the Jewish community.

While not all new Jewish rituals are linked to new ritual objects, a good many are. Some objects—such as an orange on the seder plate, a Miriam's cup, a mezuzah made from the shards of glass shattered at a wedding ceremony, even a car mezuzah—may be even more familiar than the rituals in which they are used. Consequently, we need to understand how the study of material culture can illuminate our understanding of the role objects play in new Jewish rituals.

Beginning with Objects

"I want to create a new Jewish ritual to welcome our adopted baby. What do we need to say and do? What do we need to get?"

Many assume this is how a new ritual practice emerges: Step one—someone has an idea, expresses a belief, or states a need. Step two—she or he designs a liturgy (that is, a text to be said or sung) and a ceremony. Step three: the objects needed—say, a special cup, a tambourine, a ceremonial cloth—are found or made. Step four: with all the elements

Baruch Ha-car?

If it is affixed to your car with a magnet, it's called a car mezuzah, even if it is not actually a legitimate mezuzah with parchment, but rather a container for the traveler's prayer. If it is to be carried or hung from the rearview mirror, it is called by the tongue-in-cheek title *"Baruch ha-Car."* I did not understand how such an object, evoking the traditional mezuzah hung in doorways, was meant to be used, even after I had seen it described in a Judaica catalogue:

> The Baruch Ha-Car Traveler's Prayer offers spiritual comfort for travelers along life's highways. This cylindrical capsule of solid brass and clear acrylic contains a traditional prayer for those setting out on journeys.

The traditional mezuzah belongs on the outside and inside doors of one's house—but on one's car? At first, this very idea of turning a mezuzah into a car protector seemed to me misguided. (Though I had to acknowledge that thousands of Jews wear mezuzah-shaped necklaces and find them so affirming of their Jewish identity that they never take them off.) Then one day in Colorado, I was given a ride by a rabbi I had been visiting. In his car—affixed to the door on the driver's side by a magnet—I saw my first car mezuzah in use. He explained that he spent a lot of time in his car and tended to be a "lead foot." His wife gave him the car mezuzah to remind him to drive slowly and safely, for his sake and for others. Seeing it being used meaningfully by a rabbi I admired challenged my earlier misgivings. If the presence of this new object prompted the rabbi, over and over again, to "choose life"—a central Jewish concept—was it not serving a valid and sacred ritual role?

assembled—the idea, the words, and the props—the new ritual is per-formed. In a word, spoken liturgies, texts, actions, and ritual objects are all developed or collected, and then integrated, to concretize or enact beliefs.

The creation of new ritual is usually far more complex than this orderly, belief-driven scenario. A new ritual practice can emerge *because* a concrete object has been created, borrowed, or transformed. *After* a practice has been reenacted over time, a set of beliefs might emerge. For example, a song, which is a kind of artifact, can give rise to a practice. (Here I am thinking of Debbie Friedman's rendition of the traditional healing prayer, *Mi Shebeirach.* Her song was adopted by hundreds of congregations, and its use, for many, has established a conviction that God's healing presence can be invoked and felt.) The object—in this case, the song—has what can be referred to as agency. Over time, the singing of this song causes beliefs about Jewish healing to emerge and become established.

At times, we may encounter a new object that has appeared within Jewish life and that is still calling out for a ritual and a set of beliefs to which it will be linked. Such was the case for Rabbi Stuart Kelman's Berkeley, California, congregation, Netivot Shalom. Writing in his congregational newsletter in May 2001, the rabbi reported that two new objects had appeared at his family's Passover seder that year: an orange and a cup for Miriam. He explained both their origins and how they were being used. Then another object, without an apparent place, appeared at his office. Rabbi Kelman writes:

> *A few weeks ago, Brenda Goldstein came into my office with an offer that I couldn't refuse. Brenda, as many of you know, is not only a superb shlichat tzibbur (prayer leader), but also a won-derful Hebrew calligrapher. She has been working with a famous local ceramic artist, Susan Felix, calligraphing Hebrew letters on the inner surface of some of Susan Felix's bowls. Brenda has graciously given our shul one of these creations. Now, will this bowl with Hebrew letters be used as an object for a new ritual, or will it remain simply an exquisite art object? (It resides, for safety's sake, in my office, but is available for all*

to come see.) My question to you: What kind of ritual might this bowl be used for?

I've been struggling with this for a while and the best I can come up with is to use it for some ceremony around Shavuot (Feast of Weeks). Little children might hold some sort of cloth letter in their hands (perhaps the first initial of their Hebrew name) and drop it in the bowl and say a bracha (blessing) about learning Torah, with parents then teaching their child some piece of Torah. In earlier times, honey was placed on a slate when the child first came to school as a symbol of the sweetness of learning Torah. Is this an appropriate way to physically describe our affirmation of Jewish learning in the community? Maybe it should be used around the time of bar/bat mitzvah? Other suggestions are welcome. Oranges, goblets and a bowl, each of which has/can become a new object to be part of a ritual.[1]

Thus the rabbi had, in his possession, a new ritual object created by artists that might be embraced by his community. In fact, the object might have the power to inspire the community to create a ritual practice that would enable them to struggle with change in the 21st century and create a tradition for the future. From this object, from the practice, and perhaps from texts that emerged, a belief would be set into place.

What Is Material Culture?

The term "material culture" has been defined by anthropologist James Dietz as "objects used by humans to cope with the physical world, to facilitate social intercourse, and to benefit our state of mind."[2] The objects people make (sometimes referred to as artifacts, meaning "things made by people") reveal interconnections: "A house, a carving, or a food dish reflects shared experience, community, ideas, and values connecting individuals and groups to one another and to the environment," writes Simon J. Bronner, and ... "the term 'material culture' is often used to point to the weave of objects in the everyday lives of individuals and communities."[3] While objects are created and consumed by humans they stand apart from humans, and have a life, a physical space, and a history of their own. At the same time, "despite the 'otherness' of objects, humans nevertheless project their own ideas and emotions onto them and see them as reflections of themselves."[4] Objects do give us access to the beliefs of individuals and societies. Made objects, according to Jules David Prown, "reflect, consciously or unconsciously, directly or indirectly, the beliefs of the individual who made, commissioned, purchased, or used them, and by extension, the beliefs of the larger society to which they belonged."[5]

When the study of material culture emerged as an academic field in the 1970s, scholars (anthropologists, archeologists, folklorists, and historians of religion, art, architecture, and technology) were anxious to demonstrate that material things matter, not just because they are constituted by social worlds, but also because material objects themselves serve to constitute those worlds. Currently the focus in material culture studies has shifted to *how* things matter, *to whom*, and *in what ways*.

In addition to scholars, everyday people in our daily lives contemplate material culture. We think about material culture when we shop for food and clothes, choose and give gifts, prepare meals, stitch quilts, take photographs, plant gardens, decorate houses, collect souvenirs, go house hunting. We know intimately that objects have value and meaning, and we are savvy about discerning both. We acquire expertise: we read, do research, ask around. From the consumer reports we know which car is the best buy, and because we understand how objects play out in our culture, we will also know which car carries more social prestige and what kinds of assumptions people tend to make about each other (the soccer-mom SUV, the midlife-crisis red convertible) based on the cars they drive. We know that objects can change the quality, course, and feelings of our lives (take for example, the impact of getting and wearing a diamond engagement ring). We are also well aware of changes in trends: we know that the computer and television are now the heart and hearth of family life in a way the typewriter, encyclopedia, and telephone never were.

We also experience material objects as vessels of identity and memory, and we understand that when an object becomes an heirloom or a souvenir it increases in value. We know that if we did not have the samovar our grandparents brought from Russia, we would hold less of our grandparents' lives, less of their memories, and we would therefore be less ourselves. We know that objects have intrinsic properties and rules that must be respected. Thus, scholars of material culture are especially attentive to the methods of studying objects as everyday people employ them.

Reading Material Objects

When speaking about material objects, it has often been said that they can be "read"; that is, we encounter them, interpret them, and attempt to understand them the same way we understand texts. Typically, it is the *meaning* of the objects that is read, a meaning that is culturally constructed. Objects are said to have complex, complicated stories that transmit cultural knowledge, but in codified ways. When studying a new ritual object, one must pay attention not only to what it is, what it can mean, and how it is variously used, but also to its materiality and shape, to how it moves (or is distributed) from maker to user, and to how it is used and experienced according to variables of time and place.

Material objects can be read as repositories and producers of cultural memory. They are read, as well, as the field upon which battles of memory are fought: they are a place where meanings can be contested, resisted, or repressed.

But not all scholars of material culture speak of "reading" material culture. Instead, some scholars see limitations in drawing too close an analogy between objects and texts. While objects, like texts, have meanings, both overt and symbolic, objects also have *materiality* that must be reckoned with. Like persons who have bodies, objects are embodied in matter, and that matter, so to speak, matters. As an alternative to reading material culture, Igor Kopytoff suggests we encounter objects just as we encounter the lives of real people, and seek the cultural biographies of objects. If people are constructed and constrained by society, then so are objects. Kopytoff explains his methodology:

> *In doing the biography of a thing, one would ask questions similar to those one asks about people: What, sociologically, are the biographical possibilities inherent in its "status" and in the period and culture, and how are these possibilities realized? Where does the thing come from and who made it? What has been its career so far, and what do people consider to be an ideal career for such things? What are the recognized "ages" or "periods" in the thing's "life" and what are the cultural markers for them? How does the thing's use change with its age, and what happens to it when it reaches the end of its usefulness?*[6]

Just as people in complex societies have complicated and even conflicting social identities, objects are also subject to multiple and shifting identities. New ritual objects, like people, have social lives. They have a life span, a biography that calls for narration.

Studying New Ritual through the Lens of Material Culture

Religious people are intimately acquainted with material culture: ordinary objects such as bread, wine, hats, shawls, chairs, golden rings, and roasted eggs create, express, embody, and reflect *sacredness*. For sacredness, one could substitute such words as holiness, sanctity, separateness, and specialness. Or one could use the Jewish term that describes all abstract and concrete movements toward sacredness: *kedushah*.

Gazing at new ritual through the lens of material culture, we may come to question the dualisms of religious life once taken for granted: sacred/profane, mind/body, theoretical/practical, beliefs/practices, divine/human, things/people, and of course—spiritual/material. We can discover that such dualisms do not fully and accurately describe reality or even our own experience of reality. Even if we were to define the spiritual and the material as polar opposites and were to continue to privilege the spiritual (that is, the disembodied idea, the celestial, and the cerebral) over the material, we still cannot ignore the significance of materiality in the way religion is lived. One of anthropologist Barbara Myerhoff's elderly Jewish informants tells a story, which he attributes to Martin Buber, that nicely articulates this idea:

> *It tells here about two men who are worried about the holiness of the Sabbath. "What is it that makes something holy?" they ask. They decide to make a test to see what happens when they have Sabbath on a weekday. So they make the Sabbath in the middle of the week, everything they do right, and it feels the same way as on Saturday. This is alarming, so they take the problem to the rabbi to explain. Here is what the rabbi tells them: "If you put on Sabbath clothes and Sabbath caps it is quite right that you had a feeling of Sabbath holiness. Because Sabbath clothes and Sabbath caps have the power of drawing the light of the Sabbath holiness down to earth."*[7]

Material objects are not merely substitutes for the stuff of greater weight and value that counts more or means more in the academic and even cosmic schemes of things—such as ideas and ideologies expressed in texts or beliefs held by a people, in their theological discussions, and in their dutifully recited articles of faith. I am not suggesting that as we study the objects of new rituals, we will discover that they are *more* eloquent, *more* instructive, or *more* essential than sacred texts and beliefs in constructing religiosity, establishing religious identity, or studying religions. I am suggesting, however, that the new ritual objects are equally eloquent and pivotal. John Cort once proposed that scholars of religion ask this question: What would happen if we looked at text-heavy religions and those less bound by text, with "material culture as our starting point? If we look first at the objects and base our attempts at understanding on them, will we emerge from our study with a different view of the tradition?"[8]

People living and constructing religious, spiritual lives know that objects are teachers and objects are revelatory. They know it in their very bodies. "People," writes historian of religions Colleen McDannell, "build religion into the landscape, they make and buy pious images for their homes, and they wear special reminders of the faith next to their bodies. ... It is the continual interaction with objects and images that makes one religious in a particular manner."[9]

We make objects because objects make us, and objects make us because we make objects. If this were not the case in Judaism, the central mitzvah (sacred obligation) of Passover would be reading about or contemplating bondage in Egypt; but it is not. Were the real matzah (which, by sacred obligation, one bakes or buys, displays, eats, and hides) less important than the abstract idea of matzah, Jews might read, think, discuss, and remember matzah, and neither make, use, point to, nor consume it. Rather, the experience of bondage, the memory of bondage, and the possibility of new expressions of bondage are made tangibly present in the matzah, the flat cracker that proclaims in its shape, taste, crumbling fragility, and digestive aftereffect: "This is not-bread, this is the not-bread of affliction."

The matzah matters, then, as does the box it comes in, the brand name, the country of provenance (especially when it is Israel), and the competing sale prices at Waldbaum's and the Food Emporium, published annually as full-page ads in *The New York Times*. The imprint of the rabbi's name matters, as it certifies, endorses, and extends enduring blessing to the purchased matzah. The specially chosen plate reserved for this use matters, and so does the cover placed upon it (perhaps crude but beloved, for it was made by one's child back in nursery school; perhaps costly and beautiful, designed and embroidered by artisans and representing one's good taste). And it matters where on the Passover table the matzah is placed, and who sits nearest to it, and who is selected to uncover it, point to it, bless it, divide it for others, and determine who gets it first and who gets what size. It matters who piles the matzah high with horseradish (store bought or homemade) and *haroset* (Ashkenazic style, with apples and nuts, or Sephardic style, with dates and figs) and who is chosen to hide it, who to find it, and who to subsidize the reward for its discoverer. And what an important thing the hiding and finding is, for only when the hidden matzah is retrieved can the Passover seder conclude.

The Spiritual Is Material

In Judaism, the spiritual is material. Without things, there is no Passover, only an idea of Passover. And a fuzzy idea it would be, like honor, loyalty, and remorse; perhaps like God; and more surely, like monotheism. How precisely do objects denote one's belonging, one's participation, and even one's convictions? If we look at Orthodox dating Web sites on the Internet, we will see that men submitting their personal profiles are often asked to designate the group to which they belong, or the ideology they hold, by describing an object: the particular head covering they wear—a black hat, or a *kippah* (yarmulke) made of yarn, cloth, leather, or suede. Some will volunteer when they cover their heads (all the time, at meals, for prayer); others will offer that they wear tefillin (prayer straps) when they pray. Women will designate their religious profile by objects too: they will say they wear only dresses and skirts, or will admit to wearing pants. Some women indicate if and how they intend to cover their heads after marriage: with a hat, scarf, snood, beret, or wig.

Objects also indicate the intensity of our fellow Jews' commitment and connection to certain fundamental indicators of Jewish life and help establish the particular community to which they belong. Listen to Jews interrogate each other. We do not typically ask, "Do you believe in God with all your heart and all your soul and all your might?" We will not ask, "Do you remember that God rested on the Sabbath day by keeping it holy?" Rather, we inquire about the materiality of enacted beliefs and habits of conviction: "Do you drive a car on *Shabbat*? Carry keys? In your house, do you separate your meat and milk dishes in different cabinets and have two sinks? Do you cover your head, wear a wig, put on tefillin, hang a mezuzah on your door, sleep in separate beds (to observe the laws of family purity), eat uncooked foods (like salad) at nonkosher restaurants, light menorahs, spin dreidels?" The objects tell the story.

Many of the objects that point toward and create Jewish life and identity are found and used not in the synagogue, but in the home— in Bachelard's words, "our corner of the world ... our first universe, a real cosmos in every sense of the word."[10] Within Jewish homes, objects, people, and even times of day and seasons of the year interact in a fluid process. Objects make a home Jewish by ritually animating Jewish life and by absorbing it in specifically Jewish ways. This concept is expressed in Sylvia Rothchild's autobiographical account of the Shavuot holiday, which she refers to in the Yiddish, *Shveeis*:

> *On Shveeis, the three small rooms our family of five called home became a magical place, a stage, a bower redolent with the smell of fresh green leaves, roses and peonies. My pleasure was not only in the transformation we brought about but, even more, in the seasonal discovery that it was possible to alter what was familiar and prosaic, that escape could come not only in daydreams but through physically changing things.*[11]

The Spiritual Life of Objects

Objects construct and play roles in the Jewish spiritual lives of individuals and communities. Can we then go so far as to speak of objects as having religious or spiritual lives as well?[12] Are objects spiritual agents? Independent of people who can perceive the sanctity of objects, can objects be autonomous sources of the sacred, provocateurs of sacred experience? Let us consider, for instance, the following question: is a Torah scroll holy regardless of whether someone recognizes holiness in it or attributes holiness to it? French sociologist Marcel Mauss, in his classic study of the nature of the gift and gift exchange, explains that a thing can possess spiritual power. In particular, when a thing is given as a gift, it possesses a soul, and "it follows that to make a gift of something to someone is to make a present of some part of oneself."[13] Gift giving, and endless rounds of reciprocation, represent for Mauss an intermingling of the sacred and the material: "Souls are mixed with things; things with souls. Lives are mingled together, and this is how, among things and persons so intermingled, each emerges from their own sphere and mixes together."[14]

If we could, like Mauss, imagine objects having spiritual agency, how might we speak about the spiritual lives of Jewish objects in particular? What special characteristics do Jewish objects—or objects characteristically used by Jews in predictable ways—have? We may discover that objects in the lives of Jews have complex Jewish identities: solid, ambivalent, erratic, or angst filled like the Jewish identities of people. We may also discover that just as memory recovers lost, stolen, and rejected worlds and forgotten ways of being Jewish, objects—those present, those retrieved, and even those dimly recalled—may do as well.

Traditional Classification

In order to understand the complex nature of Jewish ritual objects, it will be useful to classify them. Here I present two ways: The first is based in tradition and rooted in Jewish law; the second—a contemporary system of my own devising—is rooted both in law and in current American Jewish practices. Both approaches will guide us in studying new rituals by emphasizing emerging Jewish ritual objects.

Sociologist Samuel Heilman's engaging 1988 study, "Jews and Judaica: Who Owns and Buys What?" is an example of a traditional classification. After observing who purchases which objects at Judaica stores, Heilman classifies the objects hierarchically, from the most holy, in a traditional sense, to the most forbidden.[15] Heilman classifies four sets of Jewish objects as "holy":

1. *Klei kodesh*—holy objects. These are "sancta of the highest order," because they have the name of God written on them one or more times. They are considered sacred whether or not they are in use. Extensive rules govern how they are to be made, stored, used, handled, repaired, and disposed of through burial. Examples of *klei kodesh* are a Torah scroll or a mezuzah parchment. As we will see later in the case study on Holocaust Torahs, a Torah scroll that has flaws that cannot be repaired is less holy than one that can be used.

2. *Tashmishei kedushah*—accoutrements of the *klei kodesh,* the holy objects. These are the objects associated with the holy objects; they enclose, protect, or activate them. While in principle accou-

trements are considered more sacred when actually in use, in practice they are treated as "constantly holy." Like the *klei kodesh,* they are said to have an "inherent sanctity," and thus must be treated with special care and be used and handled in particular ways, although there are fewer and less-restrictive rules. Examples of *tashmishei kedushah* are a Torah cover that encloses the scroll of parchment, or a mezuzah case that houses the piece of parchment upon which the *Shema* is written.

3. *Tashmishei mitzvah*—ritual implements. Unlike holy objects, these objects do not have sanctity in themselves. They acquire sanctity only when they are being used as required to fulfill a mitzvah, a commanded act. Thus, outside the holiday of Sukkot, the Feast of Booths, branches of palm, myrtle, and willow that constitute a *lulav* are not considered holy. It is only when they are bundled for use on the holiday that their nature changes. Like the *klei kodesh* and the *tashmishei kedushah,* there are rules that govern which objects are acceptable for use as *tashmishei mitzvah.* For instance, the *lulav* must be composed of branches from these trees, and they must be of a certain number and quality. Heilman describes objects classified as *tashmishei mitzvah* as being "liminal," "para-sacred," and "parasitic sharers in a charisma not altogether their own."[16] Unlike the holy objects and their accoutrements, *tashmishei mitzvah* do not usually have to be handled with special care when they are not being used, because they neither contain nor enclose God's name. You could put your *lulav* on the floor or discard it in a compost pile after it has been used. A leftover matzah from your seder plate could be crumbled as farfel for soup, and leftover horseradish root could be planted in your herb garden. Nonetheless, in actual practice people so readily associate *tashmishei mitzvah* with *tashmishei kedushah* that they sometimes choose to handle them respectfully and with care. For instance, one might carry his or her *lulav* to synagogue in a protective case, and preserve it after the holiday for later use on Passover, when it can be used ceremonially to sweep away the last crumbs of leaven in one's house.

4. *Reshut*—optional ritual implements. These "quasi-sacred objects" have no inherent sanctity, as they are not required by law in order to fulfill a mitzvah or otherwise designated for a purpose by law. They are considered optional. Yet in practice, these objects enhance, embellish, or intensify the aesthetics of the performance of Jewish ritual. They participate in *hiddur mitzvah*, the glorification of the commandment. Hence, they have a sacred feel They might include a seder plate, a *tzedakah* (charity) box to hold coins, a cutting board for the *Shabbat hallah*, a scarf one wears to cover one's head while lighting *Shabbat* candles, even all the traditional foods served at *Shabbat* meals: gefilte fish, challah, kugel,[17] and chicken soup. In Heilman's estimation, the more ornamented the *reshut* object is—for instance, if it is highly decorated or made by a renowned artist—the more sacred it can seem, despite its optional status.[18]

Given that Heilman arranges his classification of holy objects in this hierarchical fashion, with the most holy at the top and the least holy at the bottom, it is not surprising that when he charts contemporary purchases of Judaica, he will claim that Jews who are most observant in practice and well versed in Jewish law are more likely to buy the "holier" holy items and use them "in context," that is, according to Jewish law and custom, and for their "original" purposes. He suggests they know the rules, follow them correctly, and know the "real" meanings behind what they are doing. For instance, if they are buying a cutting board for the *Shabbat* challah, they will also know why Jews have challah on *Shabbat* and will say the correct blessings over the bread at the right times. According to Heilman, those Jews who are not traditional in practice (Heilman refers to them with seeming derision as "liberal and free-floating in outlook") tend to buy more items in the *reshut* category, such as Star of David necklaces or pictures of Israel. Calling these objects "free floating symbols of Jewish identity," and thereby suggesting they are not the "real thing," Heilman acknowledges that many Jews find them compelling even though they might not even be connected to Jewish rituals or holidays. In fact, they might be displayed as objets d'art: "context-free object symbols that have symbolic and iconographic significance," and that may also have private, idiosyncratic meaning attributed to them.[19] What do such objects signify about their purchasers? For Heilman, only a "vague attachment" to things Jewish, an attachment that he discounts.

When Heilman presents his system as a circular model, he assigns the *center* of the circle to holier objects and to traditional Jews who are attached to holier objects that are used at the "right times" and for the "right reasons." He assigns the *periphery* of the circle to "marginally" holy objects and to those he describes as marginally observant Jews, those more open to innovation and change. All Judaica, he does say, no matter where on the line or the circle they are placed, are "symbols of social integration," serving the purpose of linking all Jews who have them for whatever reason. Nonetheless, he makes an obvious value judgment through his distinctions between center and periphery. One could argue that just because a Jewish object is also valued as an objet d'art, or just because an object's meaning may be in transition or its meaning multivalenced, one cannot necessarily assume that the object symbolizes a "vague attachment" to Judaism or that it is being used in ignorance or in repudiation of tradition.

A Contemporary Classification: Explicitly and Implicitly Jewish

The traditional system of classification presented above clearly has virtues, but it limits our understanding of new Jewish ritual objects, those that might never make it onto the "holy charts" because they have not been designated as such historically. We need a nonhierarchical system that does not identify Jews or Jewish objects as being more or less legitimate or authentic. Hence, I offer an alternative system of classification that may help us when we look at new and emerging rituals and ritual objects, such as a Miriam's cup or tambourine, or a car mezuzah. It will also help us make sense of the whole range of objects that constitute Jewish experience and construct Jewish spaces.[20] The categories that I propose—explicitly Jewish objects and implicitly Jewish objects—are more folk oriented. They consider, but do not privilege, rabbinic interpretations of Jewish law. These categories are less concerned with the user's familiarity with traditional Jewish law, with levels of ritual observance, or with conventional definitions of what constitutes Jewish identity or Jewish authenticity. Instead, they privilege actual Jewish practice, in all its expressions, and do not dismiss personal meanings.

Explicitly Jewish Objects

Explicitly Jewish objects signify that Jewish life is being intentionally constructed by the objects and through all those interactions people have with these objects. Objects included in this category are articulate, revelatory, self-evident, and unambiguous. They are simultaneously *signs* that clearly say, "a Jew inhabits this space," *props* that say, "This object is needed in Jewish life," and *catalysts* that say, "The presence of this object creates and maintains Judaism."

Explicitly Jewish objects can facilitate, instigate, and suggest Jewish ways of being. They establish Jewish identities and serve as reminders that the setting one occupies is Jewish. A woman I once interviewed described explicitly Jewish objects as the boundary keepers she sets up in order to distinguish and protect the Jewish identity she constructs in her home from the largely non-Jewish world in which her family lives. One could also say that it is not only this woman who uses the objects to create boundaries, but the objects themselves that create a demarcated Jewish world.

According to such a definition, for American Jews, explicitly Jewish objects might include: a mezuzah, a Hanukkah menorah and decorations, *Shabbat* candlesticks, a *Kiddush* cup (often silver), a prayer book, a Bible and other ancient sacred Jewish texts, a drawer of yarmulkes harvested from various celebrations, fine or folk artwork depicting shtetl or Israeli scenes, displays of Jewish holiday greeting cards, *tzedakah* boxes designated for some Jewish cause or charity, kosher wines, loaves of challah, boxes of matzah, and just about anything with Hebrew letters written on it: from an illuminated *ketubah* or a free Jewish calendar from a kosher butcher or Jewish funeral parlor, to Hebrew letter magnets in primary colors stuck onto a refrigerator, to a red-and-white can of Coca-Cola written in Hebrew, brought back as a souvenir from Israel.

Explicitly Jewish objects enter one's home in a variety of ways: as purchases, souvenirs, gifts, life-cycle mementos, inheritances, and hand-me-downs. Sometimes prayer books and Bibles are "borrowed" from synagogues, in a kind of surreptitious lifetime loan. Some objects are acquired once in a lifetime, such as a pair of silver candlesticks; others are acquired annually and are consumed or used up, such as Hanukkah candles or a Jewish calendar. Some are acquired annually, and after they have fulfilled their original purpose, they are saved and transformed into other explicitly Jewish objects. An *etrog,* for instance, is often turned into jam that is eaten on Tu b'Shevat (the New Year of trees) or into a pomander for the *Havdalah* spice-smelling blessing; a *lulav,* or a piece of the Passover *afikoman,* may be hung over a door as an amulet to increase one's blessing.

Explicitly Jewish objects can evoke important private Jewish stories that are narrated or recalled when they are seen or used. One story frequently elicited is the story of acquisition. One learns who gave the object, why they gave it, when they gave it (if it was a special occasion, like a birth, bar or bat mitzvah, or wedding), what the giving meant initially and what it means now, particularly if it affirms a continuing connection between giver and recipient. In her work on elderly Jews, Barbara Myerhoff has included such object stories, elicited by what she calls symbolic Jewish jewelry. She describes Jewish women wearing "expensive gifts from their children: golden medallions bearing grandchildren's names, 'Tree of Life' necklaces studded with real pearls, Stars of David, and the golden word '*chai,*' Hebrew for life and luck. All were announcements of connections, remembrance, and esteem."[21] An inherited object has particular resonance, the prized family heirloom, regardless of whether it is ascribed value only by the family or if it is also of value to others.

Linda Steinberg, Director of the Jewish Museum of San Francisco, writes of inherited *Kiddush* cups:

Kiddush Cups placed upon the family table, whether for Shabbat, Pesach or other special observances, particularly those cups handed down from generations past, are tangible symbols of Jewish continuity, of the enduring rituals of which they are an intrinsic part ... they represent a commitment to keep their embodied traditions vital."[22]

Another story evoked by explicitly Jewish objects is the *miracle story* of rescue or survival against great odds. Such an object bears witness to the endurance of both Jews and Judaism. An object that comes to mind is a broken silver *Shabbat* bread knife that one family hid under floorboards during the Holocaust and later retrieved—the sole tangible surviving sign of their Jewish material life in Europe. Now it is housed in a dining room on the Upper West Side of Manhattan, in effect, transforming the hutch that holds the knife into a kind of Holocaust memorial shrine or museum.

Certain explicitly Jewish objects may be considered to have a higher level of holiness (*kedushah*) than other objects in this category because of some intrinsic aspect. The mezuzah, for example, contains parchment with verses of Scripture written on it; the holiness is raised to an even higher power because these particular verses contain the written name of God. (This corresponds to the *klei kodesh*.) Some people know that the "holiness quotient" of the mezuzah would be reduced if there were a mistake or defect in the writing or a tear in the parchment. Some would argue that an object's holiness is reduced or compromised if it is used or placed improperly. In the case of the mezuzah, this could mean installation on the wrong side of the doorway, or placement either too high or too low.

Nonetheless, for other Jews, the holiness of an explicitly Jewish object is *not necessarily compromised* when the object is used in a manner incompatible, fully or partially, and consciously or not, with Jewish law. People may have strong feelings about the explicitly Jewish object's holiness and hold strong beliefs about what the object means *to them* and how it is supposed to be used in *their* scheme of things.

A former student, a Jewish soldier in the U.S. Marines, comes to mind. He always wears a silver mezuzah on a chain around his neck; it is for him a symbol of his commitment to Judaism, one that comes before *all* his other commitments. The mezuzah he describes as "very holy" is not even a mezuzah according to Jewish law, as it lacks the necessary parchment with God's name written on it. Even if it did have the proper parchment inside, according to Jewish law, it would be meaningless, curious, or even offensive when hung around someone's neck as jewelry, and not placed on a doorpost, where Jewish law says it belongs. For this soldier, however, the "mezuzah" he wears is holy, even if it is but a silver miniature of an empty mezuzah case. He has vowed that he will never take it off, so strong is his belief, and so strong is its pull on him. He says, "I live with it on, and I will die with it on."

Nonintrinsic and personal or sentimental aspects of an explicitly Jewish object can increase its felt holiness. For instance, each Friday night my mother takes the yarmulke and prayer book that belonged to her beloved father out from the cupboard and places them on a little tea cart next to her *Shabbat* candlesticks as she lights them. As it happens, she neither wears the yarmulke nor reads from the frayed prayer book—she'll cover her head with a napkin and say the prayer by heart. But because both objects evoke and represent her father's presence and remind her of how *Shabbat* once entered his home, they are, for her, Jewish objects of the highest sanctity. They are more potent and powerful than other yarmulkes and prayer books in the household that are used conventionally. In fact, when a family member is having a medical procedure or is seriously ill, my mother takes out her father's yarmulke and prayer book even when it isn't *Shabbat,* and makes a little shrine of them on the tea cart that stays on display until the danger has passed.

Thus, while explicitly Jewish objects often have codified rules and customary or traditional expectations that are connected to them, idiosyncratic, personalized usage can prevail with no dishonor intended and with the depth of private meanings added.

Those who have personalized Jewish objects in some way can readily acknowledge the distinction between what these objects "really mean" (something they believe a rabbi or Jewish scholar would know), what these objects have meant to them in the past, and what they mean to them now. They may speculate about what idiosyncratic meanings—if any—the objects will have for their descendants when they are inherited. Colleen McDannell points to these distinctions between the corporate and private meanings of religious objects in *Material Christianity* when she states that while meanings may be "articulated by a controlling institutional body with a long history of custom and tradition,"[23] these may not be able to help us "understand the personal meanings that people find in their daily use of religious objects," which may mirror neither the "intentions of the clerical elite nor express the idiosyncratic whims of the masses." In this respect, a mezuzah one purchased in Jerusalem for one's 25th anniversary will have a different valence than a mezuzah purchased from the local synagogue gift shop. The anniversary mezuzah from Israel might be seen as having greater protective power and potency when it is installed at home, precisely because it contains and activates both personal and collective memories.

Implicitly Jewish Objects

Implicitly Jewish objects, by contrast, do *not* readily reveal the Jewish work they do. It is not always clear that they designate people or places as being Jewish, as signs do. They may not announce their use or purpose in Jewish life, as props do. And they are not overt creators of Jewish ways of being and doing, as catalysts are. Still, these objects may participate in the literal fulfillment of mitzvot or, using the term coined by the rabbinic scholar Max Kadushin, they may express or achieve Jewish value concepts. Like the explicitly Jewish objects, the implicitly Jewish objects embody, create, and express *kedushah* by their presence, but do so subtly and indirectly.

Consider the books in a Jewish home—not just Jewish ones, but all books, filling shelves, covering tables, scattered in children's rooms—all attesting to a passion for learning and a reverence for the written word. Consider the foods in a Jewish home—not just the bagels, chicken soup, Hanukkah latkes, Purim hamantashen, and gefilte fish and horseradish that are readily recognized as traditional Jewish daily and holiday fare—but all of the food: a pantry and two refrigerators (one in the basement) sufficiently overstocked so family and guests can be encouraged to eat more. And consider the ubiquitous shrinelike displays of photographs in Jewish homes: children, parents, extended families assembled at what Jews call "affairs," and the sepia-toned or faded photographs of ancestors. *"L'dor va'dor"* (from one generation to another), these things announce: among Jews, one generation to another matters, family matters, love matters, marking life cycles matters, keeping connections matter, and "increasing and multiplying" matter. One might well claim, "Photographs, a well-stocked pantry, and books are not markers of Jewish homes alone!" Obviously, many non-Jews have equally well-adorned bookshelves, walls, and larders. But in a Jewish home, these objects have a particular Jewish valence, a Jewish intentionality. As an example, in many cultures, people eat braided bread. But when Jews call their braided bread "challah" and serve it on *Shabbat* and recite blessings before baking and eating it, that braided bread takes on a Jewish valence.

Implicitly Jewish objects include the material objects that can be found in many homes anywhere, but whose meanings and functions shift when they appear within Jewish contexts. A dish is a dish—but in a Jewish home, synagogue, or restaurant where kashrut (the dietary laws) are observed, the dish of a certain color or pattern placed in a particular and separate cabinet is a milchig (milk) dish, and the dish in the other cabinet is fleishig (meat). The telephone is a telephone, but for the Jew who has a sick friend living far away, the phone is a holy vessel used in the practice of *bikur holim*, the commandment to connect to the sick. All the equipment one uses in housecleaning—cleansing powder, mop, cleansing solutions, and a vacuum cleaner—is just cleaning equipment. But in the Jewish home where *Shabbat* is observed by cleaning one's home beforehand, we have in the cleaning equipment holy vessels that create and point to *Shabbat,* tangibly, experientially, and sensually. In each case, we have objects that are endowed with meaning, memory, and sacred purpose. In sacred service, they are not changed, but they have the potential to become charged, so to speak. We could say these ordinary objects compel us to engage in acts of consecration.

Implicitly Jewish objects also include those objects borrowed from other religious or secular traditions and used in distinctly Jewish ways. For example, in contemporary American Jewish practice, people are now using Christmas tree lights, Thanksgiving cornucopias, and summer poolside party decorations (usually purchased in postseason sales) to decorate their sukkot. The "previous lives" of these objects might not even be disguised. Rather, the visible shift in use is sometimes a source of festival humor, perhaps a confirmation of Jewish well-being within the broader culture. (I have seen St. Patrick's Day decorations such as shamrocks and leprechaun's hats unapologetically used in the festivities of an ultra-Orthodox wedding held in March.) Thus, Kopytoff's observation is relevant: "What is significant about the adoption of alien objects—as of alien ideas—is not the fact that they are adopted but the way they are culturally refined and put to use."[24]

New Jewish Objects as Agents of Change and Stability

However we choose to classify new Jewish objects—and ultimately, we will need to navigate between the two classifications I have presented, as neither system is complete in itself—we see that when objects are linked to new rituals, they perform various essential tasks that pave the way for the establishment of the ritual. In doing so, the objects function as both agents of change and, later, of stability.

They introduce. The new objects are concrete forms that introduce and announce the existence and availability of a new (or developing) practice to individuals and to the community. One might encounter them when attending the performance of a ritual, but they could also be found displayed on the shelf of a Judaica shop, hung on a friend's wall, or depicted as an advertisement in a Jewish magazine. New ritual objects spread the news of emerging rituals. In turn, new rituals spread awareness of the object and can inculcate desire for the object.

They retell sacred stories. The new objects provoke questions that necessitate retelling the traditional sacred narratives and coining and telling new ones: What is that thing? What is it for? Is there some special ritual I'm supposed to do with it? How did the ritual come about? Who made it up? What does it mean? How is it authentically linked to Jewish practices, stories, and things that are familiar to me?

They generate rules and spiritual possibilities. The new objects raise questions leading to discussions of rules and guidelines: How and when do you do it? Who can do it? Where do I get one for myself? What else do I need? What am I supposed to say? Wasn't it done differently somewhere else? The new objects also raise questions that require one to ponder spiritual possibilities: If I can acquire or make the object and perform the ritual, will I find it meaningful to me? Will I be changed? Will I feel connected to God and to other Jews?

They make the ritual tangible. The new objects make the rituals accessible, performable, concrete, repeatable, and transmittable from one generation to another.

They provide assurance. The new objects can make new rituals more readily acceptable to more traditional, conservative people, or those particularly anxious about innovation. In this context, objects disguise the *novelty* of a ritual by bundling it within some familiar object, something that looks and feels "traditionally" or "authentically" Jewish. They disguise the *radical nature* of a new ritual by "housing" it in an object so mundane and so innocuous that it feels nonthreatening. And they assure those who will use them that they are not transgressing any Jewish law or custom (especially relevant for those who may be less Judaically literate and who may fear making an inadvertent Jewish faux pas).

They appeal to those on the fringes. The new object can make new rituals more readily acceptable for those who may be ambivalent or altogether antagonistic toward religious rituals, old or new. In this case, the political, aesthetic, educational, or philanthropic aspects of the object may be highlighted, and its religious nature obscured.

They address communal needs. The new object responds to the developing spiritual needs of a particular community. Speaking from her own experience in a women's Rosh Hodesh group in New Haven, Judaica artist Judy Sirota Rosenthal once suggested that a new ritual object can emerge when a community chances upon an object that "works" when it needs to ritualize or commemorate some moment or important occasion.

With a good deal of methodological background in place, we now move ahead to look at the big picture. When stretched by innovation, what does Judaism look like?

NOTES:

1. See site for Netivot Shalom at http://netivotshalom.org.

2. James Dietz, *In Small Things Forgotten* (New York: Anchor Books, 1977), 35.

3. Simon Bronner, "Folk Objects," in *Folk Groups and Folklore Genres: An Introduction,* ed. Elliot Oring (Logan, UT: Utah State Press, 1986), 199.

4. Ibid., 204

5. Jules David Prown, "Mind in Matter: An Introduction to Material Culture Theory and Method," in *Material Life in America, 1600–1860,* ed. R. B. St. George (Boston: Northeastern University Press, 1988), 19.

6. Igor Kopytoff, "The Cultural Biography of Things: Commoditization as Process," in *The Social Life of Things: Commodities in Cultural Perspective,* ed. Arjun Appadurai (Cambridge: Cambridge University Press, 1986), 66–67.

7. Barbara Myerhoff, *Number Our Days* (New York: Simon and Schuster, 1978), 105.

8. John Cort, "Art, Religion and Material Culture: Some Reflections on Method," *Journal of the American Academy of Religion* (Fall 1996): 615.

9. Colleen McDannell, *Material Christianity* (New Haven: Yale University Press, 1995), 1–2.

10. Gaston Bachelard, *The Poetics of Space,* trans. Maria Jolas (New York: Orion Press, 1964), 4.

11. Judith Kates and Gail Riemer, *Reading Ruth* (New York: Ballentine, 1996), 146.

12. This provocative line of questions has been posed in conversation by Leedom Lefferts, who studies the "spiritual lives" of Thai textiles and posits that objects do possess intrinsic sacredness.

13. Marcel Mauss, *The Gift: The Form and Reason for Exchange in Archaic Societies* (New York: Norton, 2000), 11–12.

14. Ibid., 20.

15. Samuel Heilman, "Jews and Judaica: Who Owns and Buys What?" in *Persistence and Flexibility: Anthropological Perspectives on the American Jewish Experience,* ed. Walter Zenner (New York: SUNY Press, 1988), 261.

16. Ibid., 263–64.

17. According to Allan Nadler, among Hasidim of Eastern Europe "the sanctification of the kugel can serve as a metaphor for the manner in which the Hasidic movement reads holiness into the most common of mundane things." From "Holy Kugel: The Sanctification of Ashkenazic Ethnic Foods in Hasidism," in *Food and Judaism,* ed. Leonard Greenspoon et al. (Omaha: Creighton University Press, 2005), 208.

18. Heilman finds objects in this category of particular note in the contemporary context. He appears to speak condescendingly of *reshut* objects ("Jews and Judaica," p. 278):

> *Although objects of Judaica have undoubtedly been affected by the changing context of Jewish life, the greatest change by far has occurred in the domain of the ... "quasi-sacred." This is because so much of this material is associated with custom and changing tradition and because these are affected more easily by the impact of acculturation.... [I] t is safe to say that many of the objects which today are to be included among Judaica would not have been so catalogued at another time and it is not inconceivable that others will yet enter in the future while other objects will fall into disuse and become curios of a bygone era.*[1]

19. Heilman, "Jews and Judaica," 271.

20. This contemporary model of classifying Jewish objects emerged initially out of my research on how objects in Jewish homes construct Jewish space and Jewish identity. My study (1996–1998) was based on objects found in American Jewish homes in New York State and New Jersey. My initial findings of the inventories and interviews were presented as "Home Sacred Home: Inventory of a Jewish Home," in *Sh'ma* (May 30, 1997), and were later developed as "What Makes a Jewish Home Jewish," *AAR Conference* (November 1998); *Religion and Material Culture Electronic Journal* (Spring 1999); and *Crosscurrents* (Winter 1999/2000). Some of the materials in this chapter may be found in earlier versions in these essays.

21. Myerhoff, 206–7.

22. Linda Steinberg, *L'Chaim: A Kiddush Cup Invitational,* press kit (San Francisco: The Jewish Museum of San Francisco, 1997).

23. McDannell, *Material Christianity,* 17.

24. Kopytoff, "The Cultural Biography of Things," 67.

STRETCHED BY INNOVATION

Continuity Despite Change

Despite tinkering, tweaking, and radical transformation, Judaism—even when stretched by innovation—remains fundamentally intact. Jews are maintaining their figurative place along a "golden chain" of transmission. There is compelling evidence of continuity in an era characterized by what Susan Berrin, editor of *Sh'ma*, calls an "efflorescence of new rituals, created at times to mark life events traditionally unmarked and at times designated to address contemporary sensibilities and milestones ...."[1] The Torah is still taken out of the ark and read, and it is still the same story, even when women chant it, when it is chanted in English, when passages considered "difficult"[2] are whispered instead of chanted aloud, or when it is signed for the hearing impaired. While Rosh Hashanah may be celebrated at mountain or beach retreats with hiking, yoga, or singing, the New Year is still being welcomed, as it has been for generations, with prayers, the sounds of the shofar, apples and honey. Yom Kippur comes, and we're in synagogue once again. While we may now begin this holiest of days by donating canned goods and staple foods to the community soup kitchen, or by giving handwritten notes to our rabbi to burn after the holiday, we are still listening to *Kol Nidrei*, praying for forgiveness, and fasting. We are still eating matzah, even though it comes in a mind-boggling array of flavors that appeal to personal piety, individual taste, and dietary requirements (including 100% Organic Spelt Handmade Shmurah Matzah). The seder meal will take place, even if it is not at home or at a hotel, but at a trendy bistro.

Maxine Keyser on New Seder Opportunities in Philadelphia

May I recommend taking your seder to Tiramisu, where Alberto Del Bello cooks the Jewish cuisine of his native Roman neighborhood, the Trastevere. Born in the shadow of the church of St. Angelo in Pescheria, near the Portico d'Ottavia, Del Bello preserves the dishes of his childhood. For instance, homemade matzah is always served here and at his other restaurants, Il Portico and Il Tartufo. Unlike any matzah you've ever eaten, these thin disks are dusted with herbs and have an irresistibly charred flavor that keeps you coming back for more.... Tiramisu may be singular among restaurants, for the Jewish special-ties are always on the menu. But other area restaurants will be observing Passover as well. One unlikely but enthusiastic example is Michael McNally, who will be doing a seder meal at London Grill. Come prepared for the usual— good food and some surprises. Marathon On the Square will feature Passover delicacies such as matzah ball soup and fried matzah all through the holiday. Philippe Chin, the Gorgeous Goy, will have a seder-style meal for the first two nights at his elegant French digs. And Davio's power lunches will include all the requirements of Passover—i.e., matzah, soup with matzah balls, etc. ....[3]

A cup of wine is still filled for the omnipresent and indefatigable Elijah the Prophet when he makes his round of seders, even when he comes in the company of Miriam the Prophetess, who finds a water-filled cup of her own on the table.

Before sunset in some communities or at the hour of family gathering in others, *Shabbat* candles still are lit and they usher in the holiness of *Shabbat*. Relatives still come from afar to witness 12- or 13-year-old bar mitzvah boys and bat mitzvah girls dress up as adults, stand uncomfortably in front of their loved ones, and chant in Hebrew from the Torah. Now relatives are also expected to come and witness the grown men and women who have studied at length to celebrate this rite that, to them, designates Jewish legitimacy. Continuity is preserved as we perform mitzvot. We still scrutinize our lives and our relationships, making decisions according to what a mensch would do.

Judaism is sustained by our capacity to innovate while maintaining and cherishing the practices and commitments of the past. Rabbi Lawrence Kushner has expressed this notion poetically: "Torah's vitality comes from its lability.[4] Responding to the unforeseeable exigencies of each new generation ... observances and life-style customs sway and dance to the melodies of each new generation."[5]

Rituals Readily "Naturalized"

In just a few years, many of Judaism's newest rituals have lost the patina of newness. Widespread and performed with some uniformity, we take the new rituals for granted. We forget their novelty, forget they have been innovated in our lifetimes. Naming ceremonies for girls, adult b'not and b'nai mitzvah, women's seders, healing services, and women's Rosh Hodesh groups are the "naturalized" rituals that first come to mind. (I know Rosh Hodesh groups have been accepted as normative when my traditional father says my mother is out because "it's Rosh Hodesh, don't you know? She's off with her women's group. ") Yom ha-Shoah (Holocaust Remembrance Day) is not technically "new" since it has been marked since 1951, but it already feels as poignantly ancient as Tisha b'Av, however diversely it is observed.

These new rituals are what Jews do. If we fail to follow along and it has become the practice of our community, we may feel as if we are no longer members in good standing. Rituals intended to be performed just once have spread and become *minhag*, the Hebrew term describing a practice of a particular family or community that has been repeated so often (generally, three times) that one perforce must continue it. New Jewish rituals once carried out by those considered to be on the fringes of Jewish life have since become mainstream. They are held in synagogues, officiated over by rabbis using the liturgies found in their new rabbinic manuals.

The new rituals come to be labeled "traditional," as if they have been around forever, as if their origins are too shrouded in mystery to unravel, as if tampering with them could provoke cosmic retaliation. Lightening now strikes, so to speak, not for performing the new rituals, but for failing to perform them. A 30-year-old woman on the staff of my university expecting her first baby girl makes an appointment to see me in my office and asks, "What should we do? The rabbi said it's traditional for the parents to come up to the *bimah* and give a speech explaining the meaning of our daughter's name during her naming ceremony. But neither of us is comfortable speaking in public. Are we allowed to write something and hand it out?"

A college student asks me if she can depart from the "traditional, moon-themed" women's Rosh Hodesh service, because she'd like to do something a little different. I think of telling her that Rosh Hodesh has been practiced here at our university for less than 10 years. The moon-focused "script" this student has in her hands, one she thinks of as traditional and set in stone, was, as I recall, created in a mad rush one night by two of my former students. I had lent them the Rosh Hodesh texts of the 1970s and '80s that I had on file, as well as Penina Adelman's 1986 book, *Miriam's Well: Rituals for Jewish Women Around the Year,* essentially the Rosh Hodesh handbook, the source from which you sought to spark your own creativity.[6] The students stitched together the parts they liked, adding verses by Israeli poets they were reading that semester. Off they went to Kinko's, where they photocopied their script, noting on their hand-drawn cover that it was the first-ever Rosh Hodesh ceremony at the University of Virginia. (Was it, in fact? It is indeed possible there were others before our time.) They emphasized the moon theme simply because one of the women loved moons: she had moon curtains and moon ornaments in her apartment and a new crescent-shaped cookie cutter she wanted to use to make the snacks.

But I hold my tongue. Why would I delegitimize her experience of the authenticity of an inherited Rosh Hodesh ceremony, puncturing her sense of familiarity? She sees a ceremony that feels right and established; what gain is there if I point out the rudiments of its recent and pieced-together construction?

Less Familiar

Other innovations, despite their popularity in certain pockets of America, are less familiar and less widespread. These include the sewing bee shower for handcrafting a wedding *huppah;* an egalitarian, interfaith, or same-sex wedding *ketubah;* and a ceremony for young people departing for college. Miriam's cup at the Passover seder remains unfamiliar to many, as does Miriam's tambourine.

Recognizing a Stretched Judaism

What does this "stretched" Judaism look like? The expansive mode of Jewish ritual innovation has embraced Jews of all definitions, all denominations,[7] and all levels of affiliation and identification. It includes Jews who boldly affirm their belonging, those who quietly consider themselves religious, and those on the sidelines who affirm their participation in Judaism, however occasional and quirky, while simultaneously denying it, saying, "I'm not a very good Jew, but ...." We will look first to the far boundaries of innovation—keeping in mind that what is utterly novel today may be the "traditional" Judaism of tomorrow.

Big Stretches

Those who sport "Jewish" tattoos, read the magazine *Heeb: The New Jew Review,* and listen to cutting-edge Jewish music produced on the *Tzadik*: Radical Jewish Culture label[8] have something in common beyond achieving recognition for an evanescent status referred to as "New Jew cool." Here I take a leap, suggesting that even as they stretch and challenge Judaism, they are engaging in fundamentally familiar Jewish practices.

Wearing a Jewish tattoo (such as a Star of David, Hebrew words, a *hamsa* amulet, or the phrase "Never Again!") is certainly not the same as wearing a *kippah* to indicate humility before God, to proclaim observance of the commandments, and, more recently, to express pride in being Jewish. Wearing a Jewish tattoo is not the same as being circumcised, a sign of covenantal membership (though, admittedly, in both cases, it is a sign "marked" upon one's body). It does not suggest historical weight, other than the tragic historical association to the Holocaust, or evoke generations of sacred meaning. Many people are even familiar—or think they are familiar—with Jewish prohibitions against tattooing. In fact, it is intriguing how often people who know very little about Judaism and who have no interest in following Jewish laws are *certain* that tattooed Jews cannot be buried in Jewish cemeteries (a practice funeral parlors do not confirm) and will eschew tattooing for that reason.[9]

Getting Jewish tattoos is not widespread, though the phenomenon is growing among the young. Still, imagine that those who choose to mark their skin with a Star of David are designating upon their bodies their membership in the *People of Israel.* Is this practice not therefore a ritual, one inscribed upon the flesh, affirming their Jewish identity? Imagine that someone who has the word "perseverance" tattooed in Hebrew on his left arm does so not to disrespect Auschwitz victims and survivors, but to pay tribute and to display his obedience to the injunction "Never Forget"?[10]

When Jews read the magazine *Heeb,* they are obviously not engaging in *limmud Torah,* traditional sacred text study. But can we imagine that they are still wrestling with what it means to be a "people of the book" in this moment?[11] Those who listen to Jewish contemporary music may not be praying with old-world cantors or dancing to the fiddlers of the shtetl, but they are surely making a connection to Judaism with their own sounds.

Challenging Innovations

Consider other signs of Judaism being stretched by new practices, those that are less dramatic now, but were challenging (and threatening even) when first introduced. Progressive Jews are celebrating Passover by creating seders that are experimental, radical, adventure-some, and socially conscious.[12] Others are observing Passover by attending a cyber seder. (The first cyber seder was introduced in 1998 by the new music promoters, The Knitting Factory. It took place in real time at Lincoln Center and was broadcast online. Virtual partici-pants could participate by downloading haggadah materials, observ-ing the seder as it took place, and engaging in online exchanges in a chat room.[13])

Reform Jews stretch Judaism when they move away from practices of classical Reform Judaism and embrace a new traditionalism, cover-ing their heads, wearing a tallit, and using more Hebrew in their ser-vices. Conservative and Reform Jews who are also doctors stretch Judaism when they study to become certified as ritual circumcisers, *mohelim* and *mohelot*. In Seattle, the Kadima congregation has cre-ated a "Women's Torah Project," which has funded two women to learn to become Torah scribes and has commissioned them to create the first Torah written completely by women. They have also engaged women artists to create a Torah breastplate, crown, cover and wimple clasp, and pointer.[14] Liberal Jews are now holding *upsherin,* a cere-mony for a toddler's first haircut, a ritual held until recently only among traditional communities for sons when they reach the age of three and begin to wear the *tallit katan* (a four-cornered fringed gar-ment worn under one's clothes).[15]

Orthodox feminists extend boundaries when they study Talmud at schools such as The Drisha Institute, which was founded in New York in 1979 as the world's first center for women's advanced study of classical Jewish texts. Educating women at the highest levels was a radical step; equally radical was supporting women financially as they studied Torah full-time. Orthodox boundaries are extended when women choose to pray wearing a tallit, or tefillin. Some also now wear the *tallit katan.*[16]

Many Orthodox women in America are attending women's *tefillah* (prayer) groups. They usually meet monthly, on a *Shabbat* morning, to pray together, read from the Torah, and lead services. They do so with the authority and permission of several Orthodox rabbis who have been satisfied that their new practices are in full accordance with *halakhah*. The Women's Tefillah Group of Riverdale, New York, describes its monthly prayer service, begun in 1979:

> *Our tefillah is an important opportunity for women to meet the challenge of Jewish spiritual expression and become full participants in prayer. We also regard the tefillah as a learning experience to enable women to better understand prayer and make the study of Torah more meaningful. In our group women daven together, read from the Torah, and lead the services. We follow the traditional Shabbat morning services and, according to the halakhah, omit any d'varim sh'bekedushah—prayers that require a quorum of ten men. Our halakhic authority is Rabbi Avraham Weiss of the Hebrew Institute of Riverdale.*[17]

To affirm that they are keeping within the constraints of the Orthodox understanding of Jewish law, they maintain that they do not constitute a minyan, a quorum of 10 or more men. Thus, they refrain from reciting prayers that require a minyan, namely: the *Barechu*, the *Kedushah* said during the repetition of the *Amidah,* and the *Mourner's Kaddish.*

Technology has inspired much Orthodox innovation. Orthodox Jews are studying the *daf yomi* on their iPods[18] on the Long Island Railroad, turning it into a chugging *beit midrash* (house of study). *Daf yomi* is the practice, begun in 1923, of studying one page of Talmud each day so that at the end of a little more than seven years, one has completed the entire Talmud. In 2005, thousands of people celebrating the completion of the cycle of study (called *Siyum ha-Shas*) gathered simultaneously in Madison Square Garden in New York City and in the Continental Airlines Arena in New Jersey. The ceremony was broadcast live on the Internet.

Hasidic Jews are studying the *Tanya* (a central Hasidic text) on the Internet, and they are faxing and e-mailing requests for blessings to the grave of their deceased rebbe in Queens. (For Lubavitch Hasidim, the very idea that their sect could maintain itself after the 1992 death of their rebbe was a dramatic innovation in itself, stretching their self-definition.) One might think that the Hasidim began using the Internet only recently, with great reluctance. In fact, when the Lubavitch Hasidim developed their Web site, www.Chabad.org, they were among the first Jewish organizations to conduct outreach through cyberspace and to do it well. For them, it was but a continuation of harnessing new technologies for education and communication.

Even *haredim* (ultra-Orthodox Jews from a range of sects) who do not, on principle, use the Internet for fear of secular contamination, nevertheless use it for business purposes and also turn to officially approved learning sites. Some even participate in a debate on rituals and other communal issues using pseudonyms on the *haredi* blog called *B'hadrei ha-Haredim* (in the rooms of the *haredim*). To use the Internet in a kosher manner (and wouldn't anyone have trouble resisting the urge to surf the Web, even when doing so is banned?), *haredim* have developed intriguing protective strategies. Some use software that filters out inappropriate materials or permits only pre-approved sites. Others turn to *Ayinroah,* an unusual system that enforces accountability, one that models itself on *hevrusa,* the traditional system of studying Torah with a partner.

Ayinroah

According to Edward Portnoy, *Ayinroah,* meaning a watchful eye, is based on the *hevrusa* system of Talmud study:

> As their Web site states, "rabunim say that a computer is user byichud," or prohibited to use alone. The phrase, Ayinroah, is taken from Pirkei Avot, (Sayings of the Wise), chapter 2, in which it is written, "Contemplate three things, and you will not come to the hands of transgression: Know what is above you: a seeing eye, a listening ear, and all your deeds being inscribed in a book." This is exactly what the company does. It is a service wherein clients have a hevrusa, or an Internet "accountability partner," who receives an e-mail report of all sites you have visited. Inappropriate sites are

ranked according to content and listed at the top of the report. The concept behind this is that the user will be humiliated if his hevrusa finds out he has been going to inappropriate sites. If you attempt to disable the program, the partner is instantly alerted.[19]

In the area of gender, Judaism is stretched when the UJC (United Jewish Communities) organizes a gay pride mission to Israel.[20] It is being stretched because more than two dozen synagogues for gay, lesbian, bisexual, and transgender Jews and their families and friends have emerged since 1973, when the first *Shabbat* service of what would become New York City's Congregation Beth Simchat Torah met. Conservative and Reform congregations are now publicizing their outreach toward gay and lesbian Jews and their families, and two denominations now ordain gay and lesbian Jews: the Reform and Reconstructionist movements. Judaism is stretched when Sandi Simcha Dubowski, the director of the film *Trembling Before God,* a chronicle of the lives and struggles of gay and lesbian Orthodox Jews, goes on the road with his film so he can engage the Orthodox community in challenging conversations. There are the Orthodykes, a social support group for Orthodox and formerly Orthodox lesbian, bisexual, and transgender women and their families and friends, who hold "Sheitelstock," a Purim dance in New York for women, featuring "libations and hamentaschen."

In matters of *shidduchim,* matchmaking practices, ultra-Orthodox Jews seeking marriage partners are venturing outside of traditional face-to-face matchmaking by availing themselves of the Internet services of SawYouAtSinai.com, a name that plays on the idea that all Jews were present when the Torah was revealed at Mount Sinai, and hence, are already connected. The service claims to combine "traditional matchmaking and modern technology to bring you the ONLY personalized, private, and online Jewish dating site." At this site, you write your own profile and specify what you are looking for in a partner. Then you select up to three professional matchmakers (some are trained at the Matchmaking Institute in Manhattan), who browse through the profiles for you. Your potential matches are "determined by a unique combination of computer algorithms and personal matchmaker insight ...." Only when *both* partners agree to meet is their personal information shared.[21]

Other new services veer farther from tradition when the role of the matchmaker is eliminated altogether. While users are free to select and contact potential partners on their own, through these online services they will know precisely what their religious orientation is. On frumster.com, one can select a partner according to specific categories of Jewish observance: modern Orthodox *mahmir* (very strict), modern Orthodox liberal, yeshivish/black hat, Hasidish, Carlebachian (folksy), yeshivish/modern, Sephardic traditional, *shomer mitzvot* (those who keep *Shabbat* and dietary laws, at least to some extent), and traditional (a category one presumes is intentionally left vague, so as to be inclusive).

Judaism is stretched when interfaith couples and their families are no longer shunned, but are welcomed and educated by organizations such as the Jewish Outreach Institute, established in 1988.[22] It is stretched by rabbis who are becoming more willing to officiate at the marriages of interfaith couples, especially those promising to create Jewish homes and raise Jewish children.

Innovations on College Campuses

Stretching takes place on college campuses as well, reflecting the creativity of students and Jewish professionals hired to reach out to them. Before and during Passover, Hillel foundations all around the country hold an assortment of seders from which to choose. One type of seder is ubiquitous: the women's seder (it is also called a "feminist seder," but some campuses fear that the word "feminist" will limit participants to those who are overtly political about Jewish women's issues). There is also the freedom seder, a bridge-building event between African American and Jewish students, meant to celebrate diversity and multiculturalism. At Kenyon College, the event celebrates the freedom from slavery gained by African Americans during Reconstruction, as well as that of the Jews in Exodus. The traditional Jewish cuisine is combined with and complemented by distinctly African American flavors and foods. Senior James Greenwood, acting president of the Black Student Union, would not reveal the exact menu of that year's forth coming seder. "We're going to publish it as a mystery menu," Greenwood explained. "All I can tell you is that trying to get a good soul food menu and keep it kosher was an interesting challenge .... As seder invokes a tradition of music in the Jewish culture, the culturally joined freedom seder will include traditional Jewish music and African American spirituals. For both traditions, songs of slavery and lament are intertwined with those of faith and freedom." Greenwood promised that "music was and is a big part of this event." His classmate Cooper agreed, saying, "We'll have a lot of traditional music and we'll have spirituals ... it's usually really beautiful."[23]

Other college practices that stretch Passover need further explanation. What, pray tell, is a "chocolate seder"? One might think it refers to the many chocolate treats we associate with Passover: Bartons' Almond Kisses, chocolate-covered macaroons and matzot—perhaps they were the inspiration? It began as a tongue-in-cheek activity for Jewish youth groups, meant to build on the familiar strategy of using engaging pedagogic techniques to draw the interest of children toward the Passover seder. It is still performed in youth groups, and now, in Hebrew schools. College students (and Hillel staffers hired to "engage" students) brought the ritual with them to college. Students at the University of New Hampshire Hillel explain the joys of childhood regression:

> *It's a sweet, festive pre-Passover program that celebrates the traditions of a Passover seder—but with a sweet twist! A traditional Passover seder has specific menu items—matzah, bitter herbs, wine, salt water, etc. ... Our Chocolate Seder has chocolate replacements for the traditional menu items. We'll have four cups of chocolate milk instead of four cups of wine! We'll have chocolate covered matzah (unleavened bread). Our haroset (apples, nuts, wine) will contain snickers, caramel and Hershey syrup. And that's just the beginning![24]*

A Chocolate Seder

This excerpt comes from a "Chocolate Seder" published by the United Synagogue Youth Group, which includes selections from a variety of sources consulted by the editors Rachel Grossman and Stephanie Simon.

ORDER OF THE SEDER

1. *Kadesh*—Sanctify this holy day by blessing the first cup of chocolate milk.
2. *Urchatz*—Purify ourselves by washing our hands.
3. *Karpas*—Dipping of the green apple [into chocolate]
4. *Yachatz*—Break the chocolate matzah.
5. *Magid*—Tell the story of how we became free to eat chocolate.
6. *Rachatza*—Wash our hands again.
7. *Motzi* and Matzah—Blessing over the sweet treats we are going to eat.
8. *Maror*—Bittersweet chocolate to remind us of the pain of our ancestors.
9. *Korech*—The Hillel Sandwich.
10. *Shulchan Orech*—The festive treats.
11. *Tzafun*—Finding the afikomen.
12. *Barech*—A prayer of thanks for the chocolate.
13. *Hallel*—Final praises.
14. *Nirtzah*—Conclusion.

THE CHOCOLATE SEDER PLATE

Before us tonight at our Chocolate Seder sits the festive Chocolate Seder Plate. Upon it are six chocolate symbols that capture the essence of the story of Passover—in a melt-in-your-mouth sort of way.

• *Z'roa*—Drumstick. Representing the sacrificial lamb of Passover. The blood of the lamb was placed on the doorposts of Jewish homes, so that God would "pass over" those homes, sparing the children of the Jews from the tenth plague—the killing of the first-born son.

• *Beytzah*—Chocolate Egg. First of all, the egg represents the Festival Sacrifice brought to the Temple years ago at this season. Secondly, the roundness of the egg represents the continuous cycle of nature's seasons.

• *Maror*—Bitter Chocolate. This bitter chocolate represents the bitterness of our ancestors' enslavement in Egypt. It helps us to remember that although our ancestors were delivered from Egypt, we are all still enslaved in our own personal Egypt.

• *Karpas*—Green Apple. Like the sumptuous chocolate egg, the green apple symbolizes the rebirth of the world.

• *Charoset*—Chocolate Mixture. A representation of the mortar that our ancestors used as slaves in Egypt.

• Why is there an orange on the Seder plate? In the days long ago when women were just beginning to be rabbis, Susannah Heschel was travelling in Florida, the Land of Oranges. One night she spoke at a synagogue about the emerging equality of women in Jewish life—as rabbis, teachers and students of Torah, synagogue presidents, and in all other ways.

After she spoke, a man arose in wrath, red with fury, and said, "A woman belongs on the bimah as much as an orange belongs on the Seder plate!"

So ever since that day, we place an orange on the Seder plate, for it belongs there as a symbol that women belong wherever Jews carry on a sacred life.

Kadesh—The First Cup

We are about to drink the first of four cups of chocolate milk. But why four cups? In the covenant with the People of Israel, God makes four promises. The first is Ve-ho-tzei-ti: "I will bring you out from under the burdens of Egypt."

Remember, milk does the body good, giving us strong bones and a healthy smile. Let us thank the cows for their many hours of patient giving. Let us not forget the cocoa trees that grow and give us the sweetness of this chocolate. And let our minds turn to those who on this day are not blessed with the taste of chocolate. Together, we raise our first cup of chocolate milk and say:

Baruch ata Adonai, Eloheinu melekh ha-olam, borei p'ree ha-gafen u'vorei ha-chalav ha-shokolad.

Blessed are you, Adonai our God, Ruler of the universe, Creator of the Fruit of the Vine and Creator of the Chocolate Milk. (Drink the first glass of chocolate milk.)

Baruch ata Adonai, Eloheinu melekh ha-olam, shehecheyanu, v'kiyemanu, v'higiyanu lazman hazeh.

Blessed are you, Adonai our God, for giving us life, for sustaining us, and for enabling us to reach this chocolate day.[25]

One may ask, "Is the chocolate seder a silly educational game, a sacrilege, or a viable ritual?" At face value, I would call it a game, but one whose meaning may emerge as more significant at a future time. Perhaps the Passover *afikoman* began as a game to keep children engaged and then became a ritual, one eventually canonized within the text of the haggadah. (Did hiding a matzah seem silly at first? I would think so. But just as heavy theological meanings have since been attached to the hidden matzah, isn't there a slim possibility that we may yet see a future generation writing chocolate theologies?)

When I first heard about Greek seders, I assumed they were sponsored by toga-clad classics professors who would discuss the presence in the Passover seder of the ancient Greek symposium practice of reclining while eating. I would finally hear an erudite explanation of the Greek word *afikoman*. I was wrong: Greek seders are held by fraternities and sororities. One Greek seder at a Midwestern university was described as "meaningful, but short—exactly what our students wanted.... We also decorated the tables according to the plagues—we had umbrellas for hail, sunglasses for darkness, plastic bugs for locusts, etc. Students wore the sunglasses and played with the items—it definitely broke the ice and they had a blast."

The eco-seder is one I have seen held both on and off the college campus. Here we turn to Boulder, Colorado, where eco-seders, promoted by a national organization called the Coalition on the Environment and Jewish Life, augment traditional liturgy with environmental awareness. A participant at a 2003 eco-seder in Denver, Colorado, explains, "We are using all the symbols of a traditional seder ... but we just re-interpret them ecologically." Guests might be asked "to apply the mortar symbolism to modern times in the form of the concrete that 'humans now use to pave over the planet.'"[26]

The Pace of Innovation

Initially, during the 1970s and through the mid-1990s, a few months would pass before word of new rituals got out. It took longer still to see how the rituals would spread and catch on. Word traveled through letters, phone calls, magazines, and newspaper publications. Now, thanks to the Internet, the world learns of a new practice almost as soon as it is born. We also learn what people are saying, how it has been received, and any new variations being proposed. Immediately after September 11th and Hurricane Katrina, new liturgies emerged, such as this prayer by Jeffrey A. Spitzer. It was posted immediately after September 11th and was used in memorial services:

A Prayer for September 11th

Lord,
Source of Life, Creator of all flesh,
From out of the depths we call unto you.
Protect us from the hand of all our enemies.
Comfort Your children who now stand alone
without parent or brother or sister or child.

Strengthen us to stand with those orphaned by this attack on
*   our country.*
This country, our country, shelter of peace to the downtrodden,
which has gathered in millions of the peoples of the world
stands as a beacon of light and justice,
but today is dimmed with horror and tragedy.

New York and Washington, shining cities,
Diminished like Jerusalem after the destruction of the holy
  Temple,
need Your comfort, and our aid;
help us to maintain our courage and our efforts to support
  our people.

Strengthen the hands of those who defend this country,
and those who try to maintain peace against these attacks.
Teach us to speak to our children
with love and support and courage and understanding,
for we are all fearful, although their fears may not be our fears.

Gain for us a heart of wisdom,
that we may act out of compassion and thoughtfulness,
and not out of anger or prejudice.

Accept with mercy our prayers for our country and
its government for its president, judges, officials and
institutions who faithfully toil for the good of our country.

May they, with Your guidance, lead us back to lives
of peace in a land we have come to love.[27]

Immediately after Hurricane Katrina, this prayer by Rabbi Paul J. Kipnes of Congregation Or Ami, Calabasas, California circulated over the Internet, along with requests for hurricane relief:

A Prayer for Flood-Filled Days

Eloheinu v'elohei avoteinu v'imoteinu, our God and God of
our fathers and mothers, the flood waters came, wreaking
havoc upon our cities, our homes, our rescue workers, our
sense of security, and we turn to You for comfort and support.
Help us to differentiate between floods of destruction and
down-pouring of Your love and comfort.

We know that waters can destroy. In a world decimated many times before, having been submerged in waters from the Florida hurricanes, the Asian tsunami, and each of Biblical proportions, we remember the destructive abilities of these flood waters.

Recalling now that the world, though filled with Your Glory, is not equal to Your flawlessness, we strive desperately, sometimes without success, to move beyond the impulse to blame You. Keep us far from apocalyptic thoughts, for we know that You ask us to care for each other, an awesome responsibility.

We also know that we can seek You in the waters. We recall Your Loving Hand, guiding us in our infancy: From a barren rock, You brought forth water to quench our thirst, in the midst of a journey through the wilderness, You showed Miriam a myriad of wells which healed our parched throats, You guided us through Yam Suf, the Red Sea, moving us past destruction toward new life and new beginnings. Through Your love, we found our way.

Be with us now, during these deluged days. Draw us close to those harmed by these waters, hearing their cries, responding to their needs. Lead us to support those who will fix the cities, care for the displaced, who bring healing to those suffering. Though our attention spans seem so short, may we be slow to forget those who were in danger. Please bring a warm wind and hot sun from the heavenly realms to help dry up the flood waters, and may we all embrace at least one lesson spoken aloud by so many who—facing the floods—rushed to pack up their valuables:

That memories of love and of time spent with family and friends are priceless, holy and sacred. This can never be taken away. As we rush to meet the challenge of living in this imperfect world of ours, may we slow down enough to cherish those who are truly valuable—kadosh-holy—to us.

Baruch Ata Adonai, Hamavdil bein kodesh l'chol. Blessed are You, O God, who differentiates between the truly valuable and everything else.[28]

Teachers and rabbis get the word out, and so do those who call themselves ritual facilitators. Apparently, there are now hundreds of independent Jewish ritual facilitators. Some nominate themselves as "ritualists"; others are certified in the practice of "ritualcraft." They are laypeople and sometimes clergy without full-time posts who are free to travel to help affiliated, unaffiliated, inspired, or disenfranchised Jews to mark life-cycle events, in or out of the synagogue.[29]

What We Talk about When We Talk about Innovation

As practices have changed, our conversations about rituals have changed too. Whether in face-to-face conversation or online, we hear how others shaped innovations to their personal needs. We can readily post texts and images from our own experimentations onto our blogs[30] and get immediate feedback. Our conversations also chronicle new ways of struggling with old rituals. Consider this online exchange from the summer of 2005. Heartfelt and thoughtful, it concerns a topic many Jewish parents-to-be and their families are now discussing, despite the taboo against questioning this ancient practice: whether or not to circumcise their son.

Here, Sarah Chandler writes to a friend who posts her query on a Listserv that will reach learned Jews of a liberal bent. Note that Sarah isn't surprised that her request for comments is shared: she expects it! The "you" she is writing to for help is the broadest "you" possible. With only four days remaining before her four-day-old nephew, her sister's son, does or does not have a *bris,* the discussion must take place immediately:

> *dearest holy hevre (friends)*
> *i am writing to you today on my fourth day as an aunt ...*
> *my sister gave birth to a pudgy (8.5 lbs) baby boy just this past*
> *Sunday. she is STILL CONSIDERING whether or not to have a*
> *bris. she has decided however that she knows that when she*

makes the decision, it probably won't be logical, but she wants to make it with intention. SO i am asking for your help. she is looking for any information you have about why someone would and wouldn't circumcise their son. she's already heard "everyone does it, it's the mark of a Jew"—she is looking for something more meaningful. As for medical advice, there is so much both for and against that she has said it is hard to keep track. If you have any information, stories, articles, readings, anecdotes, regrets—ANYTHING that you can share with me, preferably by e-mail and preferably before Shabbat—I would greatly appreciate it. It's a big decision and she is looking for some help in making it. Even if it's a 3-sentence e-mail, "I am so glad I am circumcised! I feel connected to all the Jews!" or "Wish my parents hadn't done it"—i think it would be helpful for her to hear a range of ideas.

Sarah hears back from many people, including strangers. They include a rabbi who sends the pat responses he is accustomed to giving to couples in a quandary, a rabbinical student who attaches the papers he wrote on the topic in seminary, and an anthropologist (and Jewish mother) Lise Dobrin, who heard about the online discussion from me over bagels at a *bris* in Charlottesville, Virginia:

Hi Sarah,

My friend forwarded this after we had a discussion at a bris last week. We were talking about why this ritual has had such staying power when others don't.

All I can do is share my own tale:

We have a 5-year-old boy Elie who was circumcised in a ceremony like he was supposed to be. Though we didn't really consider NOT doing it, we gave it a lot of thought, and it was still far from easy. In fact, if you look at the pictures from the bris my husband and I look sad, crying, etc. I know they say the baby isn't finished being formed until it's been circumcised, but

I felt like we were needlessly maiming my until then perfect child. I thought at the time, this is positively barbaric, a horrible ritual. What amazed me most was that people actually did it WITHOUT a religious reason, just because everybody else did! What a stupid thing to do! I didn't find the medical reasons the least bit compelling. I think of it sort of like cutting off your earlobe (the binding of Isaac)—you can do it or not and still function just the same.

What we underwent really felt like being there with Abraham at the akedah—commanded to do something that cuts way too close to your heart, with no reason or rhyme, just to give expression to your relationship with God. Well Elie healed fine, and the trauma of the moment is long past. What I can wonder with you now though is, how would I feel if I hadn't gone along with it? Would I feel like MY feelings had come between my son and his Jewishness? And I think I'd always feel I had a lot of explaining to do (I know about this all too well because of the nontraditional choices we are making about educating our kids, which require much justification all the time). So, despite all the ugliness then, I think it bought me (and ultimately him) a certain ease and peace of mind we otherwise might not have.

Mazal tov to your sister! I wish her strength at a tough time!
Lise

Jewish ritual is no longer necessarily embraced or rejected without first engaging in a process of reflection. We might even call the current style of reflection a new spiritual practice in itself. It displays certain hallmark elements of ritual innovation of our era. These include an earnest grappling with ancient sources; a respect for inherited practices; a curiosity about the range of ideas and practices currently available; a demand for choice and personalization; and above all, a demand for personal integrity, which arises out of the authority of personal experience—what one discussant below calls "intentionality." Interestingly, as Arnold Eisen points out, contemporary rituals (like much of contemporary observance across denominations) do not depend on believing in God or obeying God's commandments. As Eisen writes, "ritual is perhaps attractive because it continues even in the absence of God's felt presence and compensates for that absence with the invocation of God's felt presence in song, text, and blessing."[31] The rituals satisfy other hungers—primarily the needs for meaning and community.[32]

We turn now to process, and grapple with how the dynamic process of ritual change allows for both resistance and acclimation.

NOTES:

1. Susan Berrin, "Inside Jewish Ritual," *Sh'ma* 35, no. 619 (March 2005).

2. Typically, these passages are misogynist or homophobic.

3. Maxine Keyser, "A Seder to Savor," *Philadelphia Citypaper.net* (April 13–20, 2000).

4. That is, its capacity for change and adaptability. While in a medical context "lability" can suggest instability, in a religious context the term can suggest a creative and sustaining vulnerability.

5. Lawrence Kushner, foreword to *The Book of Customs*, by Scott-Martin Kosofsky (San Francisco: Harper, 2004), xi.

6. In 1996, that book was already dated, and a 10th-anniversary edition was published by Biblio Press. The new edition is described as "a year-long guide to women's group celebration of Rosh Hodesh, the New Moon." Adelman develops a blend of new and traditional ritual, song, prayer, meditation and Midrash for each month, from themes linking the Jewish calendar with women's spiritual and life cycle. This 10th anniversary edition includes a preface describing current trends in Jewish women's spiritual activity in the United States. New rituals have been added for bat mitzvah, adoption, child weaning, alternative weddings, pregnancy loss, and ecological holidays.

7. American Jews conventionally have identified with particular denominations. Currently, postdenominationalism is growing: people may either feel comfortable affiliating with multiple denominations, or they may seek out communities that are nondenominational.

8. The label, featuring the work of John Zorn, describes itself as introducing "Jewish music beyond klezmer: adventurous recordings bringing Jewish identity and culture into the 21st century," http://www.tzadik.com.

9. To the best of my understanding, the biblical injunction against marking one's flesh refers to gashing the flesh as a sign of mourning for the dead, a practice kept by those people considered to be idolaters: Lev. 19:28: "You shall not make gashes in your flesh for the dead, or incise markings upon you: I am the LORD." My student Erika Meitner brought my attention to the phenomenon of Jewish tattooing.

10. This is the story of Dan Jaye of Brighton, Massachusetts, as reported in "Jews with Tattoos: What If You Wanted a Tattoo, But Your Religion Prohibited It?" by Douglas Belkin, The Boston Globe, August 15, 2004.

11. In the second edition of *Heeb: The New Jew Review*, which came out in the summer of 2002, one reader, Aaron Brown, wrote, "I just want to tell you now how much I appreciate what you are doing for Jewish people everywhere. Growing up as the only Jewish kid in the small town of Driftwood, Texas, it is a pleasure to find a publication that can help me feel proud of my heritage."

12. One popular text is the downloadable "Love and Justice in Times of War HAGGADAH ZINE," a "politically progressive/radical and anti-racist haggadah ... a source for creating a choose-your-own-adventure progressive seder," http://colours.mahost.org/events/haggadah.html.

13. Brenda Brasher, *Give Me That Online Religion* (San Francisco: Jossey-Bass, Inc., 2001), 75–78.

14. http://www.womenstorah.org.

15. Renewal Rabbi Goldie Milgram suggests in her instructions for an *upsherin*: "Have a professional present to complete the haircut so that the tresses can be properly harvested and donated to an organization that makes wigs for children with cancer such as Locks for Love." See "Upsherin: A Coming of Age Ritual for Toddlers and Their Families," *ReclaimingJudaism.org*, http://www.rebgoldie.com/upsherin.htm.

16. Haviva Ner-David, *Life on the Fringes: A Feminist Journey Towards Traditional Rabbinic Ordination* (Needham, MA: JFL Books, 2000).

17. See "Women's Tefillah" at the Hebrew Institue of Riverdale site, http://www.yerushalayim.net/shuls/hir/women.html.

18. The TorahPod or ShasPod was described by one Judaica store as "a Thirty-gigabyte (30gig) iPod loaded with 2,711 shiurim, one for each page of the Talmud. A shiur is a brief (30–60 minute) discussion by a religious teacher. Each shiur is in English mixed with Aramaic (the language of the Talmud) and some hebrew phrases. The compact iPod is not only more compact than the paper-based version of the Talmud, it is a lot smaller than the typical audio version, which runs to about 2,000 tape cassettes. A TorahPod can

be purchased for $425.... Although the TorahPod cannot be used by Ortho-
dox Jews on the Sabbath (religious laws prohibit the operation of electrical
equipment), you could still listen to your ShasPod on Friday morning and
Saturday night, thus listening to your daily Talmud lecture while avoiding the
Sabbath." Search for keyword "TorahPod" at Eichlers.com at
http://www.eichlers.com.

19. Edward Portnoy, Haredim and the Internet, MODIYA Project,
<http://modiyanyu.edu/handle/1964/265.

20. Its goal is to address "specific interests of the Lesbian, Gay, Bi-sexual
and Transgender (LGBT) community, while also providing participants with
the unique UJC Missions experience, an understanding of the annual Federation campaign, and its importance in community building." See the United
Jewish Communities site at http://www.ujc.org/content_display.html?Arti-
cleID=143114.

21. See SawYouAtSinai.com at http://www.seeyouatsinai.com.

22. Their mission is "to empower and help the Jewish community welcome and fully embrace all members of interfaith families into Jewish life....
We seek to be a resource and advocate, dedicated to raising awareness in the
Jewish community of opportunities inherent in welcoming individuals, couples and families impacted on by interfaith marriage." See The Jewish Outreach Institute mission statement at http://www.joi.org/about/mission.shtml.

23. Mike Ludders, "Joint Seder Celebrates Freedom," *The Kenyon Colle-
gian*, March 28, 2002.

24. For current information about the University of New Hampshire Hillel, see http://www.unh.edu/hillel.

25. From the Chocolate Seder, edited by Rachel Grossman and Stephanie
Simon of METNY USY, United Synagogue Youth, http://www.USY.org/your
usy/pbank/results.asp?id=273.

26. From Julie Marshall, "Eco-Seder Augments Traditional Liturgy with
Environmental Awareness," Jews of the Earth, http://www.jote.org/articles/
passover.html.

27. Originally published on *JewzNewz: The Online Center for Crisis,
Updates, Sense-making and Comfort*, http://www.jewznewz.com.

28. Published at Website for Kol Ami, The Northern Reconstructionist
Community, http://www.kolaminvrc.org/Prayers.

29. Rachel Bodie and Julie Natz, "Inspiring Jewish Ritual," *Sh'ma* 36, no.
619 (March 2005). See also *Jewish Milestones*, at http://www.jewishmile-
stones.org. Of ritualists making their services available, I am most intrigued
by Rabbi Jamie S. Korngold, the "Adventure Rabbi," who, in the wilderness of

Colorado, "is ready and able to serve the needs of [the nation's 70 million] unaffiliated Jews. We offer an invigorating approach to Judaism, and have the ability to customize retreats and life-cycle events to suit your needs." See the Adventure Rabbi site at http://www.adventurerabbi.com.

30. A blog, or Web log, is a personal journal posted on the Internet. It is characteristically written in a confessional, detailed voice, used formerly for the most intimate or private exchanges.

31. Arnold Eisen, *Rethinking Modern Judaism: Ritual, Commandment and Community* (Chicago: University of Chicago Press, 1998), 256.

32. Ibid., 262–63.

CHANGE: RESISTING AND ACCLIMATING

The Threat of Novelty

As the late Judah Goldin, scholar of postbiblical literature, once wrote, "To change we are all subject, perhaps most profoundly when we offer greatest resistance; adaptation, on the other hand, requires genius."[1] All religions with deep historical roots are works in progress, and Judaism is no exception. However much one fears novelty, new religious practices—like the older, ancient ones—will be created. They will be repeated, and transmitted. Some will even become "tradition."

As sociologist Wade Clark Roof reminds us, "Religion is socially produced, or more accurately, we might say it is constantly being reproduced. Far from being handed down from the heavens, religious symbols, beliefs, and practices are created and then maintained, revised, and modified by the often self-conscious actions of human beings."[2]

At the same time, as religious historian Terrence W. Tilley suggests, the mere fact that rituals are made—artistically constructed by a people and a culture—does not necessarily deny or denigrate the presence of divinity, the commandment of certain behaviors by God, or the holiness of ritual practice.[3]

Any number of factors change religious practices, including what Roof calls "changing interpretations of religious heritage, social location and influences, new leadership, groups contending for power and control."[4] Author and ritual innovator E. M. Broner understands that performing new rituals, even as they serve to repair, heal, and reclaim tradition, can still feel both dangerous and paradoxical to those performing them. She quotes Barbara Meyerhoff, who explains that rituals may seem "dangerous because when we are not convinced by a ritual we may become aware of ourselves as having made them up, thence on to the paralyzing realization, that we have made up all our truths; our ceremonies, our most precious conceptions and convictions—are mere memory."[5]

From New to Familiar

Every Jewish practice and ritual object was once "newish," but was never *totally* brand-new. It may have its roots and may already have circulated in Jewish or even non-Jewish practice. How did it become part of Jewish spiritual life? It was adapted, borrowed, appropriated, redesigned, or derived. We have seen such phenomena occur in our own time. Eight days of Hanukkah presents were, in an earlier incarnation, Christmas presents. And would Hanukkah decorations for the home have emerged without the enticing domestic charm and commercial festivities of Christmas? The annual Salute to Israel Parade—an important ritual of pride and belonging for many Jews—is a variation of the St. Patrick's Day Parade, Macy's Thanksgiving Day Parade, and every other parade that marches down the streets of New York. The makers of the patchwork wedding *huppah* evoke the American quilting bee.

A New Wedding Ritual

Many a close friend or relative of a bride or groom is now spending the months before a wedding overseeing the creation of a patchwork *huppah*. Family and friends (Jewish or not—this practice does not require "tribal credentials") are invited to embroider or decorate a patch of fabric for the couple's *huppah,* which can later be hung and reused as a family heirloom. Patch contributors—women or men—gather at a quilting-bee wedding shower to piece the quilt together and ceremoniously offer the bride and groom their blessings and wisdom. They may also recite benedictions at the wedding itself. This practice reflects the prominent role in new rituals of the impulse to personalize and to create community.

But such shifts of context and rites of adaptation are not solely a modern phenomenon. In ancient times, matzah was not "invented" for Passover use. It was flat bread, already familiar and available to Jews, that became specifically designated for this holiday. Before the shofar was assigned its symbolic role in the new year, Jews were already using it for other purposes, such as calls of warning and calls to war. The Greek loan word *afikoman,* the matzah hidden and eaten as dessert at the Passover seder, recalls an ancient Greek practice of eating dessert at a different location at the end of a feast, like a progressive meal. The eight-branched Hanukkah menorah was a variation of the seven-branched temple menorah.

This process of ritual development is in keeping with historian Eric Hobsbawm's familiar formulation of the term "invented tradition." Invented tradition refers to "a set of ritual or symbolic practices, normally governed by overtly or tacitly accepted rules, which seek to inculcate certain values and norms of behavior by repetition, and which automatically imply continuity with the past."[6] In Hobsbawm's formulation, inventors of new tradition dip into the vast repositories of any culture's rituals and symbols, obscuring the intended "break in continuity."[7] Through emphasizing the link to the past, it becomes possible simultaneously to disguise and legitimize innovation.

Talmudic Innovation

If ours is not the first generation to invent ritual, it is also not the first to voice anxiety about ritual change, or to resist it on principle, before finally making our peace with it. The Talmud documents liturgical innovations that might have been considered idiosyncratic or anomalous when they were written and redacted.

Some talmudic innovations were retained and remain in use. Familiar examples include the blessings recited over natural phenomena and social events. They include blessings upon seeing exceptionally beautiful people, trees, or fields; when encountering a place where you were once miraculously saved from a disaster; and when you hear good or bad news. These are provided in many a prayer book.

Other talmudic innovations have fallen out of use. Consider this practice of facilitating the birth of beautiful children: It was customary for Rabbis to sit outside the ritual bath (mikveh) and to advise entering women how to immerse themselves properly. It was the practice (at least as it was told) of the extravagantly handsome Rabbi Yochanan to sit outside the mikveh, so that as women exited, they would behold him before returning home to their husbands to resume sexual relations that night. As it was believed that the state of mind during conception influenced the formation of one's child, the lingering image of beautiful Yochanan would surely result in a beautiful child.[8]

Other ancient practices endure as sacred texts that have been codified in the Mishnah or Talmud. Sometimes they are drafted into service to ground and inspire new practices.[9] Consider the following dream practices, drawn from Tractate *Berachot* of the Babylonian Talmud; this text that offers an excellent glimpse of the "smorgasbord Judaism" that characterized the world of early Rabbinic Judaism. (Note that we cannot know how the ritual was actually practiced, or if it was even practiced at all.)

A ritual for a nightmare: A person who had a troubling dream was advised to assemble three companions to constitute a dream court. The dreamer would assert, contrary to fact, that he or she had good dream. The companions would affirm the

falsehood, that a good dream was had, and would follow with
a litany of Torah verses, evidencing historical precedent for
divine rescue, transformations from sorrow to joy, and the
granting of peace. Those who had dreams that left them per-
plexed turned either to a Rabbi or paid for the services of a pro-
fessional dream interpreter.[10]

Talmudic innovations that we still practice and those that only remain
on paper together constitute the Jewish cultural wealth we call the
"oral tradition." We should remember that however vast the repository
of talmudic memory, it is but partial. It is not an inventory of *every*
Jewish practice observed in antiquity. Why were some ancient innovations excluded from Jewish written memory? I imagine the following possibilities:

The Rabbis rarely debated the merits of popular practices in
which they did not engage. (This may explain why we hear so little in
talmudic discourse of women's practices.) At the same time, they did
occasionally discuss certain practices that they found to be objection-
able, but that had potential lifesaving or healing attributes. Interestingly enough, many of these healing practices were attributed to the
Amorite people; in fact, the term used for such practices is *mipnei*
darkei ha-Emori (literally, according to the ways of the Amorites)—a
term with a decidedly negative connotation.[11]

But the Rabbis went further than merely tolerating such innovations: in claiming that a given practice was performed as a matter of
life or death, the Rabbis legitimated innovative practices that were
becoming popular among the general public. As Judah Goldin
reminds us, both the Babylonian and Palestinian Talmuds "declare
that whatever heals is *not* to be regarded as *mipnei darkei ha-Emori.*"[12]
Indeed, Goldin teaches, we should not underestimate the combination of what he calls "elasticity, patchwork, downright inconsistence
and contrariness" that often characterizes the Rabbinic approach to
religious practice and doctrine. Whether the Rabbis resigned themselves to innovation or accepted it gladly, it is clear that they approved
many practices and doctrines that pointed clearly to reconciliations
between what Goldin terms "conflicting interests inside a pattern of

indoctrination and there is never a loss for a prooftext to validate what desire can't resist."[13]

When they failed to defeat a new practice, the Rabbis moved to authenticate and professionalize it. For instance, failing to prohibit the use of amulets, the Rabbis ruled that an amulet could be used *if* a professional amulet writer wrote it and *if* the amulet had been proven effective.[14] The ultimate strategy, in talmudic times, was privileging *minhag,* customs that had already taken hold, and creating some jurisdiction over them.

Erwin Goodenough's oeuvre on Jewish symbols in the Greco-Roman period traces precedents for such intercultural borrowings of ritual objects and practices. Goodenough asks: "Why did the Jews suddenly want to put symbols of fish, bread, and especially wine on their graves and synagogues [compared to the symbols he considers distinctively Jewish in nature and origin, such as the menorah or the shofar], and what did they tell themselves and one another when they did so?"[15]

The Rabbis of the Talmud rarely came out and sanctioned overt borrowings from the non-Jewish world, but they were unable to prevent such borrowings, these "obvious invasions from the outside."[16] Powerless to forbid them, the Rabbis nevertheless spoke out against the borrowers: "What sort of Jews could have borrowed these art forms—art forms, indeed, especially associated with pagan gods and their cults—and why did Jews want them?"[17] Alternatively, the Rabbis would justify the borrowings, straining to find (or fabricate) "authentically Jewish" earlier origins in sacred texts.

In other words, the Rabbis would try to sanction an overt borrowing by maintaining that what appeared to be a new practice was indigenous all along.

Any culture that prefers tradition to innovation and experimentation has complex strategies to obscure the novelty of a borrowed ritual object. As Goodenough explains, "The most successful religious reformers have invariably insisted that they were bringing in nothing new, but rather were discovering the true meaning inherent from the first in the symbols of the religion they were reforming."[18]

Judaism never delighted in the inevitability of change, says Goldin. Nonetheless, many internal cultural mechanisms have been formally established to deal with necessary change, especially when such changes necessitate reframing both Jewish law and practice.

The classical vocabulary includes:

1. Legal mechanisms: *takkanot* (enactments), *gezerot* (decrees), *hifsikan* (suspended practice)

2. Technical principles that justify particular adaptations: *mipnei darkhei shalom* (legislation made for the sake of general welfare) and *mipnei tikun olam* (legislation made for the maintenance of good relations in society)

3. Reading practices: midrash (the interpretation and reinterpretation of classical texts over the generations), a practice of rereading sacred texts that allows for adaptations that are experienced as being ever continuous with the past and still relevant for the moment[19]

Ascribing "new Jewish explanations to old observances" is still a common Jewish practice, because a symbol adjusts "itself to new situations by giving to the old value a new explanation."[20] When David Roskies describes the "artful fashioning of ... new tradition"[21] in the works of both 19th- and early 20th-century Yiddish writers, he notes that this process continues into modernity: "In the cultural as in the legal realm, every innovation was legitimated on the grounds that it had been there to begin with."[22]

Is Anyone in Charge Now?

When new Jewish rituals emerge in contemporary America, they seem to "erupt." That is, they are messy and chaotic. While rabbis and laypeople have endless informal discussions about ritual innovation, no one is really in charge of approving or classifying new rituals. There is no "National Board of Rabbis, Pious and Powerful Layeaders, and Scholars of Jewish Ritual and Liturgy" that meets to review rituals. (If there were, however, I imagine they would need to go out into the field of the Jewish world, asking questions such as these:

Which rituals are still working well? Which need updating? Which need major overhaul? Which Jewish rituals have, in effect, been archived, and what practices, now fallen into desuetude, are worth resurrecting? They might determine which rituals need to be created from scratch, and which new practices from the various denominations—of other religious traditions, even—are the most inspiring. They might look to secular culture for promising possibilities for Jewish ritual renewal.)[23]

Still, there are some efforts to impose order. Each denomination has a central location for its leaders to discuss matters of ritual concern. Of course, for better or worse, organizations move slowly. For instance, it was not until 2002 that the rabbis of the Conservative movement's law committee voted that women may count in a minyan and be *shlichot tzibbur* (prayer leaders).[24] The decision was the outcome of a discussion begun in 1972.

Other groups act more quickly, but their leadership lags behind. In 2003, Reform rabbi Peter Knobel headed a Central Conference of American Rabbis committee to create a guide to same-sex weddings. The committee had been formed more than two years earlier, "when the Reform organization approved the right of its members to officiate at such rituals, but is only now becoming active, said Rabbi Knobel...."[25] Same-sex commitment ceremonies had been performed for over 15 years. Only *after* they became mainstream did the "official" rabbinic discussion commence.[26] It is not unreasonable to postulate that these drawn-out rabbinical discussions are out of synch with the fast-paced lives of real people. Perhaps that is a blessing in disguise.

In synagogues, there are ritual committees, but based on my own experience, few are willing to champion change before it reaches the pews. Typically, the ritual committee preserves the status quo. Theirs is not to innovate but to maintain. They discuss distribution of honors and *aliyot,* seating on the High Holy Days, decorations and décor, ushers and greeters, kashrut and catering, and they determine the nature of the relationship between the rabbi, the cantor, and the ritual committee. But no one is *really* in charge of determining what intellectual, financial, and spiritual resources ought to address rituals that are absent or functioning weakly. When it comes to new ritual, the key players might be rabbis, but the real movers and shakers are the good people of the town square, creating, improvising, and voting with their feet.

Rabbinic Power and Folk Power

The 1998 issue of *Moreh Derech,* the manual for Conservative rabbis published by the Rabbinical Assembly, alludes to the power of the people as it intersects with rabbinic power. Conservative rabbis are advised to acknowledge the prevalent sensibility of *amcha* (the people—a term that can express condescension), and to embrace the inevitability of ritual innovation and eventual adaptation:

> *During times of both stability and change, the rabbi represents continuity with the past. As rabbis, we need to utilize the tradition in such a way that it continues to speak cogently to the generation at hand. And so this manual has been designed to bring Jewish tradition and amcha (the people) together. We must focus on the people we want to reach, using Jewish tradition to transform nature into history, accidents into meaningful events, and experiences into sacred moments.*[27]

The spirit of popular innovation and flexibility is further emphatically evoked in the manual's specific instructions for the ceremony welcoming a newborn baby girl:

> *The welcome of a baby girl into the Jewish community with a ceremony that deliberately affirms her inclusion in the covenant is a ritual that is barely a generation old and is still evolving. A ceremony is usually held within the first month after the baby's birth. Many models and ceremonies have been developed. Some use the structure, texts, and concepts of the brit milah (circumcision) as a starting point.... The following ceremony offers three options within a single structure.... This*

> *multiple-choice arrangement has been provided to satisfy a range of liturgical and aesthetic preferences, but more importantly, to reflect the reality that liturgical history is still being written. While it seems clear that the simchat bat ceremony is here to stay, the final form has not been canonized.... All those who use these rituals are partners in their creation.*[28]

The language of this entry is worth scrutinizing. Even though the ritual appears in a rabbinical manual, an authorative text for an established, set practice, we are told that the ritual presented is, in the scheme of Jewish history, practically brand-new. Furthermore, it is still in flux, and we can expect this to be the case for a while. There is no familiar model you can turn to, one that participants will recognize from past experience and feel at home with: no one can obscure the fact that this is a work in progress. Whatever format you choose for the ritual, you will be part of an innovation that is still developing.

These selections from a rabbinical manual would suggest that rabbis are in charge of innovation, and that it is their prerogative to give their congregants the opportunity to collaborate with them. Rabbis do innovate, some brilliantly: many of the ritual innovations in Debra Orenstein's anthology, *Lifecycles: Jewish Women on Life Passages & Personal Milestones,* were created by the first generation of women to be ordained as rabbis. But rabbis, as we have seen, are not the sole source of innovation. Today, rabbinic innovation follows popular innovation, just as it did in the past.

Rabbis are unable to direct or curtail the ritual innovations of *amcha,* the people, especially when many practices (like baby namings, bar mitzvah parties, or wedding ceremonies) take place outside synagogues. When these practices become familiar and entrenched, rabbis (just as they did in the past) may claim that the innovations were theirs all along, and that they will now be their gatekeepers, setting rules and standards. Numerous ritual practices we now consider highly traditional were once considered inappropriate by many rabbis. For instance, when married women wanted to wear wigs as a sign of modesty, rabbis of the late 19th century argued against it, preferring the less attractive hat, kerchief, or shawl. For the rabbis, the wigs were lewd and provocative borrowings from secular culture. But the wig-wearing women prevailed, especially as more of them could afford wigs. Now, wearing wigs is *the* sign of the highest standards of modesty and piety in certain communities, and the rabbis would be the first to pronounce the practice de rigueur.

A more recent example is the interfaith wedding ceremony. These days, Conservative or Orthodox clergy do not perform interfaith weddings, and the professional bodies to which Reform rabbis belong also discourage it. Still, many liberal rabbis, either with or without clergy of other faiths co-officiating, preside over interfaith weddings. Often, it is because they have been persuaded by Jews who argue that non-traditional ceremonies *can* legitimately honor the role Judaism plays and may play in the life of the couple, and the rabbis agree to sculpt and participate in such ceremonies.[29]

As we have seen, the surrender of rabbinical will to public practice is nothing new. In the Talmud, when the Rabbis contemplated ritual behaviors they were unsure of, they advised each other, *"Puk hazei mai amma davar."*[30] Look around, and see what the people are actually doing. Then legislate it.

The creative impulse and the creative religious genius of a community reside in the lives of real, everyday people. Sensitive religious leaders know this. Robert Orsi, historian of Christianity as it is lived by Americans, offers a perspective that can illuminate how we understand grassroots innovation in Judaism. Says Orsi: "People appropriate religious idioms as they need them, in response to particular circumstances. All religious ideas and impulses are of the moment, invented, taken, borrowed, and improvised at the intersections of life."[31] Lived religion offers people the possibility of shaping and improvising their lives and theologies in response to their changing circumstances. Religious creations contain "libratory possibilities," and the oppressed and powerless find a stage upon which to declare their freedom, resist, rebel, subvert, and transgress.

Within the field of Jewish studies, Ellen Frankel calls the oral transmission of people's practices "folk Torah."[32] Laura Geller, upon realizing that her own lived experience *is* Jewish experience, calls it the "Torah of our lives."[33] Rabbi Lawrence Kusher explains that "what the Jews wind up doing as they attempt to negotiate, comprehend, and live by God's laws" is not only significant; it "attains independent and authentic religious status." In Kushner's understanding, if "Scripture is from the top down (from God to the Jews) ..." then the customs Jew invent and elaborate "... are from the bottom up (from the Jews to God). The Torah tells Jews about God, the *minhagim* tell God about the Jews."[34] Both, intertwined, have sacred status.

Resisting Innovation: A Case Study

Each era seizes upon some innovations that raise Jewish communal anxiety more than others. The earliest innovations of Reform Judaism in Germany caused intense consternation. Still earlier, Hasidic practices fueled much passionate debate. Of the new rituals that have been introduced in the last 30 years, those created by women have met the strongest initial resistance—this was particularly so in the early years, when women's entry into the rabbinate was a topic of heated debate. That the very practices that so threatened the status quo have become widely adopted, not only in America, but wherever Jews live, is ironic. (Of course, it's also highly ironic that Hasidism, Reform Judaism, and Jewish feminism—all movements that once seemed so threatening—are now described as dynamic forces that have reinvigorated Judaism.)

Why were the new practices initially so worrisome?

To understand resistance to ritual innovation, let us consider one modern case: the story of a young Orthodox rabbi who was threatened by the beginnings of some Jewish women's ritual innovations.

By current standards and sensibilities, the innovations that made Rabbi Meiselman fret in the 1970s seem innocuous, hardly more provocative and bold than the idea of women voting or wearing pants. Here is what worried him: Orthodox women in America had begun studying Torah and Talmud at advanced levels, praying together and having *aliyot* (Torah honors). They were reading the Torah and dancing with Torah scrolls on Simchat Torah. Families were marking the births and b'not mitzvah of their daughters. In nearly all of these cases, I should add, the women involved had proceeded only *after* securing the approval of rabbis who had determined that the practices were in accordance with Orthodox readings of *halakhah*. About such rituals, Meiselman wrote, "The introduction of new rituals may not be forbidden, but it is certainly an exercise in futility, a series of meaningless activities."[35] Note that Meiselman was aware he could not argue that the rituals defied or degraded Jewish law.

However commendable it is to thank God and celebrate the birth of a daughter or a young woman's bat mitzvah, Meiselman claimed, "it completely mocks the entire structure of Judaism to invest these celebrations with specific and detailed rituals."[36] In his view, a "ridiculous ceremony" such as the *britah* (the feminine form of *brit* or *bris*) held on the eighth day of a girl's life, "destroys the meaning" of the male rituals and "is not necessary to make women feel significant." He further claimed, "To pursue ritual creativity is to deny divine obligation as the source of all meaning in religious activity"; it is a "meaningless form of spiritual autoeroticism."[37] Women may not dance with Torah scrolls on Simchat Torah, he argued, because it has not been an age-old synagogue practice: "the introduction of this practice would be a violation of synagogue etiquette,"[38] not to mention a sexual provocation that distracts male worshippers from their concentration. As for women who wish to wear a tallit, it is a "tool for an ego trip or for the advancement of a ... political movement."[39]

Yet, in spite of these objections, such practices have entered mainstream modern Orthodoxy. Some are even practiced in ultra-Orthodox sects. Unfamiliar with their contentious history, many people under the age of 25 will assume that such practices have gone on among Orthodox Jews for generations, and that they are, in fact, "natural." Rivka Haut, a founder of the Women's Tefillah Group, offered the following observations in a letter sent to the activists of Women of the Wall. Her intention was to inspire perseverance during a particularly frustrating period of the women's struggle to fight for the right to pray properly, as a group of women, at the Western Wall. Haut's remarks chronicle one innovation, the Women's Tefillah Group, which gained acceptance within Orthodoxy during her lifetime:

> *When women's tefillah groups began, 25 to 30 years ago, we were met with fierce opposition. All over the Orthodox world we were accused of strange practices, of plotting to destroy*

Judaism. The attacks were often quite personal. We were small groups with little support.

This past Shabbat, I was at my daughter's home in Maryland. There is a women's tefillah that meets every month for Shabbat Mincha [afternoon services]. The shul, which is mainstream, not at all radical, encourages the women's tefillah group, which meets in the beit midrash [library]. The rabbi's wife attends. The rabbi continually urges them to meet more often than once a month, as the group gets women to attend Mincha services, which they do not ordinarily do.

Two women in the community who are not members of the women's tefillah group asked the group if they could have aliyot when their children became engaged to each other. The two cried when receiving their aliyot, held hands with each other, and hugged everyone with great joy. It was very moving.

I was offered an aliyah. My daughter is the gabbait [officiant]. My six-year-old granddaughter stood with me by the Torah. So there we were: three generations. My generation fought for women's tefillah group. My daughter attended as a young girl, but few of her friends came.... But for my granddaughter, there is nothing unusual about women's tefillah group. She has been in one since her birth. There were lots of young girls of all ages there. It is their religious tradition.

True, this took years. But, in Jewish history, what is 30 years? We have achieved such a major change in such a short time! Although the years seemed to drag, and change seemed slow in coming, in reality we accomplished a revolution in the Orthodox synagogue.[40]

How did this ritual persist, survive, and flourish? I suspect these are some of the reasons: Women were persistent in coming to the *tefillah* groups over a long period of time and in a variety of locales. The generation of new initiators refused to allow strong and organized efforts to malign their worship, or to discourage or stop them. When they were denied synagogue space, they worshipped in private settings. They organized. They publicized their efforts through newsletters and assisted groups of women around the world to set up prayer groups of their own; education was a priority. On the home front, they engaged their families in the practice, bringing their daughters along with them, month after month, and their mothers too. The women understood that they were embarrassing their daughters by standing out, for what teenager wants her mother to be different? They did their best to assure them that their initiative was both ethically compelling and fully compatible with Jewish law (if not with standard Jewish custom). They negotiated with their husbands and sons when they worried that the practice would take away from the good feeling of going to synagogue all together: "It is just one *Shabbat* a month," many explained. They were cheered on by feminist Jews in the liberal movements who may have visited *tefillah* groups to express their support. The practice became habit. Now the daughters and granddaughters who were "born into" the practice, those who cannot imagine a time when such a practice did not exist, are its newest leaders.

Given the ready and widespread acceptance of these practices today, why did this rabbi take such exception when they were first introduced? Why did he dig in his heels, and pronounce dire warnings? He admitted he could not claim that new practices had never been introduced into Judaism. He could not even claim, based on his own legal reasoning, that these particular innovations were either technically impermissible or prohibited by standard interpretations of *halakhah*.

The practices were new. Fearful and without legal or rational ground to stand on, he cursed innovation: "Futile!" "Meaningless!"

Others, past and present, have hurled invectives of their own at new practices they have encountered. They claim innovation desecrates a precious tradition and endangers the community. Innovation pollutes the tradition with beliefs and practices of the secular world or of foreign faiths. Even one innovation opens the door for the entire tradition to be altered and abandoned. The innovators are themselves pernicious and dangerous. They lead us down a slippery slope. A cadre of the learned and pious must come forth to stand guard and remain resolute. Who but the faithful can guard the integrity of the tradition against the threat of those who claim to improve upon it? Who else can hear and protect God's will?

Meiselman wrote in a period when many changes were being introduced to improve the role of Jewish women in study, prayer, and leadership. His comments were meant to make people resist and fear such change, to persuade them that feminism was a secular fad. His call to stand steadfast did not prevent the gradual unfolding of change, though it (and other such calls) did protract the process—the discussions, the negotiations, and the establishment of those facts on the ground that paved the way for new practices to become acceptable.

The Rabbis of the Talmud knew that resistance is a natural response to change. Still, they encouraged people to *renew* their Jewish observance through innovation, at least in prayer, so as to connect personally with God. In regard to the *Amidah*, the central prayer of every Jewish service, they ruled that those who *do not* innovate by making a personal request have not offered proper supplication. I relate well to Rabbi Zeiri, who found this requirement altogether too challenging: "I am able to innovate in my prayer, but I am afraid to do so, for I risk losing my place."[41] Valuing change extends beyond prayer: regarding bad fortune, the rabbis urged, *"Mishaneh makom, mishaneh mazal"* (When you change your place, you change your fate). I believe they meant this literally, suggesting the blessings of a fresh start in a new place. But they also meant it spiritually, suggesting that even if you stayed put, you could reorient yourself and alter the outcome of your life.

As intolerant of rabbinic misogyny as I am, I surprise myself by understanding Meiselman. I know that like daily routines, religious rituals hold us together, keeping us, figuratively, "in place." I am writing these words on the first days of a sabbatical in Cambridge, England, and I realize that I have been rattled by the small changes in my daily life. No *New York Times,* no Cheerios, no cat on my lap? Even with my husband and daughter living here, even with acquaintances who wave to me as we pass on the street, even as a visiting member of High Table at Newnham College, I long for home, with its predictable and familiar daily rituals. Of course I will fashion new morning rituals for Cambridge that will soon become automatic, even dear to me. And within a week, I am eating rugged Scottish oats and bicycling across the fen to the university. My new morning routine won't change the core of my identity, but I also know that I will indeed be changed in small ways by new practices that I might retain after I return home.

However open people might be to changing where they live, who they live with, and their jobs, I know they are less open to change—even pleasant, comforting change—in their religious practice. Change, in a word, alters us and alters our world. Those like Meiselman who worried about the religious changes of the 1970s, worried that they would rob Judaism of its coherence. And given the common fear that Judaism's legacy is always fragile and on the verge of disappearing, one can almost understand a stubborn resistance to any change whatsoever.

The Banality of Change

At the same time, as Rochelle Millen writes, "changes in religious ritual, observance, and law occur all the time" in Judaism and in all living religions. They can emerge from the best of intentions, such as "to make things better." And with the passage of time, and lapses in memory, we inevitably discover that "customary practices today will not necessarily be customary practices tomorrow."[42] Even the most conservative of Jewish law keepers acknowledge that change happens, and that when new practices are embraced by the community, they carry weight. In fact, a widely accepted principle is that when a *minhag* is widely observed, it can override *halakhah.* This is true even if the *minhag* is observed in just one particular city, in one community, or in one's parents' household.

The process of acclimation in religion follows the process of acclimation in daily life. Changes in our customs or habits feel strange at first. Then they are tolerated, next they seem familiar, and soon enough they may become beloved. Eventually, they may come to hold our world together. Our personal or cultural memory of a time when the new custom did not exist or when it was first introduced grows fuzzy and is eventually erased. A new memory is constructed, and we say to ourselves, this custom has existed for as long as we can remember. It feels rooted in the most ancient practices and affirms and honors our connections to our ancestors and their most sacred commitments. It defines one's Jewish identity. As one Israeli mother, now raising her son in a Reform congregation in Virginia, told me: "When I first came to this synagogue and saw men and women praying together, I was shocked. This is not what I saw my parents do; they pray with the *mechitzah*. But I kept coming back because I made friends, and much more quickly than I would have believed, I got used to how they pray. My son grew up in this congregation and knows nothing else. To him, men and women praying together is normal. A woman wearing a tallit and *kippah* is normal. It is what Jews do. When we go to Israel to visit, and he goes to the shul with his grandfather, he is shocked."

If we think of rituals as the habitual, patterned, familiar, and automatic acts we perform, and if we think of rituals as the maps we turn to for direction when we go adrift or when we are unhinged by loss, confusion, or complicated life transitions, then the idea of ritual innovation seems paradoxical. How can rituals also be brand-new, freshly invented, strange, provocative, and destabilizing?

Despite our resistance, we do tolerate change when it feels so continuous with the past that we hardly even notice its novelty. When we witness a ritual change once or twice and it seems not as bad as we anticipated, we overcome our initial shock or anger. As one elderly member of a Conservative congregation said on the day I started *leyning* (chanting) from the Torah, "I never thought I'd see a woman reading Torah, but now I've seen it, it's not bad." He shook my hand and said, "I could get used to it."

Religious rituals work, in many ways, as hypnotic suggestion. When you are told by your religious tradition that you are married, you, your partner, and all others are convinced that you are. When you are told that your departed are now with God in heaven, you might be persuaded, even if only on a metaphorical level, that they are. Ritual innovation also works hypnotically, and with a twist. If I am acknowledged as an authority figure in my tradition and I possess the convincing dramatic skills of a good ritual expert, I can claim that a new ritual is just as potent and effective as an old one. If I suggest that the ritual is not new at all but is rather a truer, better, more accurate representation of our deeply held beliefs and claims of the past, you may be persuaded to believe that it is so. What's more, you may believe me when I say that you may very soon forget that this new ritual was once an unsettling innovation. Even if you resist my claims now, your experiences will eventually persuade you to accept them as true.

Time, in part, makes this sleight of hand possible. The passage of time transforms the invention that initially characterizes all rituals into a recognized, deeply felt authenticity. It is important to realize that authenticity in religious traditions is a feeling, not a fact. Lapsed time changes the valence of a ritual, giving it weight and steadiness that support it, in all its guises and variations. Even whimsical rituals—such as going into the field to greet the *Shabbat* bride, or inviting the invisible Prophet Elijah into every Jewish home on Passover and pouring him a cup of wine—possess this quality. So do curious rituals we have accumulated along the way, such as *tashlikh,* emptying one's pockets of sins into a body of water on Rosh Hashanah; or *kapporot,* the ritual of atoning for one's sins before Yom Kippur by twirling a rooster or hen over one's head, then donating it to the poor. Time makes these and other rituals real and plausible. It makes them, in their own way, ordinary. Add individual and group memory to the mix, and as Rabbi Steven Greenberg once told me, these new ritual expressions "become communal, and in time, the ones that stick, like always and forever, become a part of the inherited tradition." With the passage of time comes the forgetfulness that facilitates cultural change. We forget that the ritual once made us uncomfortable. We forget that once, we knew neither the rules, nor how we were supposed to feel anticipating or performing the ritual. We know only this: a given ritual is one we perform now, and we probably have been doing so since the beginning of time.[43]

The Artistry of Innovation

We can compare innovations in Jewish ritual to innovations in the arts. They emerge because individuals, alone or in collaboration, are compelled to express themselves, creating objects and experiences that are beautiful or arresting, insightful, unnerving, or important. Some say they surely come by the grace of God; for others that is a feeling more than certain fact.

Neither ritual nor artistic innovations emerge in isolation, free from constraints, free of history. Ritualists, like artists, draw upon "materials, concepts, references, and themes" of the past, and are linked to what art historian Johanna Drucker calls, in the context of artistic innovation, "a continuity of ideas from earlier movements."[44]

There is one key difference. Artists may flaunt their break with conventions and constraints of the past as they step into the future. (Granted, while they may eventually be praised by critics and embraced by audiences, artists may also initially hear their radical new work described as "bad art.") Jewish ritual innovators, by contrast, must maintain that their creations are strongly tied to the past. Otherwise, what they present may not just be called bad religion—but may be seen as heretical, as not even Jewish.[45]

Thus, the bolder and more radical the ritual, the more emphatically the Jewish ritual innovator claims, "This is what Jews have always done. This is consistent with 'the true spirit' of our ancient practices." Or (and this takes great imagination and even greater chutzpah, but it has been a frequent strategy of Jewish innovation—witness the midrash, the Mishnah, and the Talmud, all of what is called "the oral Torah"), "It was all revealed at Mount Sinai."

Maimonides

Maimonides, in his Mishneh Torah, does not go this far. He distinguishes the 613 mitzvot, which can clearly be derived from the Torah, from the innovations that came later. These include reading the Book of Esther on Purim, lighting the Hanukkah candles, and fasting on the Ninth of Av, all practices innovated by prophets, scribes, or courts, and accepted by many people. These new practices, Maimonides says, are permitted and are to be followed not because they come as a belated divine revelation, heard by some, but because they praise the name of God and reveal God's presence in history to the generations.

The Jewish ritual innovator who cares to circumvent doubt, discomfort, shunning, ridicule, or even something akin to excommunication will boldly highlight the presence of the old within the new. Tropes of Jewish memory will be echoed: The covenant! The Exodus from Egypt! Standing at Mount Sinai! Familiar Jewish symbols will be displayed: the shofar! The megillah! The sound of Judaic languages will be heard: *Baruch ata ...! Mazel tov!*

Guardians of Continuity, Agents of Change

Jewish tradition reflects a dance between two partners with opposing impulses. I think of them as the guardian of continuity and the agent of change. The guardian of continuity is motivated by loyalty to ancestors, respect for things untainted, the belief that God's will is reflected in the ancient documents of the Written and Oral Law, and the desire to maintain cohesion among Jews dispersed worldwide through a consistent repertoire of shared practices. The guardian, nursing a mythic, dreamlike belief that the tradition was once perfect in antiquity, acts to maintain things as they always have been and forever will be.

The agent of change, on the other hand, takes steps to honor the commitment to tradition by carefully, systematically, and ingeniously refreshing that tradition for a new age so that it can remain both precious and practical. The agent of change, not beholden to mythic history, but lovingly respectful of it, carefully studies the old and ancient remembered forms of Judaism. The agent knows that we do not practice Judaism as our grandparents did. Our grandparents did not practice Judaism as the Jews of the 18th and 19th centuries did. Jews of the medieval period did not practice the Judaism of the Babylonian exile, and Jews living in the time of the First and Second Temples were not practicing the Judaism of our biblical Patriarchs and Matriarchs.

The guardian of continuity demands to know, "Will your innovation survive the test of time?"

The agent of change knows that it is impossible to predict how a new ritual will play out, and can live with the uncertainty. It often depends on chance, the vagaries of fashions that do or don't catch on. Who would have thought the crocheted *kippah* would have become so popular? Who would have thought that the choice men and women made among a variety of head coverings would come to designate not just one's humility before God, but also the level of one's Jewish observance and the community with which one is affiliated?

The agent of change knows this: some ritual innovations of contemporary Judaism will endure. Some will endure as practices, and others will endure, as they did in the past, as part of our rich historical narrative, the remembered Torah of our lives.

The guardian of continuity may be a religious authority or a layperson who feels obligated to maintain and protect a tradition perceived as perfect. The agent of change may be a religious authority bold enough to risk taking the initiative, or a layperson compelled and empowered to repair, reform, or reconstruct.

That Jewish sacred texts often support the voices of the guardian partner is not surprising. The ancient texts and their reverberations are often heard most vociferously in the face of incipient change. In the early 19th century, Hungarian rabbi Moshe Sofer wished to protect the traditional Judaism he knew from the earliest reformers, who were proposing to create a synagogue of male and female voices and to eliminate Hebrew prayer. He proclaimed: "That which is new is prohibited by the Torah."[46]

Yet sacred texts also support the agents of change. Here, we see the Psalmist claim that God delights in innovation, a fresh and original new prayer:

Sing a new song to the Lord,
renew yourselves all people on earth.
(Psalm 96)

Many sacred texts report innovations and alternatives to conventional practice without any disparagement. The Talmud reports that the house of Hillel lit their menorah by adding the lights from right to left and by lighting them from left to right; the house of Shammai lit the opposite way. Before Hanukkah was established as an annual, postbiblical practice, no one was lighting eight-branched menorahs, either from right to left or from left to right. The familiar menorah had seven branches. The reason the Talmud asks, "What is Hanukkah?" (Babylonian Talmud *Shabbat*) is precisely because not everyone knew what the new holiday was about or agreed about how it was supposed to be observed. What was the lighting supposed to signify? Right to left or left to right? Whose version was one to follow? It was a matter of debate, and our ancestors worked out which practices felt appropriately holy. (Would the houses of Hillel and Shammai, who both lit their menorahs with oil outside their homes, recognize the menorahs we now place on our windowsills—especially the Mickey Mouse ones—or make sense of our multicolored wax candles?)

Jewish tradition does not prefer either the guardian of continuity or the agent of change. It embraces the tension of their intermingling. This flexibility is vividly reflected in the chant that accompanies the return of the Torah to the ark after it has been read.

Help us to turn to you, and we shall return,
Renew our lives as in the days of old.[47]

The words are both poignant and paradoxical, blurring the past and the future, and mingling nostalgia and prophecy. The course of action it proposes—simultaneous restoration and renewal—is logically impossible. Only divine cooperation, it seems, makes it plausible.

Let us not imagine the guardians of continuity and the agents of change in opposition to each other. Instead, let us imagine that we can simultaneously embrace the impulse to maintain and protect along with the impulse to refresh and revise. We can believe it is important to perform and venerate inherited rituals, even if we cannot articulate why. We can simultaneously acknowledge that the world we live in is perpetually changing—through scientific and geographical discoveries; philosophic enlightenments; political, ethical, medical, and technical innovations. We can hold a vague nostalgia for "the way things used to be," and still prefer to keep up with change rather than resist it. As E. M. Broner writes, "The ultimate purpose of ritual is twofold and contradictory: to maintain the status quo, to step in place, and, conversely, to change, to alter."[48] In this respect, religion itself is simultaneously conservative (wanting to keep the wisdom of the past in place) and subversive (wanting to create a world that is much better than the one we inhabit.)

Mary Douglas once wrote, "Ritual makes visible external signs of internal states."[49] The truth is that rituals *can* have this capacity when they are working well. When rituals make visible our internal states, expressing things we deeply feel and experience, then they are said to "work." Rituals that work effectively have the power to move, heal, order, recognize, or change us. Older rituals can work especially well when they speak to our current condition and offer comfort. They tell us there is nothing so very unique or new about our current situation. When we perform the same ceremony that other fearful parents, long before us, once performed to protect their children, we feel less distraught about the fears we have for our own children, and less alone. If a ceremony worked for those before us who felt the same way we do, we trust it will work for us too. Inevitably, as time passes and situations change, our own internal states are not always made visible by the rituals our ancestors performed. Without transformations, the rituals will not externalize what we are experiencing inside. And so, we must invent.

But what have we invented, and how—drawing upon methods of narrative and material culture study—might we encounter this creativity? In the coming chapters, I offer case studies that will reveal answers to these questions. We will be looking at three new and distinctive ritual practices. I have selected them because they reflect different sectors of the Jewish population and because in each, an object is so essential to the practice. The case studies include the Miriam's tambourine innovated by Lubavitch women, the Holocaust torahs that have been enshrined in American congregations, and the wedding booklets penned by couples of various demoninations for their marriages or commitment ceremonies.

NOTES:

1. Judah Goldin, "Of Change and Adaptation in Judaism," in *Studies in Midrash and Related Literature* (Philadelphia: The Jewish Publication Society, 1988), 215. This essay was originally delivered in 1964.

2. Wade Clark Roof, *Spiritual Marketplace: Baby Boomers and the Remaking of American Religion* (Princeton: Princeton University Press, 2001), 79.

3. Terrence W. Tilley, *Inventing Catholic Tradition* (Maryknoll, NY: Orbis Books, 2000).

4. Roof, 79. While these changes still happen in observable social spaces, in the encounters of individuals, communities, and organizations, Roof notes that the production of religion also takes place through "faceless" Internet exchanges.

5. E. M. Broner, *Bringing Home the Light: A Jewish Woman's Handbook of Rituals* (San Francisco: Council Oaks Books, 1999), 2.

6. Eric Hobsbawm and Terrance Ranger, eds., *The Invention of Tradition* (Cambridge: Cambridge University Press, 1983), 1.

7. Ibid., 7.

8. Babylonian Talmud, *Bava Metzi'a* 84a.

9. See Vanessa Ochs with Elizabeth Ochs, *The Jewish Dreambook* (Woodstock, VT: Jewish Lights Publishing, 2004).

10. Babylonian Talmud, *Berachot* 55b.

11. Judah Goldin, "The Magic of Magic and Superstition," in *Studies in Midrash and Related Literature* (Philadelphia: The Jewish Publication Society, 1988), 339. According to Judah Goldin, many of these problematic, though healing, practices may even have had Roman origins.

12. Ibid., 340. Addressing the folk healing practices enumerated in the Talmud—many of which were the medicine of their day—Goldin writes that when the ancient Rabbis couldn't forbid a practice, they attempted to outwit it: "Some embarrassing practices they left alone, doubtless out of prudence ... because there was something like precedence for them in ancient Jewish custom. And I can't resist guessing that there must have been practices that surely irritated them, but they simply shut their eyes to them and must have muttered under their breath the equivalent of, 'Oh, to hell with it.' Or they cleverly converted what may have been magical spells to begin with into religious prayers and thus removed the sting of superstition from them. Or it might be that they would sanction a superstition which they themselves accepted by endowing it with a religious value" (344–45). Goldin illustrates the rabbinic phenomenon of "If you can't beat them, join them" with the example of *Tashlikh*, a post-talmudic practice that rabbis protested even while acknowledging that, "But clearly the folk won't give it up" (347). Rabbi Moses Isserles writing in the 16th century, declares that "even a mere custom *(minhag)* of Israel is Torah," and goes on to explain how going to a body of water on Rosh Hashanah allows one to contemplate the truth of the creation of the universe and to recognize the existence of God (347).

13. Ibid., 351.

14. Babylonian Talmud, *Shabbat* 61. We would need to keep in mind that every professional amulet writer or maker of herbal amulets was once a novice with unproven skills.

15. Erwin Goodenough, *Jewish Symbols in the Greco Roman Period,* edited and abridged by Jacob Neusner (Princeton: Princeton University Press, 1988), 9.

16. Ibid., x.

17. Ibid., viii.

18. Ibid., 19.

19. Ibid., 220.

20. Ibid., 19.

21. David Roskies, *A Bridge of Longing: The Lost Art of Yiddish Storytelling* (Boston: Harvard University Press, 1995), 5.

22. Roskies, 6.

23. For a brief time, innovating new Jewish ritual became my day job. In the late 1990s I was hired by a Jewish think tank called CLAL, the National Jewish Center for Learning and Leadership, as an anthropologist to perform an American Jewish cultural inventory. I was to notice how Judaism was meeting the spiritual needs of American Jews in new ways and to tabulate needs that were unmet. My colleagues and I set out to fill those gaps by creating new practices, which we tried out around the country in different settings. Our work was calculated not to appear too groundbreaking. Practices designed were based on a traditional Jewish template, using meditations, actions, blessings, and teachings. No practice intentionally violated a traditional definition of Jewish law. This work was eventually published as *The Book of Jewish Sacred Practices: CLAL's Guide to Everyday and Holiday Rituals and Blessings*, ed. Irwin Kula and Vanessa L. Ochs (Woodstock, VT: Jewish Lights Publishing, 2001).

24. Rabbi David Fine, "Women and the Minyan," Committee on Jewish Law and Standards of the Rabbinical Assembly, OH 55:1.200; online at the Rabbinical Assembly Website under *Teshuvot,* at http://www.rabbinical assembly.org/law/teshuvot_public.html.

25. Debra Nussbaum Cohen, "Gay Rituals Going Mainstream," *The Jewish Week,* August 1, 2003.

26. Ibid. This is the *official* discussion that is taking place. Informal discussions among all liberal rabbis have taken place all along.

27. *Moreh Derech—The Rabbinical Assembly Rabbi's Manual* (New York: The Rabbinical Assembly, 1998), xix.

28. Ibid., 29–30.

29. Jacques Cukierhorn, "What about Now? Accepting the Challenge of Intermarriage," *Issues of the American Council of Judaism* (Summer 2005).

30. Babylonian Talmud *Berachot* 45a, *Eruvin* 14b.

31. Robert Orsi, "Everyday Miracles: The Study of Lived Religion," in *Lived Religion in America: Toward a History of Practice*, David Hall, ed., (Princeton: Princeton University Press, 1977), 8.

32. Ellen Frankel and Betsy Platkin Teutsch, *The Encyclopedia of Jewish Symbols* (Northvale, NJ: Jason Aronson, Inc., 1992), 4–6.

33. Laura Geller, "Encountering the Divine Presence," in *Four Centuries of Jewish Women's Spirituality*, ed. Dianne Ashton and Ellen M. Umansky (Boston: Beacon Press, 1992), 244.

34. Lawrence Kushner, foreword to *The Book of Customs*, by Scott-Martin Kosofsky (San Francisco: Harper, 2004), xi.

35. Moshe Meiselman, *Jewish Women in Jewish Law* (New York: Ktav, 1978), 60ff.

36. Ibid., 61.

37. Ibid., 62.

38. Ibid., 146.

39. Ibid., 154.

40. Rivka Haut, personal communication.

41. Babylonian Talmud, *Berachot* 29b.

42. Rachelle Millen, *Women, Birth, and Death in Jewish Law and Practice* (Waltham: Brandeis University Press/University Press of New England, 2004), 127.

43. A similar process characterizes the way the general public reacts to medical innovations. At first, we may be unnerved or even outraged—as with organ transplants, artificial hearts, or assisted conception. But eventually, when the innovations have proven themselves successful over and over again, we not only accept them, but often forget how they once caused us to flinch.

44. Johanna Drucker, *Sweet Dreams* (Chicago: University of Chicago Press, 2005), xiii.

45. I try to explain to an ultra-Orthodox friend of mine that I am writing about new Jewish rituals. "You may know that they are new," he says, "but I know that they are not Jewish."

46. Millen, *Women, Birth, and Death*, 129.

47. *Sim Shalom* prayer book, edited and with translations by Jules Harlow (New York: The Rabbinical Assembly, 1985), 426.

48. Broner, *Bringing Home the Light*, 3.

49. Mary Douglas, *Purity and Danger* (New York: Pelican Books, 1970), 52.

CASE STUDY ONE:
MIRIAM'S TAMBOURINE

I first noticed tambourines in the homes of Lubavitch Hasidic women, though it was not initially clear to me that I was seeing what was for these women an important new ritual object: a "Miriam's tambourine."[1] I saw the tambourines first in Morristown, New Jersey—then my hometown and the home of the Lubavitch Rabbinical College of America. I was doing fieldwork between March and July of 1994, a period just before and after the death of the Lubavitcher Rebbe, Menachem Mendel Schneerson. In those days, most of the Lubavitch women I encountered in Morristown and in Crown Heights, the Lubavitch headquarters, believed their Rebbe would not die, but rather would emerge—"rise up" was the expression they used—as the Messiah of their community.

The tambourines, I discovered over time, had spiritual agency. Owning them, decorating them, or just having them around channeled anxiety, released creative energy, and mobilized the community of Lubavitch women worldwide. Through the tambourines, Lubavitch women identified with the biblical Miriam and the confident ancient

Israelite women who gracefully had saved the day when their husbands quarreled, complained, despaired, and withdrew from procreation under Pharaoh's edicts. If a woman had a tambourine of her own, she could better tell the story of Miriam's faithfulness. In telling the story, she would not just remember it, but *experience herself* as an incarnation of Miriam, a woman of great faith in bleak times. The tambourine eased women across a threatening transition, guiding and assuring them, and most of all affirming God's presence and beneficence.

I saw the Lubavitch women, in the context of their leader's impending death, asserting themselves as ritual and spiritual experts. As theirs is a community in which men are meant to be more visible in public and women have more agency in the private realm, the tambourines enabled the women to expand their roles without risk: Behind sweetly decorated tambourines, they asserted their spiritual leadership at a traumatic time, and held their families and community together. Through their tambourines—in virtuoso, lived religious performances—they maintained faith and community during a crisis.

Passover 1994

Ignoring their exhaustion, stepping beyond their anxiety about all the cleaning and the tasks that remained to be done, Lubavitch women prepared for Passover in the spring of 1994 with particular exhilaration because of their certainty that the Messianic Age was approaching. Recent acts of violence had given the Lubavitch women I knew the sense that they were living in nightmarish times, a period of overwhelming tragedy and suffering, just the kind of times that were supposed to precede the coming of the Messiah. On February 25, Baruch Goldstein had massacred Palestinians worshipping in Hebron. Days later, in a seeming act of revenge on the other side of the world, Rashad Baz had opened fire on a convoy of Lubavitch students, killing Ari Halberstam and severely injuring his friend Nachum Sasonkin as they drove back over the Brooklyn Bridge after praying for the Rebbe at Beth Israel Hospital. There was Ari's funeral, with hundreds coming to mourn. This was all on top of an earlier wound the community still felt, the killing of one of their yeshivah students, Yankel Rosenbaum, during riots in Crown Heights in 1991. Lubavitch leaders declared that at such moments of intense darkness, when everything seemed to be falling apart, a coming light could be glimpsed. This classic Jewish narrative felt especially descriptive of the present moment.

During this time, the Lubavitch women I knew were especially energetic, hopeful, and geared up, as though they were expectant mothers hovering over delivery dates. Many said they believed that just as the Children of Israel had been redeemed from bondage in Egypt on account of the righteous women of that generation, so would the Jews of today be brought out of *golus*[2] (physical and spiritual exile) and into *ge'ulo* (the Messianic Age) on account of the righteous women of their own generation. They believed they themselves had the potential and the responsibility to bring the Messiah. It was a matter of believing deeply, praying, spreading the belief, doing *mitzvos* (commandments), reaching out to the world, and spreading light, goodness, and Torah.

Lubavitch women regularly told me that redemption was imminent because of righteous women. The primary source for their conviction was the midrash on Exodus. They knew this text well, from their study both of primary texts and of the Rebbe's discourses, at various formal and informal study sessions. (Many people suppose incorrectly that Lubavitch women and girls are neither encouraged nor permitted to study sacred texts. While they do not study as intensively as the men and rarely study the Talmud—though the Rebbe permitted them to do so—they are learned in Torah and Hasidic texts.)

The midrash reads:

> *Israel was redeemed from Egypt on account of the righteous women of that generation. What did they do? When they went to draw water, God deposited little fishes (as aphrodisiacs) in their pitchers, so that they found them half filled with water and half with fishes. These they brought to their husbands. They put on two pots, one for hot water and one for fish, and they used to feed them, wash them, anoint them, and give them to drink, and they cohabited with them between the mounds in*

the field .... As soon as they became pregnant, they went back to their homes; and when the time came for their parturition, they went into the field and gave birth under the apple-tree .... God then sent an angel from on high to cleanse and beautify them .... When God revealed Himself by the sea, they [the women] recognized Him first. (Exodus Rabbah 1:12)

Miriam's Cup

Miriam's cup is a new Passover ritual that also explicitly honors Miriam, highlighting her role in the Exodus story and invoking her healing and creative presence. Miriam's cup *(kos Miriam)* initially emerged in the context of women's Rosh Hodesh groups. The cup then began appearing at feminist and women's seders, and by 2000, it was finding its place at many family and community seders as well. Miriam's cup is now encountered as a venerable tradition and not as a newfangled gesture, easy to dismiss, or as a ritual of interest only to women. In *A Night of Questions: A Passover Haggadah*,[3] the Miriam's cup ritual is included in the body of the text along with the more familiar rituals; its relative novelty is not emphasized. For most, Miriam's cup, filled with water, or collectively filled with water from each person's cup, symbolizes that like Elijah, Miriam "visits" the seder meal. Several blessings for the water and liturgical evocations of Miriam are emerging, but a standard practice has yet to emerge. The ritualwell.org Web site offers this blessing for Miriam's cup, one that is commonly used:

זֹאת כּוֹס מִרְיָם, כּוֹס מַיִם חַיִּים. זֵכֶר לִיצִיאַת מִצְרָיִם:

Zot Kos Miryam, kos mayim chayim. Zeicher l'tzi-at Mitztrayim.

This is the cup of Miriam, the cup of living waters.

Let us remember the Exodus from Egypt. These are the living waters, God's gift to Miriam, which gave new life to Israel as we struggled with ourselves in the wilderness. Blessed are You God, Who brings us from the narrows into the wilderness, sustains us with endless possibilities, and enables us to reach a new place.[4]

MUSEUM EXHIBITS OF MIRIAM'S CUP

Exhibits of Miriam's cups in Jewish museums have also spread the ritual of Miriam's cup. In many instances, artists were invited to create Miriam's cups. For many of the artists, the process of text study, making a Miriam's cup, and reflecting in writing upon their personal experiences was transformative.

The first Miriam's cup invitational exhibit, organized by Ma'yan, a Jewish women's center in New York City, was held at Hebrew Union College-Jewish Institute of Religion in 1997 and was called Drawing from the Source: Miriam, Women's Creativity and New Ritual.[5] Ma'yan invited 175 Jewish women artists around the world to design a cup for Miriam. Some artists had never heard of Miriam's cup until they were sent the materials to guide their creation—and now they were being asked to act as ritual experts, making an object to be used in a sacred setting.

Anticipating that God would perform a miracle for them, Miriam and the Israelite women brought along their timbrels (tambourines) as they left Egypt, to use them in celebration; and the miracle—the parting of the sea—indeed transpired. Quoting the medieval exegete Rashi, Lubavitch women said this prescient gesture demonstrated the exemplary faith and foresight not just of biblical women, but of all Jewish women, including themselves.

Just before Passover, while I was visiting Ita Morris, a Lubavitch woman who lived a few blocks away from my house in Morristown, a boy arrived to deliver her tambourine and collect $10 for it. I asked Ita how the idea for the tambourines had come about. She supposed that it had originated in Morristown with Mrs. Lebovic, the boy's mother, a well-known Lubavitch matchmaker: "She had the idea that all the women should have tambourines. She ordered them so all the women will be ready to sing and dance when the Rebbe gets up. It's said that the women brought about the redemption from Egypt. In their merit, the Jews were redeemed. In our merit ...."

Ita trailed off, the connection between the women of antiquity and the present-day Lubavitch women being familiar to us both.

Later that evening, I joined a prayer meeting in the finished basement of a private home in Morristown. The women were preparing to listen to a prayer session broadcast from Crown Heights over speakerphone. While we waited, many women wrote checks for tambourines, plain ones that Mrs. Lebovic pulled out of a large cardboard box.

Over the phone, we heard a man ask what more could be done to hasten the coming of the Messiah. "We must have *simcho*, joy," the speaker urged. "We should begin with an actual action."

Eager to determine what constituted an "actual action" and to engage in one, a young woman in our group, the wife of a rabbinical student, said, "Let's get out our tambourines!" Even with all the newly purchased tambourines on hand, no one took up the young woman's suggestion.

The women, continuing to listen, were exhorted to carry on giving strength to their husbands and children; the speaker reminded them that historically, when men were ready to give up, the women held the day.

A second, especially energetic younger woman in our midst announced, "We should go to Crown Heights! I'm ready to go, the tank is full of gas. Should we sing and dance?" Still, no one left for Crown Heights at that moment to perform an "actual action"; no one sang or danced that night. No one "did" anything at all with her tambourine.

Indeed, I wondered: what did one do with one's tambourine, other than have it on hand? Maybe that alone was the "doing"—not unlike the ritual preparation of one's soul before Rosh Hashana for the new year, which is an invisible rather than overt "actual action." Certainly, just having the tambourine on hand was what the Israelite women crossing the sea had done. Their virtue lay not in their final celebration, but in their faithful anticipation that it would come. Perhaps having the tambourines on hand and anticipating that they would one day be used "for real" constituted the tambourine ritual.

The collective wisdom of this group was that this was *not yet* the right moment for the tambourines to be brought into action. The speaker affirmed this idea when he said that the women should keep doing their part in bringing the redemption by expanding their outreach efforts. Referring to the campaign to encourage young Jewish girls to light candles on Friday nights, he asked rhetorically, "Will it take just one more Jewish *maideleh* lighting *Shabbos* candles?" Have your tambourines ready, the speaker said, accessible and on hand. I noticed that a ritual that had been created by the women was so quickly becoming regulated by the men and that this regulation took the literal form of their being silenced.

At the evening's end, before the women recited *tehillim* (psalms), a much respected older woman in the Morristown group guided them with a *kavono* (a sacred intention): "Try to imagine that women all over the world are saying this." It seemed to me that this spiritual direction was given particularly to the two younger women, who wanted so badly to "do" something concrete with their tambourines.

As a gesture of solidarity, I bought a tambourine for myself and brought it home. When I saw it on my coffee table the next morning, two thoughts came simultaneously to mind. The first was cynical: "Look what desperation leads people to do!" The second surprised me: "It's good I have gotten a tambourine for myself and my daughters, in case it ends up being useful in the coming days. I wouldn't want to be caught without one." That second thought evaporated rapidly, but before it did, I was able fleetingly to experience some of the hopefulness embraced by the Lubavitch women.

I soon learned that tambourine buying and decorating were not restricted to Morristown and did not originate with Mrs. Lebovic. Lubavitch mothers and daughters all over the world were buying tambourines so that they would be prepared to rejoice like Miriam when the Rebbe announced himself as the Messiah. In fact, the tambourines had officially been introduced two years earlier when representatives of a Lubavitch women's group presented the Rebbe with a tambourine to convey their belief that it was he, as the Messiah, who would herald the redemption. The night before, hundreds of women had gathered in Brooklyn to dance with tambourines in celebration of the coming redemption.

Mrs. Lebovic had gotten the idea of selling both plain and decorated tambourines as a fund-raiser from a California woman she had met back in February at a Lubavitch women's conference in Brooklyn. She knew that thousands of tambourines made in Pakistan had been distributed in Crown Heights, and women were decorating them with puff paints, sequins, beads, silk flowers, ribbons, and the Hebrew words welcoming the King Messiah. A smaller plastic tambourine had been manufactured for children, and the Lubavitch women in Israel had their own version. In the Midwest, a Lubavitch women's group calling themselves the Project of Women for Redemption had affixed a photocopy of relevant texts on the back of each tambourine they distributed, ending with the Rebbe's own words: "Now, as then, the Jewish woman's yearning for *Moshiach*—a yearning which runs deeper than that of their menfolk and inspires and uplifts it—will form the dominant strain in the melody of redemption."

I asked Miriam Swerdlov, a respected Lubavitch women's teacher from Crown Heights, if she had a tambourine of her own. I was surprised that in our previous discussions, she had never mentioned anything about tambourines. I imagined she might be critical of the practice. "Of course I have one!" she answered over the phone and added, jokingly, "My *name* is Miriam."

"Do your daughters have tambourines?" I asked.

"We're a five-tambourine family. You know historically what the point of the tambourines is?"

I did, and she reminded me.

"When men came out of *Mitzrayim* [Egypt], they said, 'I don't believe it till I see it.' Like, 'Till the check clears the bank, then I'll know.' We women took the tambourines. We are the same people, the same *neshomos* [souls] that went out of *Mitzrayim*."

Had any women rehearsed what they would actually do with their tambourines, in terms of playing them or performing particular songs or dances, I asked? Given that Lubavitch women do sometimes hold women's musical performances—staged, for the sake of modesty, for women alone—I knew this was possible.

"Some women painted them and made them pretty," answered Miriam. "It's not one of my great talents in life. Some ladies put ribbons on them, all sorts of things." Miriam indicated that my questions about the tambourines were about superficial manifestations of belief. I had not gotten their point, even if I thought I had. In a plaintive voice full of longing, she said, "*Moshiach* is coming, he has to, he has to. The whole world is at the end of its rope."

What did Basha Oka, who handled public relations in Crown Heights for the Lubavitch women's organization Neshei Ubnos Chabad, think the tambourines were about? She told me:

We are the reincarnation of the women who left Mitzrayim. The tambourines aren't a fetish. They're a way to find our way into expressing our faith that the Rebbe's words will come true. The tambourines are an expression of our belief. Miriam and the women had faith it was all going to work. Imagine how scary it was then: Going out of Egypt at night into a desert, no food, and no water! It required courage and bravery. By taking along tambourines, the women showed they believed they would eventually rejoice. They went through a hard test. When you pass a hard test, the rewards are great. Women have a more intimate connection, a deepened understanding of spiritual reality. It is the women's role to bring about the dawning of a spiritual age. The men are discouraged, but the women are to push—like the birth pangs that are associated with the coming of the Moshiach .... This current generation is like the generation that left Egypt. Women are now in the same role. The men now, like the men then, are discouraged, but the women have a sense of where we're going. The Rebbe has given respect to the women of Lubavitch. We are filled with energy and learning. We are very actualized women because of the Rebbe's confidence and trust in us. We have miracles coming before our eyes. Open your eyes and see. Maybe it seems extraordinary, but this is happening. The Moshiach will speak, and the world will listen.

Likening the Israelites' experience of leaving Egypt for freedom to a baby's struggle through a narrow, arduous birth canal is a familiar interpretive strategy. The prominence of birth imagery suggested, for many, that women intuitively understood the move from exile to redemption, in a way that men could not.

Had Lubavitch women living right now, in this generation, done something in particular that would bring the Messiah, or were they about to do something? A Lubavitch woman friend in Morristown told me, "Women in particular have been saying that the Rebbe is *Moshiach*. While it's not our business to figure out God's plan, this is not a delusion or a mistake."

Many weeks passed, and June 8, I belatedly received a press release faxed from *Neshei Ubnos Chabad*. Entitled "Jewish Women Ready Tambourines for Rebbe's Recovery," it announced an event sponsored by an organization called Rejoice for the Redemption, held at a junior high school building near Beth Israel Hospital. The organization, "heeding the prophecy of the Lubavitcher Rebbe that the Messianic Era is on the way," would provide a banquet, a *"Moshiach in the Media"* video, and a tambourine lesson. The significance of the tambourines was explained in the press release:

> *According to the book of Exodus, the women's faith in Moses and the Almighty was so strong that they carried tambourines with them in anticipation of greater miracles as they left Egypt. Jewish mystical sources refer to this current generation as a reincarnation of those redeemed under Moses. Thus, like their forbears, many Jewish women today own tambourines, some bedecked with paint, sequins and ribbons. In communities across the country, these humble instruments have become a symbol of trust in the Rebbe's words and belief that the great events of the Messianic Era are imminent. The hallmarks of this new age are universal peace and goodness, and the open revelation of the existence of G-d.*

Here, the tambourine was a symbol not just of the women's belief that the Rebbe would bring the Messianic Age, but also of their belief that the Rebbe—in his own words—had confirmed that he was the Messiah. The humble tambourine, the voice-masking prop of the faithful women, represented this bold claim: that the signs of the times *could* be read, without doubt, as indications of the approaching redemption.

The Lubavitch women of Morristown had traveled to the event together by bus, I learned. It was, as one woman described it, "a celebration of ... faith through singing and dancing." They attended a workshop on tambourine decorating, and all the way back home, they sang *nigunim*. This was permitted, since the bus driver was a woman.

The Death of the Rebbe

Then what was not going to happen simply happened. The Rebbe died in the middle of the night on June 12. This event was announced in Crown Heights by three wailing sirens. Some mistook the sound of the siren for that of a shofar announcing the redemption. People dressed quickly. Many had been leaving their best clothes at the foot of their beds for months now, so they could dress properly to greet the *Moshiach*. Some had even taken to sleeping fully dressed. Now stunned and anguished women and men poured into the synagogue at 770 Eastern Parkway, central headquarters of the Lubavitch movement in Crown Heights to pray, the women in the balcony, the men down below. In the streets outside 770, I was told, women danced through the night with their tambourines, singing to greet the Rebbe as Messiah, despite his physical death. One woman from Morristown described her immediate reaction:

> *When the Rebbe's wife died, you knew how to comport yourself. But now, when it was time to tell the children, I started to choke. I said that the Rebbe's heart had stopped, which meant he was physically gone. My six-year-old asked, "Does that mean Moshiach isn't coming?" I said that Moshiach is definitely coming, but the children knew that for themselves, as they hadn't departed from their emuno [faith].*

The funeral was held on Sunday, the very next day, in accordance with Jewish practice. In the hours before it, according to *The Jewish Week*, young men danced in a small circle outside 770, and many more danced inside. "[A] dozen young girls from a Crown Heights yeshivah loudly waved tambourines on the front steps of a dormitory building" across the street, an action that drew disapproval from some adults. One girl explained that she had bought the tambourine "as part of a Lubavitch project to emulate the prophet Miriam, who led the Hebrew women, freed from Egyptian slavery, through the Red Sea with timbrels. 'We're doing the same thing.'"[6]

In Allan Nadler's account, we learn that he was amazed to see "young Lubavitchers singing, dancing and drinking vodka directly across the street from ... where the body of their beloved rabbi was lying .... Even more stunning was a small group of women encouraging the men with tambourines."[7] Was this vision reminiscent of the biblical women seducing their husbands with little fishes, or did it evoke many Eves with fruits leading men to sin? Nadler, surprised by the singing and dancing—Jewish law forbids song at funerals and requires mourners to abstain from music—overheard Lubavitch women debating the propriety of dancing at this time. Those in favor of it explained that this was the beginning of redemption, and momentarily the Rebbe would rise up and take them all to Israel.

Reporter Toby Axelrod described the women standing outside 770:

[As] the sunlight that poured through the rain—their raised voices were against nature, for a miracle. "Women have the kind of belief that changes reality," said Tzvia .... "Men are more realists." ... "The women declare about the Messiah, not the men," proclaimed Tovi, and Uzit shook a tambourine ... "because women never had any doubt."

Later, Axelrod reported,

[W]hen someone told the women to leave the platform to make room for politicians, several said they would stand their ground. "I think we are a little closer to the Rebbe than Mayor Giuliani ...," said one woman. "I don't want a good place to see a box," said another. "I want a good place to see a miracle. A box is a box is a box."[8]

That afternoon, at each moment of the funerary proceedings, before men and women could file separately past the Rebbe's casket at 770, before the casket was then carried out and the women screamed a shattering *"Yehi ...!"* (the King Messiah chant), and before the casket was then brought to the Old Montefiore Cemetery in Cambria Heights in Queens, many women expressed their belief that the events would come to a halt, and the Rebbe would be resurrected then and there as the Messiah. Some told me that they thought the Hasidic trademark, *simcho*—their joy in the face of even the bleakest realities—would help make that happen. A woman named Mirele, a musician and mother, said that the women and men who rejoiced were told by rabbis that this was no time for dancing. Miriam and the women, they were reminded, played their tambourines *after* the sea had been crossed, not before. On Sunday evening after the funeral, as dazed and shocked men and women, having paid their respects at the grave site, either prayed inside 770 or milled about in the plaza outside, I saw that women had left their tambourines lying about on the ledge of the women's balcony. Some were stuffed into baby strollers, or sticking out of hastily packed suitcases and diaper bags. The many tambourines I saw were silent. I had been told that Lubavitch women had entrusted tambourines to the Rebbe's nurses in Beth Israel Hospital, so that immediately upon his "rising," the sound of tambourines would be heard, even if non-Jewish nurses played them. I imagined those tambourines were also lying still. There was not much *simcho* in the air. I felt none at all.

Was it the men who had suppressed the *simcho* that could have been activated by the women's tambourines? Or had the women laid down their tambourines autonomously, understanding that the time for their use was still to come?

After the Funeral

Death did not alter the belief of Lubavitch women who knew their Rebbe would be revealed as the Messiah. Just after the funeral, one mother of nine expressed a common viewpoint: "I am sure the Rebbe will reveal himself! Nobody thought he would die. We are sad but excited, because we're all going to see the revelation. I hope it happens right now, because we have suffered enough."

Lubavitch women gathered each evening during the week of mourning, listening to the various rabbis in their home communities advise them about what to do now. (All the Lubavitchers, not just the women, were given detailed instructions; on the Lubavitch Listserv, the information was called "Directives to do now.") There were instructions for conduct, disclosure of emotion, praying, reciting psalms, studying, lighting memorial candles, giving to charity, telling stories about the Rebbe, and pursuing the Rebbe's missions.

At a gathering at the Chabad house in Morristown (which also happened to be Ita Morris's house), a rabbi told the women sitting around a long dining-room table that it was unfortunate that events happened as they did, and the death was not anticipated, but that's what God did. The passing of a righteous man was more tragic than the destruction of the holy Temple. But even if the Rebbe was no longer present in his body, his soul was present with his people, for would a righteous man desert his people? "Our father is with us, praying for us." As Lubavitch watchers might have anticipated, the women were told that even though they may have done everything they could to prepare for the Messiah, there was still room for a last drop of self-improvement. No dancing, the rabbi cautioned the women again and again, lest anyone even consider it.

Not one woman present appeared to be on the verge of shutting down. Despite their sadness, they were as effervescent as ever. They had been listening politely to the rabbi, for Lubavitch women, not unlike other women of faith, know well how to appear to heed the prescriptions of their male clergy and then take only what is relevant to them. They knew themselves to be fully capable of dreaming up and actualizing a spiritual and political agenda of their own. Their Rebbe knew this about them, and they loved him for it.

In this period following the Rebbe's death, Lubavitch women continued to gravitate toward Miriam in their textual references. Basha Oka explained: "We are the reincarnation of the women who left Egypt." Another woman declared that at the funeral "the women were the strength and the men went to pieces. The Rebbe told us countless times that women would lead the redemption. The Rebbe has given us such empowerment!"

Tambourines were still being sold and decorated. Turning to Rashi, the women continued to identify with those ancestors whose enormous faith had equipped them to divine that they would soon be celebrating the miracle of God's rescue. They had role models. As they told it, the Israelite men, who could *not* look into the future, were more prone to despair. Just like their own men.

They remained composed. "In this moment of ultimate disorientation," said one woman, "we are still aware of our mission to educate the world in love and peace." Their work would continue, "performing deeds of goodness and kindness so as to bring on the redemption."

Toward the end of a gathering later that summer, Mrs. Lebovic came in with new tambourines designed by artists she had commissioned. The proceeds would go toward a *hachnosas kallah* fund, monies to help a poor bride. She said she knew the women would *kvell* (express delight) when they saw the decorated tambourines, and *kvell* they did. The tambourines facilitated the articulation of new theological understandings and reaffirmed familiar ones: Redemption would still come, eventually, and God would provide sustenance for carrying on, as always.

For Mrs. Lebovic, I believe, the tambourines remained a tangible reminder of the faith of Miriam and a woman's ability to do what she has to do to sustain life, even when it is tempting to stop functioning. They were a sign that one could believe in a joyous future despite the painful present. One woman purchasing a tambourine said, "The tambourines show that whatever happens, we're looking forward to good times, and our connection to God isn't contingent on always seeing the revealed good." Another woman said she had planned tambourine decorating for her daughter's birthday party. Yet another said that at her daughter's wedding, the women brought their tambourines and did "a little dance act" for the bride. Later that July, an article about Mrs. Lebovic and her tambourines that appeared in the Newark *Star-Ledger* clarified how the tambourines were to be used. "The instruments need not be used at any time in relation to the redemption," Mrs. Lebovic is reported to have said. "It's not a religious duty to shake them. Some people just hang the tambourines up, using them as ornaments for their homes."[9]

This remark is significant. First, it suggests a growing acceptance of redemption's delay. Second, it begins to answer the question of what women were supposed to do with their tambourines now that the Messianic Age seemed less imminent. Mrs. Lebovic seems to have to established guidelines for practice: (1) shaking tambourines does not necessarily mean redemption has come; (2) there is no prescribed way or time for their shaking (unlike the shaking of the *lulav* on

Sukkot, for example); and (3) until the redemption seems more likely, it is proper to keep them visible, hung on the wall as ornaments.

Mrs. Lebovic quickly sold one of the tambourines bearing an image of the ancient Temple in Jerusalem for $36. She suggested it be used as a wall hanging and not as an instrument. With her tambourines decorated with crowns, musical notes, and cut-out pictures of the Rebbe circled with sequins, glitter, gems, ribbons, and silk flowers, Lebovic brought *simcho* back into this room in Morristown. *Simcho* was being restored to New York, Massachusetts, Florida, and even Russia, where tambourines were also being shipped and sold to women's groups. As purchased ritual objects, meant for decoration, they had become agents of remoralization.

Mrs. Lebovic later explained how the tambourines enabled her to reframe this complicated episode in her community. Her words, recorded in detail, reflect how the tambourines were still making sense shortly after the Rebbe's death, even though they had not been used, as originally envisioned, to announce and celebrate the moment the Rebbe simultaneously died and was revealed as the Messiah:

The Moshiach is still coming. That hasn't changed. We're going to have to wait and see how he will come. There's no doubt that there will be wondrous miracles. Women have a different perspective; we have faith within. Hazal [the ancient learned Rabbis)] gave credit to the nashim tzidkaniyos [the righteous women], all those that took tambourines through Miriam's inspiration. Miriam dared to approach her father. [This is a reference to a well-known midrash in which Miriam rebukes her father for divorcing his wife so as not to have more babies who would be killed by Pharaoh's edict. It was Miriam who convinced her father to remarry Yochebed and beget Moses.] Wasn't this more difficult than the task of Moses, who approached Pharaoh? In Egypt, the men gave up marital unions, but the women said, "Now we have it rough, but we have to go on!" They gave their husbands little fishes to entice them, to get them interested in the worthiness of family life and pursuing normalcy, because they believed the world wouldn't end. God rewards this kind of faith that manifests itself in action. The women didn't give up; they wanted to show their belief in redemption. They dressed their families Jewishly, they gave them Hebrew names, they didn't assimilate into Egyptian culture.

I'm trying to perceive what might have happened. Leaving Egypt, there was still a lot to be despondent about; they didn't know manna would fall. Miriam took her tambourine. We will need it. We're going through it now. There will be such a need to celebrate God's benevolence. They were ready. It was natural for women to want to show gratitude. They anticipated future miracles; we find that trait in women. The nation went into the desert without an infrastructure, but the women knew the world would be sustained.

I take my inspiration from Miriam and thank God the tambourines came my way and gave me the wherewithal. The tambourines are tangible; they are a humble instrument of music. They help symbolize the faith of Miriam and her generation of women. Women are created to be mothers, so we have it in ourselves to carry on no matter what, and to see the potential long-range outcome, just as a mother would see the future for her child. If a woman knows it is the time to dance, she dances. Moshiach will appear in some way, either through resurrection ... or we'll see. We are prepared. I know God is running the show; with my tambourine, I am ready for what God will give us in the interim and to get ready to celebrate when the redemption comes, and to help our brothers and sisters to carry on.

Tambourines and the Passage of Time

Years have passed, and Lubavitch women still wait. They no longer habitually toss their tambourines into backpacks and baby strollers.

But sometimes the tambourines get carried from place to place, and they seem to function, like the ritual *tzitzis* worn by men, as reminders of sacred obligations that are carried around on one's body. The tambourines "proclaim" in every moment of one's life that one has to act in such a way as to hasten redemption. They announce that one has to carry oneself, continually and in every situation, as if the Messianic Age could commence in an instant.

Tambourines can still be found on shelves or hung on walls; Lubavitch girls are encouraged to have and decorate one of their own. In the April 3, 1998, issue of *L'Chaim,* a publication of the Lubavitch Youth Organization, Esther Melamud related:

> *Whenever we set up a table, whether at the local J.C.C. or in a supermarket, in addition to brochures about various mitzvot,*[10] *such as keeping kosher, lighting Shabbat candles, having mezuzot on one's doors, we also publicize the Rebbe's message that the time of the Redemption has arrived and that Moshiach's coming is imminent. As part of the display we have a beautifully decorated tambourine .... Everyone always asks us about the tambourine. I remember once when an older woman was so excited by what we said about the Redemption and its imminence that she took the tambourine in her hand and started dancing with it.*

After the fourth anniversary of the Rebbe's death had been commemorated by thousands of Lubavitchers at the Montefiore Cemetery with quiet prayer, the Third International *Moshiach* Congress was held in Crown Heights. Jim Yardley interviewed a 33-year-old woman who counted herself among the Messianists, those who persisted in publicizing the message of the Messiah's still-imminent arrival. Rivky Shvey spent Thursday selling Messiah posters, tapes, candy bars, and tambourines. Just as Moses led the Jews through the Red Sea, Ms. Shvey said, she kept a small tambourine in her carrying bag in readiness for the arrival of the Messiah. "Just in case I'm on the subway when *Moshiach* comes," Ms. Shvey said, "I'll have one."[11]

With the passage of time, the tambourines of the Lubavitch women seem more and more like the tambourines of Miriam and the women in Scripture: potent symbols from a time that already has the feel of an era long ago, simultaneously slightly larger and slightly smaller than life. They are being safeguarded so that they will be ready for celebrating redemption.

In the summer of 1999, I spent one Sunday morning in Crown Heights searching for a decorated tambourine. I went inside gift stores, Jewish bookstores, and stores specializing in ritual items. Nearly giving up, I went to a toy store, and was sent from there to the small office and shop of *Tsivos Hashem* (God's Army), which sold Jewish learning items that would appeal to young children. Two tambourines hung on the wall; I paid $15 for the smaller one. My tambourine was painted sky blue. In the center was a tiny cameo-shaped picture of the Rebbe, outlined in gold glitter paint. Over his head were the Hebrew words *Boruch habo melech moshiach*—"Welcome King Messiah!" Under the image of the Rebbe were two olive branches drawn in green and red glitter paint, and between them a fabric rosette was attached with glue. White lace and sequins covered the wooden frame of the tambourine. It was very delicate, very pretty.

A friend, seeing that tambourine displayed on a shelf in my house and noticing the rosette, lace, and sequins, remarked, "That tambourine's not for using, is it?"

"It's not meant for playing," I explained. "But it *is* meant for using—one uses it by having it, by explaining what it's about. In that sense, it's being used right now."

NOTES:

1. A longer, somewhat different version of this case study appeared as "Waiting for the Messiah, a Tambourine in Her Hand," in *Nashim* 9 (Spring 2005).

2. Hebrew terms are transliterated throughout this article according to the Ashkenazic pronunciation widely used among Lubavitchers. It differs in several ways from the pronunciation of modern Hebrew.

3. Rabbis Joy Levitt and Michael Strassfeld, eds., *A Night of Questions: A Passover Haggadah* (Reconstructionist Press, 2000).

4. See the *ritualwell.org* Web site at http://www.ritualwell.org. For information on Miram's cup, look under "Holidays > Passover > On the seder table" subheadings.

5. Other exhibits that followed include: L'Chaim: A Kiddush Cup Invitational, at the Jewish Museum of San Francisco (1997–1998); and Updating Ceremonial Objects: A Cup for Miriam, at the Nathan D. Rosen Museum Gallery and Adolph and Rose Levis Jewish Community Center of Boca Raton, Florida (1999).

6. Steve Lipman, "What Do We Do? How Do We Carry On?" *The Jewish Week*, June 17–23, 1994, 26.

7. Allan Nadler, "King of Kings Country," *The New Republic* (July 11, 1994).

8. Toby Axelrod, "A Faith Supreme," *The Jewish Week*, June 17–23, 1994, 28.

9. Jenny Park, "Lubavitch Women's Faith in Messiah Hasn't Been Shaken," *The Star-Ledger*, July 11, 1994.

10. In this publication, Hebrew words were transliterated according to their pronunciation in modern Hebrew.

11. Park, "Lubavitch Women's Faith."

CASE STUDY TWO:
THE HOLOCAUST TORAH

N early every faith has standard rituals of purification or reconsecration that restore holiness to sacred objects that have
been desecrated or compromised. In Judaism, there is a ritual practice for holy books that contain the name of God but can no
longer be used because they are damaged. These traditionally have
been stored in a repository called a *genizah*. When an object such as a
Torah scroll cannot be repaired and made "kosher," so to speak, it will
be accorded a burial. But in the case of the Holocaust, the desecration
of Torah scrolls was so extreme and atrocious that familiar methods
of restoring holiness were insufficient.

"Rescuing" or "Adopting" a Torah Scroll

In response, a new practice has slowly emerged: "rescuing" or "adopt-
ing" Torah scrolls that were pillaged from communities annihilated
in the Holocaust, and giving them a place of honor in living congre-

gations. This memorial ritual—often initiated by an individual member of an American synagogue—points to the possibility that order and dignity can be restored to such Torahs. It honors, as well, those who perished in the Holocaust and memorializes those towns where Jewish life once flourished. Because many of these scrolls are beyond repair, with parchment torn and letters effaced, they cannot be read from in a synagogue. Through the new ritual of rescue and rededication, they receive a distinctive holy status as they become designated "Holocaust Torahs." Each synagogue that acquires one of these Torahs becomes—by virtue of housing this inanimate yet highly personal relic—a small scale and distinctly local Holocaust memorial, recalling the destruction of European Jewry and affirming the intention to remember.

Most new rituals and ritual objects raise concerns, and the Holocaust Torah is no exception. It is a sacred cultural object that is decontextualized—taken out of its natural environment—and is put to a different use from the one originally intended for it. Many will be familiar with the dilemma of the decontextualized object in the case of sacred African or Native American objects taken from their communities and placed in art or cultural museums where they serve new functions and acquire new meanings. Holocaust scholar Oren Baruch Stier writes that displacing an object linked to the Holocaust raises distinct ethical issues "... about the meaning of property and its propriety, the treatment of sacred objects, fetishization ... mystification, and mythologization."[1] As we shall see, those who wrestle with the very idea of the Holocaust Torah ask if the desire to remember those who perished in the Holocaust through various memorializing activities (such as creating museums, monuments, and artworks), however praiseworthy such initiatives might be, justifies turning material objects—such as defaced Torah scrolls, yellow stars, or Holocaust-era railway cars—into symbols that are exhibited so that they may serve as testimonies. Does the desire for effective Holocaust education justify depriving a Torah scroll of a traditional burial so that it might become the memorial shrine we need? If we cannot keep the survivors among us alive so we can keep hearing their stories, does that permit us to enshrine a rescued Torah scroll within a lively synagogue, with the hope that its presence alone will be sufficiently eloquent to tell the story of the Holocaust for generations to come?

Rescuing Jewish Sacred Objects

When the violent forces of nature or inhumanity destroy or uproot a sacred object from the place in which it belongs, some interpret this as a sign of God's absence. Jewish books scorched in a fire, synagogues defaced or shattered by bombings, lead some to ask, "Where is God now?" But when sacred objects are rescued and restored and are returned to use once again, they can point toward divine presence and the survival of faith. Hearing the story of Torah scrolls being rescued can restore hope and strengthen faith. We will go on, some will conclude. We can move on from here and be sustained, just as we have been sustained in the past. The rescued sacred object—even if compromised beyond repair—becomes doubly sacred. It has become a repository of the community's memory, telling a story of trials and endurance.[2]

A recent example of the function of the rescued sacred object as a repository of memory and faith was made poignantly clear in the days after Hurricane Katrina, when Jews from across the United States and from Israel rushed to Louisiana to rescue threatened Torah scrolls. Solomon Moore, writing in *The Los Angeles Times,* tells the story of Congregation Beth Israel, a flooded synagogue on the northern edge of New Orleans, a few blocks from Lake Pontchartrain:

> *[The rabbi, Yisroel Shiff,] called Rabbi Isaac Leider, who had spent five years in Israel with the search-and-rescue squad Zak'a, performing sacramental cleanup duties at bus bombings and other sites. Leider—who also volunteered his services at the World Trade Center, the TWA Flight 800 crash site, and other tragedies—now works with a Jewish ambulance service in New York City and New Jersey.... Leider and the rescue team climbed aboard a pair of rubber rafts with outboard motors and started toward the synagogue through flooded streets, barred in places by brambles and rusting cars.... The synagogue was still swamped by 4 feet of water. Wearing waist-high rubber waders and a yarmulke, Leider followed the rescue squad*

into the synagogue and made his way to the sanctuary.... Lei-
der inched his way through aisles filled with saturated seat
cushions, broken glass, and overturned pews and podiums. The
rabbi waded to the front of the hall and opened the ark that
held six Torah scrolls. He also found a white prayer shawl and
the silver adornments for the scrolls. He cradled them in his
arms and made his way toward the rafts.[3]

Chabad emissaries in New Orleans tell the story of their Torah scrolls, which were rescued and taken to Houston, Texas:

James O'Bonnell, an intrepid and dedicated volunteer from
Metro New York Search and Rescue, working closely with
Chabad's rescue mission, braved danger to salvage five Torah
Scrolls from the Chabad center in New Orleans. "James was
heroic in his daring," says Sharfstein. When an additional two
Torahs from the Chabad synagogue in Metairie were saved yes-
terday, rescue workers held an impromptu, small celebration.[4]

Throughout Jewish history, protecting a Torah scroll has been the symbolic equivalent of protecting the entire Jewish people, protecting the Jewish soul. Of course, when a human life is endangered, one immediately rushes to rescue the person first. But once life has been saved, rescuing the Torah scroll is the next highest priority, for the Torah is the symbol of all of Jewish peoplehood, history, and faith. It is said that one who rescues a Torah preserves Judaism.

Rededicating a Holocaust Torah

The ritual of rededicating a Holocaust Torah has galvanized the energies of many an American Jewish community, teaching the values of Torah study and remembrance. It is an especially riveting ritual for those who affirm their Judaism through their commitment to Holocaust remembrance. While some may say of such people, "Holocaust remembrance is their religion," suggesting a faith born of grief, anger, and the impulse to perpetuate victimhood, it can also be said that the "religion" of Holocaust remembrance can connote a spirituality kindled by a sacred vow and a solemn pact with those who died in the Holocaust. A key emblem of such spirituality is the creation of tangible monuments that sustain memory.

This is the story of one Holocaust Torah whose holiness was restored. The story is set in Congregation Beth Israel (CBI) of Charlottesville, Virginia.

In 1999, the congregation acquired a Torah scroll on permanent loan from the Czech Memorial Scrolls Trust. It had been confiscated by the Nazis from the town of Frydek-Mistek, along with hundreds of others from the former Jewish communities of Bohemia and Moravia. The Czech Memorial Scrolls Trust had rescued these scrolls in 1964, and since then, many have been distributed to Jewish communities around the world in order to memorialize those lost communities.[5]

My study of the Torah rededication ritual is based primarily on texts generated from within the congregation: a narrative, a sermon, and a prayer. I have had the advantage of interviewing the individuals who composed the texts as well as members of the family involved in rescuing the Torah. I have also seen the Holocaust Torah in place over several years, and have watched newcomers linger before it and inspect it.

Unlike most narratives of new rituals (such as the orange on the seder plate, or the song of the Jews in the Woods) that are complex, the narrative of this particular ritual seems particularly straightforward.[6] Our first text is a narrative that Rob Capon, an investor, entrepreneur, amateur astronomer, and active member of Congregation Beth Israel, wrote for the synagogue Web site.[7] Being a straightforward man, he titled this account of how the congregation came to possess this Torah scroll and make it holy once again, "How CBI Acquired the Holocaust Memorial Torah Scroll."[8]

Initially, acquiring a Holocaust Torah was not anyone's objective. The original intention was to purchase an additional Torah scroll for the congregation to use on holidays. This important detail indicates that it is possible to stumble by chance into a new ritual practice, one that ultimately provides an important lesson in dedication to Judaism for a family and a community. An opportunity arose to innovate, we shall see, and it was seized, first by Capon, then—with some reservations—by his rabbi, his family, and the congregation.

Like many a ritual innovation, this one began with a conversation. As Rabbi Alexander recalls, Capon, a pillar of the Jewish community who is pleased to use his abundant energies to spearhead projects for the communal good, had asked the rabbi after a board meeting what was on his "wish list" for the synagogue. Rabbi Alexander mentioned they needed an additional Torah scroll for the synagogue's small sanctuary. It would be especially useful on a festival such as Simchat Torah, when the designated readings come from three different sections of the Torah and would otherwise require—in the middle of the service—a good deal of scrolling to get to the right place.

Capon is someone who likes to make other people's wishes come true. Characteristically, he got to work immediately on the project. Capon writes:

> *Neither of us had expertise on the acquisition of such a scroll, but I agreed to research the matter further. This chance discussion launched journeys to New York and London that led to the acquisition of two Torah scrolls, a scroll for the sanctuary as well as a 200-year-old Holocaust Memorial Scroll from Czechoslovakia.*

Capon, who was not daunted by his inexperience in such matters, turned to the Internet and carefully researched exactly how one went about acquiring a Torah:

> *I quickly learned that purchasing a scroll would not be easy. There is apparently a market in stolen Torah scrolls, and the UAHC [the Reform movement's Union of American Hebrew Congregations] has put out an advisory that congregations should proceed with caution. It is also important to ensure that a purchased scroll is kosher, which means that the text of the Torah be absolutely without flaw, and that it meets a number of other criteria. Unfortunately, Torah scrolls that are not kosher are sometimes misrepresented.*

With a donation secured to finance the purchases and with leads provided by the UAHC, and with renowned Torah scribe and historian Dr. Eric Ray engaged as a consultant, Capon arranged for Rabbi Alexander and himself to fly to New York for a day to examine Torah scrolls. Based on that visit, Rabbi Alexander decided to acquire a scroll for the synagogue from the Jay Levine Company. The scroll had a well-known history, which was reassuring: it had come from a synagogue in Pennsylvania that was closing its doors. The scroll was written in Vilnius, Lithuania, at the turn of the 20th century. Dr. Ray described the scroll as a masterwork of a particularly accomplished scribe and estimated that the scroll took seven years to write.

Just as the story of how a Torah is secured for the synagogue concludes, the narrative of the Holocaust Memorial Scroll begins. In the course of his Internet research, quite by chance, Capon learned of an opportunity:

A number of synagogue Web pages made reference to a Holocaust Memorial Scroll on permanent loan from the Memorial Scrolls Trust at Westminster Synagogue in London. The trust has a Web page that provided contact information, so I telephoned the cochairman of the trust, Mrs. Ruth Shaffer, and inquired on behalf of CBI.

The trust owns 1,564 Torah scrolls that were purchased by an English philanthropist from the Czech government in 1964. The scrolls had been placed by the Nazis in the Prague Synagogue as a "memorial to a defunct race."

For over 20 years, the scrolls had lain unused and unattended in a Prague synagogue that had been converted into a warehouse, and they were deteriorating. They were a part of the huge collection of Jewish ritual objects confiscated by Hitler to be used in his planned "museum of an extinct race."

According to the trust, many of the 1,564 Torah scrolls that had been placed in the Westminster Synagogue had come from hundreds of Czech Jewish communities that had perished in

the war and have since been adopted by communities in
Europe and the United States "as memorials to a tragic past
but at the same time to be read and studied by a new genera-
tion of Jews, the guarantors of Jewish survival and rebirth."

Mrs. Shaffer advised me that approximately 100 scrolls
remained, all in poor condition, and she instructed me on how
to make application for CBI to obtain a scroll on the basis of a
permanent loan. An application was made that included
information all about CBI, including photographs of the syna-
gogue, a copy of the bulletin, and even a synagogue cookbook.
Several weeks later, I received a fax from the trust that CBI was
qualified to obtain a scroll, but only on the condition that a
representative travel to London to make the selection.

Rabbi Alexander recalls that when Capon broached the idea of acquiring one of these Torah scrolls, he was unsettled by the idea. Was it
appropriate to acquire a Holocaust Torah that could not be made fit
for use? To use James Young's terms, the rabbi knew that "icons of
memory" could too easily harden into "idols of remembrance."[9] There
was, the rabbi knew well, a traditional Jewish practice available for
Torahs beyond repair—and that was burial. Moreover, if the rabbi
agreed that the congregation could receive such a Holocaust Torah—
essentially a new sacred object, like but not exactly like a Torah—what
were the guidelines for its use and display?

Rabbi Joel Roth of the Jewish Theological Seminary explains that
the Conservative movement had to resolve this dilemma for many of
its rabbis who found themselves in a position similar to Rabbi
Alexander. They did so by submitting the issue to the movement's
Committee on Jewish Law and Standards for its input. Roth explains
the situation:

A congregation acquires a Holocaust Torah and wants to put it
on display. The rabbi is faced with a dilemma. On the one
hand, the rabbi knows the Torah should be buried.... On the
other hand, there might be legitimate halakhic reasons to

forego the burial and allow the display as a memorial to the victims of the Holocaust and their destroyed communities. Allowing the display would raise further questions: Are there restrictions on where or how the Torah could be displayed? Would it have to be displayed closed or might it be open? If it could be open, must it be open to a specific passage or is any place acceptable? The rabbi turns to the usual sources and, finding no definitive answers, submits the questions to the Committee on Jewish Law and Standards. The halakhic arguments for forgoing burial, particularly in view of the desire to memorialize the Holocaust, are overwhelming. The primary reason we must bury a disqualified Torah is to prevent its inadvertent use. The two responsa raised in our first meeting offer evidence that if provisions are made, making it improbable, unlikely, or impossible that the Torah would be used, it need not be buried. When Rabbi Finkelstein gave the Torah to President Truman, it was with the express understanding that it would be displayed in the Truman Library or in a museum. In this case, once the Torah is placed in the display case, its inadvertent use is out of the question. Further, putting the Torah on display serves as a permanent reminder of the tragedy of the Holocaust.... With only one abstention, the committee votes unanimously in favor of permitting the display of the Torah, and the case of the Holocaust Torah ends with an uncommon outcome.[10]

Rabbi Alexander was eventually persuaded of the educational merits of acquiring a Holocaust Torah; Roth had presented compelling arguments that resonated with him and many other rabbis. First, a "disqualified" Torah that is on display will surely not be used inadvertently. Secondly, it could serve an important educational purpose—allowing generations to come to be reminded dramatically of the "tragedy of the Holocaust." Such a Torah, if buried, could not be an eloquent and horrible reminder: it would simply disappear.

We return to Capon's narrative. As he recalled:

I had applied to Mrs. Shaffer for a scroll, and had received word that CBI could have a scroll, but only if I was willing to travel to London to select one. Mrs. Shaffer explained that the only scrolls that remained were damaged, and the burden of choosing had become too difficult for her. I have always wondered if there might be more to it than that, but never asked Mrs. Shaffer to elaborate. I wondered if this requirement was her way of determining whether the applicant was truly committed to obtaining and caring for a scroll, and the trip was the final gauge of one's commitment.

Capon was free to go to the Westminster Synagogue to acquire a Czech Torah scroll, for as it happened, he was scheduled—again, just by chance—to take a business trip to London. Moreover, as it was off-season, it occurred to Capon

that it wouldn't be expensive to bring Rose [his wife] and the kids ... [and] my business trip turned into a family expedition. Rose and I thought the chance for the kids to participate in the project would be an opportunity of a lifetime, and reasoned that a week in London would be at least as educational as a week in school. So we took them out of school, and they joined me for the trip.

Rose Capon—also a pillar of the local Jewish community, active in Hadassah—tells the story of the family's role a little differently, which I discovered when I asked if she had been comfortable with Rob's idea of involving their young children—Howard was 11 and Miriam was 6 at the time—in a project that was linked to the Holocaust. Rose told me:

Rob said that when he was in London, he would try to see Mrs. Schaffer. I said, "We have to go with you." I saw the trip as a responsibility and an honor. I wanted to be part of it and I wanted the kids to be part of it. I felt the Jewish community had been buried and this was among the last living things. I thought of the Torahs lying there in state in London. They needed to be part of a living community.

Rob Capon's written narrative of the family's journey continues:

When we arrived at Westminster, Mrs. Shaffer took us to the scroll room, where we had the opportunity to handle and examine scrolls. I cannot begin to describe how moving it was to see the burnt and damaged remains of 100 scrolls from the Holocaust. We saw scrolls that had been damaged by smoke, flame, and water. Several scrolls were wrapped in a tallit, a measure to help protect them during the tumult of the Holocaust. Try to imagine the scene in which such a scroll is wrapped in a tallit in the midst of war and civil unrest. A number of scrolls had a Nazi identification number written on the rollers, so that the scrolls could be identified in the Nazi collection. Our hands quickly became covered with the soot and dust.[11]

We had been at Westminster for several hours, and had not yet seen a Torah in good condition, when Howard spotted scroll number 12 tucked away in a corner. The scroll was in relatively good condition, although it was not kosher by virtue of extensive damage to approximately five percent of its columns. The rollers were in good condition, and are light brown in color. The documentation of the scroll describes it as being c. 1790, and having come from the neighboring towns of Frydek-Mistek, a combined Jewish community of approximately 432 members in 1930. Mrs. Shaffer furnished us with a one-page history of the congregation, excerpted from a book about the history of the Jewish people in Czechoslovakia. We know that the Nazis destroyed the synagogue in 1939, but that the Jewish cemetery remains in Frydek. The scroll has a Nazi identification number 37031 written on the lower right handle.

We took extensive photographs of scroll number 12, along with two other scrolls, and presented the materials to the synagogue board for a final decision. The Board delegated the decision to Rabbi Alexander, who concurred with the recommendation to adopt scroll 12. The scroll was shipped from London, following the preparation of export licenses and the fabrication of a wooden shipping crate. The scroll cannot be used in regular services because it is not kosher. However, the Holocaust Memorial Scrolls have been given special dispensation to be used in services on Yom Hashoah. The scrolls may also be used for teaching purposes, and in this manner are "living" memorials.

Rose, Howard, Miriam, and I feel very privileged to have participated in the process of acquiring the Westminster Memorial Scroll. It is our hope that the scroll adds richness to our already rich and diverse educational and cultural program at Congregation Beth Israel.

Dedicating and Ritualizing the Use of the Scroll

The scroll was packaged and sent to the United States, and Rob Capon drove to Dulles Airport to pick it up and bring it home. As Rose tells the story, when Rob brought the Torah into their home in Charlottesville, they both decided it was wrong for their family to unpack it alone. "We need a minyan," Rose remembers thinking at the time. Only afterward did she reflect on her instant decision that a particular ritual needed to be crafted, practically on the spot, in order to welcome this Torah. "Why did we think that? What did we know? We made the ceremony up as we went along." Acting spontaneously, but certainly drawing on the "Jewish ritual toolbox" to which they had access, they called friends from the synagogue to come and help with the unpacking and to welcome the Holocaust Memorial Scroll. Once a group was gathered, it was spontaneous, but it seemed logical enough to unroll the scroll on the dining-room table. It was only then that the extent of its damage became more poignantly apparent.

Rose recalls how the rest of the new ritual—one held in the private space of a home—fell into place as new "players" came to participate, bringing Jewish ritual sensibilities of their own.

> *Yacob Haimes, then the synagogue president, said, "I wonder if I can read from it?" … Yacob looked at me and asked, "Do you have a yahrzeit candle?" We did, and we lit it. It was the most moving spiritual experience I have ever had. Being in that group of people, it was almost like we were resuscitating that Torah that lay on the table. It had been through so much. It was as if we were saving the life of a forgotten community.*

When Rabbi Alexander, who had been on sabbatical during that time, returned to the congregation, an official ceremony was held in the synagogue. It was called a "reconsecration," and Rabbi Alexander offered a sermon on the occasion.

Welcoming the Holocaust Torah

Some congregations, holding ceremonies to welcome Holocaust Torahs into their midst, have referred to them as a *Hachnassat Sefer Torah* (welcoming of the Torah scroll). Temple Emanuel in Cherry Hill, New Jersey, called their ceremony, held before Simchat Torah in 1999, a *siyum*, a celebration of completion, as their Holocaust Torah has been completely restored. Five hundred members of their community gathered as a scribe wrote the final words on the scroll before the service. This congregation, like others, uses the occasion of a Holocaust Torah's restoration to teach its children and adult members about the art and spiritual practice of being a *sofer*, a Torah scribe.

Below is the text of Rabbi Alexander's sermon at the reconsecration ceremony. As you will see, he does not try to hide from the congregation that at first he had been uncomfortable with this new ritual object: a Torah scroll used in a wholly new way. In fact, he pointedly decides to share his own journey of acclimation, and the very process he describes becomes an educational opportunity in itself for the congregation. And we learn that the journey, and taking the risk of being open to a new ritual practice, held unforeseen blessings of its own. Having the Holocaust Torah in their midst, he discovered, could serve as a goad for others not just to remember the Holocaust but also to intensify their being faithful to the "traditions of our ancestors," and to embrace a Jewish life that was positive, vigorous, and serious.

The Reconsecration of Holocaust Memorial Scroll No. 12

Rabbi Daniel Alexander

This Torah scroll, which we dedicate today, what meaning has it? As some of you know ... this rabbi had to overcome considerable reluctance before reaching the enthusiastic embrace of the concept of our synagogue becoming a home for this or any Torah scroll whose use would be other than regular ritual reading. I think it may be instructive to explain both the reluctance and the enthusiastic embrace.

There were three obstacles that had to be overcome, and they were:

1. Like other written items containing the name of God, Jewish tradition has long-standing rules and regulations for the proper and respectful treatment of such items when they are no longer fit for use. Thus, prayer books,

Humashim (Bibles), sacred works of oral tradition—that have become worn, even photocopied sheets containing the name of God—all of these are referred to as Shemot—meaning writings with God's name. They are never simply tossed into the trash, but are placed into archival storage—*genizot*—until they can be ritually buried in a Jewish cemetery. If even a Xeroxed sheet with a *bracha* (blessing) on it must be handled with such care, how much more so must a sefer Torah (Torah scroll) which can no longer be used nor restored but handled with care and respect—not only because it contains God's name but because of its symbolic value as embodiment of the ancient covenant between God and the people Israel. Should such a Torah be put on display when display is not the traditional norm for handling defective scrolls?

2. The reason we were able to obtain this scroll, the reason the Capon family was able to obtain it for us, was because 1,564 scrolls had been pillaged by the Nazis and deposited in the Mishle Synagogue in Prague—with other ritual objects—intended all together to become part of the museum to the vanquished race. Those scrolls were later lovingly transported to the Westminster Synagogue where they have been carefully preserved, catalogued, and distributed to worthy institutions throughout the world, their own communities of origin no longer in existence.

    To me, it has become axiomatic that, in Emil Fackenheim's famous formulation, we must not hand Hitler posthumous victories. If we are to display this scroll, we must be certain that we are not, in any way, shape, or form, doing what Hitler intended to do.

3. Here I risk giving offense, but so be it. I have on occasion visited a home where the hosts proudly show me some

ritual item on display: a *Kiddush* cup from grandfather, a set of candlesticks from some great aunt. Similarly, I have been in synagogues with museum displays that include tefillin, *tallitot*, or *Havdalah* spice boxes, and the like. What saddens me about all of these displays is the implication that these items are no longer used. The sadness is even greater if the implication corresponds to fact in that particular home or in that particular synagogue. To me it is a deep source of sadness when Jews relegate to museum displays living objects of ritual power as if they were merely remnants of a distant and archaic past, one we only wish to remember behind a glass. Forgive me, but *tallitot* are for praying with, as are those weird-looking tefillin. Spice boxes are for use in saying good-bye to *Shabbat*. *Kiddush* cups are for the sanctification of this day, still a living and meaningful option for a Jew living in 1999 in north-central Virginia. Basically, Torah scrolls are for our communal ritual reenactments of the Sinai experience and the chain of its transmission through the generations. These rituals and the objects that we employ to undertake them, constitute the core of meaningful Jewish living in our time. It pains me to see them displayed as if they are fossilized remnants from a disconnected past.

Those were the obstacles I needed to get by in order to feel as I do that the acquisition of this Torah—with its unique and sorrowful past—is a great blessing. To display this Torah in a synagogue that pulsates with life as does ours is not to do what Hitler intended, but the opposite. Westminster Torah Scroll #12 now joins its story to the story of our small but dynamic and growing community. It becomes for us a tangible, visible means to accomplish an essential but difficult task: to remember a time in recent history full of unspeakably evil deeds and unbearable catastrophe—

without being overcome by the same. As such, to display it as a memorial, to use it to teach that most difficult of historical periods, to read from it on the rare ritual memorial occasions that allow—is to treat it with high honor and appropriate respect.

This tattooed Torah scroll, what meaning has it? It should recall for us a specific Jewish community. That twin town, Frydek-Mistek, straddles the Ostravice River, with Frydek on the northern, Silesian bank and Mistek on the southern, Moravian bank. Jews lived in both towns but shared one small synagogue, located in Frydek. The census of 1930 revealed 430 Jews. Today, only the Hebrew cemetery, established in 1882, and the synagogue, now used for prayer by Seventh Day Adventists, remain as visible signs of an eradicated Jewish community.

We remember that community of Jews—similar in size to our own. Rather, we remember that there was a community in that hilly country some 20 kilometers from the Czechoslovak-Polish border. In truth we know little about the Jews of Frydek-Mistek.... All we really know is that we now possess a Torah scroll, once a means for their expression of allegiance to God and the Jewish faith.

This tattooed, partially defective scroll, what meaning has it? The Torah insists—as a matter of unshakeable principle—that we remember, that we remember both the beneficent and the evil that has befallen our people. *"Zachor et yom ha-Shabbat l'kadsho"* (Remember the Sabbath day to keep it holy)! On the one hand, our tradition bids us to remember *Shabbat* and its creation as a divine act of love and as a sign of the unique covenant between God and the people Israel.

On the other hand, our tradition teaches: *"Zachor et ma asah l'cha Amalek"* (Remember what Amalek did to you)! Remember the evil deeds of Amalek and Amalek's descendants, among them, Haman and Hitler—who sought to dehumanize us and destroy us. *Shabbat* we remember "to make it holy" and to make the holy and sacred part of our lives. Amalek we remember so that we may do everything in our power to prevent his evil goals from being achieved.

It is immensely important that this memorial scroll help us not only to recall the dark and chaotic period of Holocaust night but that it stir us. It is essential that it allow us an awareness of the darkness and gloom and death and that awareness give way to a positive, life-embracing, faithful Jewish response. The Torah passage that we will hear shortly (Deut. 4:30–40) begins with an acknowledgment of gloom: *"Ba'tzar l'cha um'tza-ucha kol had'varim ha-eleh ..."* (In your distress, when all these things had come upon you ...). It concludes with an awareness of divine sovereignty—a verse incorporated into the prayer *Alenu*—and the ongoing covenantal bond between God and Israel. As in our Passover seders, we begin with degradation and end with praise—as we must.

Ultimately, our Jewish response to the horror of the Holocaust must be a commitment to remember—in spite of the many forces that would wish and have tried to snuff it out. It is wonderfully coincidental that we schedule this dedication on *Shabbat* Emor, a *Shabbat* during which a 13-year old Jewish boy will, like his father before him and like Jewish boys for generations—ascend the *bimah* tomorrow as a bar mitzvah— as a full member of our prayer quorum, as a faithful member of the people Israel. There is no better response to Holocaust night than that.

To the enemies of our people, we best respond by positive determination to remain faithful to the traditions of our ancestors, by becoming bar mitzvah and bat mitzvah, by creating Jewish families, by engaging in the study of Torah and the practice of religious ritual, and by performing deeds that bring honor to God and our people.

May this scroll that we dedicate this *Shabbat* serve as a reminder of the community from which it came and of the many who perished during the days of the Holocaust. And may it goad us to live lives that hallow the name of the Almighty. *Ken yi'hi ratzon.* May it be God's will.

Rabbi Alexander offered this "Prayer of Reconsecration" for the service:

Eloheinu v'Elohei avotenu v'imotenu, Our God and God of our ancestors, You through whose light all creation issues and subsists, with all our hearts we thank You for this sacred scroll, this shining oracle, which now comes to illumine our synagogue and our lives. With Your divine help we will guard this sacred treasure. May its presence remain among us, a lasting memorial to the martyrs of our people in the tragedy of the age. Before the throne of Your universal and everlasting love, may the souls of the pious whose eyes once scanned this sacred scroll, be bound up in the bond of life. O God, who knows the way of all children, bless all those who have labored for the rescue and restoration of the sacred scrolls of which this sacred scroll is one. And now, O Eternal One, and in the long years to come, may our contemplation of this sacred scroll enlighten our eyes and fire our imagination, that we may more zealously serve humankind, and glorify Your holy name. To these ends we reconsecrate this sacred scroll, for memorial in Congregation Beth Israel. O God, bless our purpose, and accept our humble praise.[12]

The Holocaust Torah scroll is now kept in an alcove in the back of the small sanctuary, over shelves where prayer books are stored, displayed in a modest wooden case with a glass front. The Torah, locked in the case and standing upright, is rolled slightly open. One can see that since it was written in the 1800s, its letters have become worn and smudged in places, and the parchment has been patched up numerous times. On the adjacent wall, there is a framed certificate indicating that this is a Holocaust Torah, and a small brass plaque at the bottom indicates that the Capon family obtained the Torah for the synagogue. The display case, it says, was their gift.

Transmitting a New Ritual through Children's Literature

The Tattooed Torah, written by Marvell Ginsburg and illustrated by Martin Lemelman, was published (UAHC Press) in 1983. Created for elementary school children, the book tells the story of the rescue and restoration of a little Torah from Brno, Czechoslovakia. Underplaying the violence of the Holocaust and emphasizing the joy of the Torah's rescue, the book is said to teach "the Holocaust not only as a period of destruction but also as an opportunity for redemption." The text of this story features a layperson called Mr. Weil in the crucial role of researcher and redeemer, who is reminiscent of Capon. He is an American Jewish man seeking to find a small Torah, light enough for young children to hold. Learning that Torahs are available in London at the Westminster Synagogue, Mr. Weil, just like Rob Capon, goes to London; meets Mrs. Schaffer; and sees the damaged Torah stored on wooden racks. Weil selects a Torah that children can hold and carries it back with him on the airplane. Back home, he has a red mantle made for the Torah, decorated with the word *Zachor,* "remember." At a service honoring the new Torah, all the children process with it and hear Mr. Weil tell the story of this "tattooed Torah."

The Future of the Holocaust Torah

At this moment, like Congregation Beth Israel in Charlottesville, most American congregations housing Holocaust Torahs are mining their educational use. The "rescuers" like the Capons, those whose spiritual energies were most galvanized by the project, are still proudly narrating their stories of trips to London, many posting them on their synagogue Web sites, as Capon did. The Torahs are displayed and are sometimes read from on Yom ha-Shoah. In many instances, Holocaust survivors from Czechoslovakia have even traveled to the American synagogues housing "their" Torahs, and have shared memories and forged bonds. Adult and youth groups are taking congregational trips to the communities in Czechoslovakia where "their" scrolls come from, worshipping in the sanctuaries where they were once housed. Some groups have taken their scroll with them, for a return visit. These visits have led to commitments to preserve these old synagogues.

But what will become of any congregation's Holocaust Torah once the zealous members who championed its "rescue" lose some of their enthusiasm or are no longer there? What memory of the Holocaust— if any—will those Holocaust Torahs displayed in glass cases in American synagogues be mediating? Will this Holocaust Torah eventually become a relic, just as Rabbi Alexander feared? And almost worse: what if, as James Young has written, "the initial impulse to memorialize events like the Holocaust may actually spring from an opposite and equal desire to forget them"?[13]

It seems as if the Czech Scrolls Memorial Trust has indeed anticipated the possibility of a future in which American congregants in decades to come will strain to make sense of the Holocaust Torahs displayed in their presence. As one response, the Czech Torah Network was created to connect over 1,500 synagogues and religious institutions that have Czech Torah Scrolls on permanent loan. The trust has already held two conferences for delegates of congregations in America that have been entrusted with the scrolls. After the Spring 2005 conference, the trust made the following statement:

> *Valuable information regarding tracing the original scroll congregations was shared. Although there are over one thousand Czech Torah Scrolls in the USA, most have been with congregations for over 20 years. Those members responsible for bringing these scrolls to their congregation have, in many cases, moved on and the present leadership is sometimes unaware of the "forgotten Holocaust survivor" sitting in their ark. The CTN was able to revive awareness and explore making these scrolls a meaningful and symbolic link to the past. People left with*

excitement and enthusiasm about connecting with their
[T]orah and the town and people who once used it.[14]

For the moment, in the town of Charlottesville, does memory suffice? What do the Capon children remember of their journey, after only a handful of years have passed? Granted, Miriam was but 6. She is 14 when we speak of the family trip to London, and she herself acknowledges she was probably too young to grasp why all the Torahs were there, why it was all so terrible for her parents to see, and why there was so much ceremonializing going on, first in their house when the scroll arrived, and then later, in a more official way, at the synagogue. Yet given the funeral pall Miriam made for her bat mitzvah project, I could not but remark how very young Miriam was to have already learned a deep Jewish lesson taught by this new ritual object, the Holocaust Torah, and the new ritual of reconsecrating it: death creates opportunities for sanctification. Might we not imagine that this awareness has come, in part, from Miriam's family's trip to London, from helping carefully to unpack the crate holding the Torah scroll that arrived in her own home and seeing it unfolded on her dining-room table? Because Howard was 11 at the time, his memory of the experience is more vivid. He was, after all, permitted to be the one to "discover" the Torah his family would eventually bring home. Now a college student, he shares his memories as he thinks back upon that day in London:

> *Just being in that room with the Torahs made you want to cry. It was very powerful. You grow up and go to synagogue and see how the Torah is treated so delicately and with reverence. To see them there, in racks, rotting away ... you're not ready for it, even at an age when you're just beginning to understand the significance of things. You'd handle the scrolls and wash your hands from the filth and the water would run brown. You choked back tears. I felt really proud to be the one going to London to do this.*

For both children, for their families, for an entire congregation: having a Holocaust Torah in their midst to which sanctity had been restored had become a new sign for the generations—in Hebrew, an *ot*—that when there was *menschlikhkeit,* holiness could be sustained.

How to Be a Mensch: Mitzvah Projects

In this case study, I narrate the story of the new rituals around Holocaust Torahs from the perspective of one family, the Capons. For them, acquiring the Holocaust Torah would become linked to another new family ritual that was beginning to put down roots: the philanthropic or social action project that typically occurs in the years close to a child's bar or bat mitzvah, a time when a child is on the cusp of a higher level of moral and intellectual apprehension. At this time many families are especially open to embarking on a project that models high standards of commitment, both to maintaining the Jewish heritage and being involved in the larger community. It is a time as well when many families will invite Judaism to take a more central role in their lives.

The philanthropic or social action project might engage all members of the family, sometimes across several generations. As part of the bar or bat mitzvah ceremony, the family might speak of their project or, if it surrounds a ritual object, they may make a public presentation of that object to their community. In the case of the Capons, the family worked together to procure a meaningful Jewish object, a Torah scroll, and several years later their daughter Miriam created an object for synagogue use, a hand-crafted funeral pall, with the assistance of her family.

No name has yet to emerge for such individual family "mitzvah projects" that parents are spearheading in order to set a good and dramatic example. I might call it "modeling *menschlikhkeit*," being a human being of the highest moral standards. The family projects can be linked to other new spiritual practices of an active nature performed by children and synagogues: mitzvah projects and mitzvah days.

Mitzvah projects. Many synagogues require bar and bat mitzvah students to carry out yearlong "mitzvah projects" or "*tzedakah* (social action) projects." They might tutor, volunteer at a senior center, or collect money for charity. The beneficiaries might be Jewish, but that is not a requirement. The goal is to restore the "mitzvah" (the doing of good deeds) to the bar/bat mitzvah ceremony, which can get overly focused on

a lavish party and other accoutrements. Examples of recent mitzvah projects reported in the *Detroit Jewish News* include these: Jacob Brian
Brody donated "hundreds of children's books to Reader to Reader's Hurricane Katrina Book Drive, which helped to restock elementary libraries
affected by the hurricane." Alexander Barron Loewenstein "organized a
baseball equipment drive and collected hundreds of bats, baseballs, and
helmets to benefit Think Detroit, a nonprofit agency that organizes youth
sports leagues in Detroit." Alexandra Logan Pierce participated in the
Celiac Walk " to help raise funds and create awareness for people who
suffer from severe wheat allergies." Elizabeth Ivy Shore donated 15
inches of hair to Locks of Love.[15]

Mitzvah Days. Synagogues hold annual "mitzvah days"—opportunities
for adults and children to spend a Sunday performing multiple hands-on
charitable acts in their communities. Typically the day will start in the synagogue with an informal ceremony setting the mood and framing the charitable acts in Jewish language, as mitzvot. The mitzvah day Web site of
Congregation Emanu El of Houston, Texas, explains that their congregation:

> holds service to the community to be among the highest values of its
> ancient tradition. We have a long history of devotion to repairing the
> broken fragments of society and serving the needs of the less fortu-
> nate. As it says in the Torah, God's spirit is with us in every righteous
> deed. Established at Emanu El in 1992, Mitzvah Day is a congrega-
> tion community service day created to encourage our members to
> go out into the community to make a difference in the lives of others.
> Over 35 projects are chosen by our Project Ideas Committee,
> selected from needs across all community borders. You can choose
> among construction, landscaping, visiting the elderly or infirm,
> chaperoning young children or at risk teens on field trips, making
> greeting cards, working at the children's carnival, and more. We
> also collect donations of good used clothing, baby needs, nonper-
> ishable food, and new toys. We sort, package, and distribute these
> donations to agencies in need. On Mitzvah Day, we have very brief
> opening ceremonies at 8:30 A.M. in our sanctuary. Donuts, coffee,

juice, and a special Mitzvah Day T-shirt will be available for every-
one in Feld Hall. You can help by bringing a needed item to Temple.
Also, you can perform your first mitzvah of the day and participate
in our blood drive held at Temple[16]

NOTES:

1. Oren Baruch Stier, "Different Trains: Holocaust Artifacts and the Ideologies of Remembrance," *Holocaust and Genocide Studies* 19, no. 1 (2005).

2. I thank Kim Lawton, of the PBS series *Religion and Ethics Newsweekly*, for asking me the questions about rescued sacred objects that inspired my thinking on this subject.

3. Solomon Moore, "Religious Rescues: Squad of Rabbis Wades in Water to Save Religious Symbols after Hurricane," *The Los Angeles Times*, September 24, 2005.

4. "Search and Rescue Efforts Shift Gears," found at Chabad Lubavitch Global Network Web site, http://www.lubavitch.com, September 9, 2005 (no longer available at this site).

5. Hundreds of Czech Torahs have been rescued and distributed by The Czech Memorial Scrolls Centre of London, England. See The Czech Torah Network, A Holocaust Education Project, at http://www.czechtorah.org. A number of stories about congregations that adopted Torahs are available on their Web site. The most extensive account, "The Woodacre Torah," which tells the entire life story of an acquired Torah, is told imaginatively by Suzanne Sadowsky and is available on the Web site of Gan HaLev, an independent congregation of the San Geronimo Valley, at http://www.ganhalev.org/torah/the_woodacre_torah.html.

6. Robert Capon, *"How CBI Acquired the Holocaust Memorial Torah Scroll,"* Congregation Beth Israel Web site, http://www.cbicville.org/about/scrollstory.html.

7. I am also a member of Congregation Beth Israel synagogue. .

8. Robert Capon, "How CBI Acquired the Holocaust Memorial Torah Scroll," http://www.cbicville.org/about/scrollstory.html.

9. James Young, *The Texture of Memory: Holocaust Memorials and Meaning* (New Haven: Yale University Press, 1993), 14.

10. Joel Roth, "The Case of the Holocaust Torah," *JTS Magazine* 7, No. 1 (Fall 1997). It seems worth noting that the rabbinic discussion does *not* mention the fact that the idea of having a Holocaust Torah is often initiated by congregants.

11. Rabbi Sid Schwartz, in a dedication ceremony at his congregation, Adat Shalom, describes his own observations of these Torah Scolls that he describes as having been "orphaned": "Indeed, the Torahs that were brought to Westminster Synagogue bore every evidence of the terror and tragedy of the Holocaust from which they were saved. Some were charred from fire. Some mildewed from the elements. Some were stained with blood. Some were wrapped in clothing, presumably an attempt to protect them by the last Jew to touch it. Some were wrapped in *talitot,* the Jewish prayer shawl in which traditional Jews are buried. And in some were found handwritten notes, desperate pleas from Jews who knew that they would perish. They entrusted a Torah with their final words, hoping that it would survive them and bear their testimony to the world." Adat Shalom, March 11, 2000, http://adatshalom.net/torahstory4.html.

12. Those interested in the variations of new liturgy will note a different blessing, composed by Rabbi Sid Schwartz for his congregation's rededication ceremony. This is a modified version of the prayer invoked by Rabbi Harold Reinhart of Westminster Synagogue in London upon the dedication of the first Holocaust Torah on June 2, 1968 (from Adat Shalom Web site, http://adatshalom.net/torahstory4.html):

Dear God, source and sustainer of all creation. We thank you for this sefer Torah *that now comes to illumine our sanctuary and our lives. We consider it a sacred treasure. May its presence in our midst serve as a memorial to the martyrs of our people who perished in the Holocaust. We pray that the souls of the pious whose eyes once looked upon this Torah, be remembered for good and that we, who survive them, insure that they did not die in vain. As we bring this Torah into our community and into the spiritual home that we are building together, we pray that we may be worthy of the history which this scroll represents. May each of us deepen our commitment to a life of Torah, living lives that bring honor to the Jewish people and advance the cause of peace and justice in the world at large. To this end do we dedicate this Holocaust Torah for use at Adat Shalom Reconstructionist Congregation this fourth day of Adar II, 5760,* shabbat Peku-day, *March 11, 2000.*

When a Holocaust Torah was dedicated at Congregation Beth Tikvah-B'nai Jeshurun in Erdenheim, Pennsylvania, in 2004, Bruce Engleman, who spearheaded the project as a tribute to the memory of his parents, said:

> *We have the great privilege of adopting this Holocaust Torah and dedicating it in memory of my parents. When it is taken out of the ark tomorrow morning, and my daughter Sara reads from it, it will be used as it was intended for the first time in more than 60 years ... BUT even more special, I believe, is the fact that, surely, this Torah scroll from Luze has never celebrated a bat mitzvah. In becoming its custodians, there is an element of melancholy as well as an element of great joy and celebration.* Melancholy, *because when you see it in the case that we will build in the lobby, it will always serve as a chilling reminder of the millions of Jews who lost their lives tragically ... only because they were Jews.* Joy and celebration, *because in rededicating this Torah for use in as vibrant a Jewish community as BTBJ, we are reminded of the Jewish people's tenacity for survival. Finally, being custodians of this sacred scroll becomes a powerful reminder to us of our responsibility to take Judaism seriously and to pass this legacy on to the next generation.*

From "About—Our Holocaust Torah," Beth Tikvah—B'nai Jeshrun Web site, http://www.btbj.org/HolocaustTorah.asp.

13. James Young, *The Texture of Memory: Holocaust Memorials and Meaning* (New Haven: Yale University Press, 1993), 5.

14. From The Czech Torah Network, A Holocaust Education Project, http://www.czechtorah.org/events.php.<en>

15. "Life cycles: Bar/Bat Mitzvahs—October 15, 2005 Edition," *jNonlin*, http://www.jnonline.us/.

16. Mitzvah Day 2004, http://www.mitzvahday.org (site accessed May 1, 2004; information no longer available at site).

CASE STUDY THREE:
THE WEDDING BOOKLET

Marriage requires compromise, and wedding planning offers boot-camp preparation as a couple decides whether their wedding will be an intimate ceremony or a gala affair, her rabbi or his, a klezmer band or a string quartet, the marinated chicken breast served on a bed of basmati rice garnished with asparagus, or the seared aged fillet of beef served with tomato Provençal, *haricots verts,* and *pomme noisettes.* And that is but the beginning, for each family brings its own customs and expectations, and emotions may come to a rapid boil as decisions create either elation or wounded feelings.

To this daunting array of decisions, the question, "How will we do the ceremony?" is now added. If rabbis and Jewish etiquette books once stipulated the one and only "right" way to perform a "traditional" Jewish wedding, they no longer do so. The design of the ceremony is subject to negotiation, and couples are debating what legal and customary elements that constitute a Jewish wedding ceremony will feel legitimate and acceptable to them.

Many couples have created a wedding booklet to explain their choices in designing the ritual components of their Jewish marriage ceremony. The wedding booklet is placed in the hands of guests as the ceremony begins, and strains of Hebrew love songs play. It may serve to calm emotions, present a spirit of resolve, and to answer the question, "What kind of a Jewish wedding is this?"

Here are just some of the ceremonial decisions couples are making and documenting in their wedding booklets:

1. In the veiling ceremony (*bedeken*) that precedes the wedding, do we accept the conventional symbolic interpretation of this gesture—that the groom, in lowering the bride's veil, is checking that he has not been deceived, as Jacob was by Leah? Or, would we prefer that the veiling symbolize "the privacy and individuality of the *kallah* (bride) that must be protected despite the intimacy of marriage"?[1] Or, finding neither interpretation compatible with an egalitarian worldview, do we create a new ceremony and a new interpretation? To represent that we are entering this marriage with open eyes and with a commitment to "continuously care for one another,"[2] might the groom dress the bride in her veil, and the bride help the groom into his *kitel*, a traditional white robe?

2. Do we accept the Orthodox rabbi's insistence that having a double ring ceremony will invalidate the practice of *kinyan* (acquisition), in which the groom's giving and the bride's acceptance of the ring symbolize that the groom has acquired the bride? Or do we find a way for the bride to give the groom a ring of his own as well, explaining that the first ring "symbolizes the Jewish legal aspects of what is taking place" and the second ring, given by the bride to the groom, will "stand for the love and emotional commitment that is of equal importance in sealing our marriage"?[3]

3. After the ceremony, do we chose not to observe *yichud,* a time for the bride and groom to spend a few moments alone together, in seclusion, because we shun a ritual that echoes the practice of consummating a marriage immediately and providing evidence of the bride's virginity? Or do we observe it because "*yichud* reminds

us of the importance of taking time together, of creating a safe and loving home for each other"?[4]

The privilege of entering into debate is not limited to those couples with rich Jewish educations or with access to a rabbi's ear. Any couple, armed with a Jewish wedding guidebook and a collection of wedding booklets saved from their friends' weddings, can feel empowered to "renew the old and sanctify the new" as they custom design their ceremony, making it their own, and making it Jewish, on their terms. Many—and I will call them "the selectors"—will do so without fearing that their choices are about to endanger the legitimacy of their rite of passage. Without hesitation, they claim freedom of choice in *these* religious matters as their right, even though I doubt they would be so bold as to suggest changes in, say, the Rosh Hashanah or Yom Kippur liturgies. Their fearlessness in matrimonial matters does not come out of bravado or callousness in the face of an inherited tradition. Since few of them want to use this occasion to transform Judaism into a spiritual or political agenda, they may even be oblivious to the role they are playing in shaping the trajectory of Jewish practice. For them, Jewish law and generations of practice have provided them with a collection of old-fashioned traditions that are charming enough to trot out and juggle around for this special occasion. "Getting to choose" is just what people are doing: designing the ceremony seems no different than designing the reception.

But there are couples, and I'll call them "agents of change," who are acutely aware that their wedding choices are intentional interpretations of past practices, and that the resulting redesigns or rejections can have consequence. They feel the gravity of the role they play, and realize their wedding has become, like it or not, an occasion on which to address social imbalances in Judaism. Do brides and grooms generally agree that this is the time and the place to affirm or challenge communal norms? Not always, or not in equal measure, and this is a common source of tension. This is especially so when the bride and groom differ in their understanding of how much binding authority *halakhah* has over them and differ too in their willingness to subject their families to novelty at a time when what they have come to witness is "a traditional ceremony." "I just can't deal with them," I have heard many a couple say, meaning there may be more familial fallout than either feels equipped to handle, and judiciousness is advised. Or, with resignation following a heated debate, "Let's just do the ritual."

The extent of transformation deemed necessary varies. Some couples seek only to achieve a greater level of personal comfort, so that their own integrity is honored alongside that of the tradition. For some, astute tweaking that makes overtures toward egalitarianism will suffice. Others believe that if they are to have a Jewish wedding, they must enter into battle with a set of infuriating and outdated patriarchal practices that still hold sway over them, for these traditions possess what Tamara Cohen (a well-known Jewish feminist writer, activist, and educator) calls an "authenticating power." (These are invariably the couples confessing, in their wedding booklets, that they have been wrestling with the tradition until the eleventh hour, and only the arrival of the wedding day itself could nudge them toward closure.) They will emerge victorious if they can succeed in manipulating the old forms, extracting their powerful essences, and rebuilding them so they can still hold meaning. Such couples know the rules of rabbinic reasoning. They can parse the centuries of rabbinic debate and enter thoughtfully into the discourse. They are ready to activate mechanisms for change within the system by virtue of the fact on the ground they are about to embody and enact.

The New Jewish Wedding

For guidance, many Jewish couples planning their weddings will turn to Anita Diamant's popular book *The New Jewish Wedding*. It reflects and endorses the spirit of invention, providing both the permission and the information that gird a couple with sufficient agency to become architects of their own wedding. When Diamant's book first appeared in 1985, she wrote that taking charge of one's own wedding was not "an exercise in nostalgia or an affirmation of orthodoxy but [is] about an evolving and dramatic synthesis of modern sensibilities and Jewish tradition."[5] Imagining a readership of liberal and potentially disenfranchised Jews, she offered resources that would provide "alternative visions of what Jewish weddings in America today can be and what they have in fact already become."[6] She directed couples to view the diverse Jewish wedding traditions that have developed wherever Jews have lived as a generous resource of inspiring choices, an impetus for brainstorming and creativity, revivals, and reinventions: "It is a dynamic and flexible tradition," she wrote reassuringly, "and it is yours to explore and recreate."[7] It is significant that 16 years later, Diamant already needed to revise and update her book. In a preface to the new 2001 edition, she describes the earlier edition as a "*minhag* book—a description of contemporary customs."[8] But the new (or newly recovered) wedding customs of the 1980s—introducing klezmer music, engaging a calligrapher to write one's *ketubah*, or donating a percentage of the food costs to charity—all once "vaguely experimental," had become mainstream. Demographics had changed too, and under the *huppah*, there were the new faces that her book would welcome, especially non-Jews marrying Jews in Jewish ceremonies and same-sex couples. In 2001, Diamant could only conclude: "Today the Jewish wedding is a great example of the vitality and dynamism of a living Jewish culture, sparkling with fresh artistic expression, spiritual authenticity, and joy."[9]

Wedding Booklets

Much of the ritual innovation one now encounters at a Jewish wedding is documented, as I have mentioned, in the wedding booklet distributed to guests as they take their places at the ceremony. The Jewish wedding booklet is a variation on the wedding program that many American couples, religious and secular, will provide as keepsakes for their wedding guests. The wedding program—homemade or commercially produced on a variety of cardstocks, some covered in vellum or tied with satin ribbon—follows a standard template, though in register it can range from folksy to formal. Typically, it details the order of the service (according, of course, to the faith tradition), indicating when audience response is appropriate. It introduces the members of the bridal party, in the order of their appearance, and sometimes, like a playbill, gives a brief biography and explains their importance to the couple. It might include words of tribute as a memorial to departed family members.

While such programs of modest scope are distributed at some Jewish weddings, it is the more elaborate wedding booklet that is becoming standard for couples wishing to explain the Jewish traditions from their point of view, and to highlight their particular interpretation of them. Couples lavish attention on the content and style of their booklets, and the "agents of change" are especially deliberate.[10]

Wedding guests can no longer rely upon their own cultural memory to convince themselves that what they are witnessing is a legitimate Jewish marriage, for what they are seeing may be quite new. Guests have not been asked to preapprove the new ritual—for opening up a new ritual for discussion ultimately invites not only debate but also disapproval. In the wedding booklet, the ceremony is presented to guests as a *fait accompli*. Ritual legitimacy will be defined by the performance of the new wedding booklet text before them. The ritual might not feel old, but at least it will feel "real." If the couple plays by the rules they have established in the wedding booklet, then most of their guests will concede that by this newly articulated definition of the ritual and its meanings, they are married. Leafing through the booklet before the ceremony begins, or reading along as it progresses, wedding guests learn about the rituals unfolding before them and tacitly accept them, forming a temporarily cohesive witnessing community. It is the wedding booklet that allows guests to feel as if they are witnessing a ritual that is familiar and beloved to them.

We can easily imagine a time when a wedding booklet was unnecessary. Perhaps the bride and groom's family came from the same town. The people walking up the aisle with the bride and groom were their parents—there weren't stepparents, parents' partners, stepsiblings and half-siblings to sort through. Everyone was Jewish and everyone knew the ritual. The bride would circle the groom and would hold out her finger to receive a ring. The groom would break a glass, and that would signal shouts of *"Mazel tov!"* Knowing who was who, what would happen next, and what it all meant, one could keep up with the emotional cadences of the ceremony. You could imagine what others were feeling, and you knew what you were supposed to feel too—when it was time for anticipation, and then relief and joy.

Now the guests assembled at a Jewish wedding are likely to be an *ad hoc* community that runs the "gamut of ideologies, observances, and denominational affiliations."[11] Now, two brides or two grooms may be walking down the aisle. The couple may choose to make multiple separate circlings and joint promenades, and the bride may be stomping on her own glass. How are guests to know exactly what is going on and how it conforms to or deviates from traditional practice? They need a wedding booklet—a ritual object that will serve to identify, interpret, and, finally, legitimize the ritual action of the marriage ceremony.

How to Write a Wedding Booklet

Diamant commends the writing of a wedding booklet in both editions of *The New Jewish Wedding*. It will put guests who are not Jewish or who do not understand Hebrew at ease, helping them to navigate the ceremony and feel included. Those thoroughly unfamiliar with Jewish weddings, she advises, will be grateful to receive theirs in advance of the ceremony. (This is a gesture meant to diffuse some of the added tensions brought, in particular, by non-Jewish relatives coming to a ceremony that will be mainly Jewish in format.) For those who are well versed in Jewish traditions, the booklet provides a different kindness: it obviates the need for lengthy midceremony explanations from the officiant, which might "make the ceremony feel watered down to the point of Protestantism."[12]

The booklet is not, Diamant claims, a new custom meant to create confusion or discomfort. Rather, it comes to soothe: it might include a letter of welcome and an English translation of the *ketubah*, obviating the need to read it aloud in English, which would bring its archaic premises more prominently to people's attention. There could be acknowledgments to friends and family, memorials to the beloved deceased whose absences are palpably present, definitions of Hebrew terms, explanations of terms and customs, and a general guide to the ceremony.

How do most couples know what to include in their booklets? Most will rely on Diamant's suggestions, or they will select what they have admired in the wedding booklets of their friends. As one bride put it:

Ever since I was a little girl, I dreamed of one day circling my groom under the huppah seven times. Then I learned it symbolized that he was supposed to be the center of my world, and I didn't like that. But I read in my cousin's wedding booklet that it could symbolize the sacred space we would create together in our home. I really liked that, so we put that explanation in our wedding booklet, and I could do the seven circles like I wanted.

Diamant insists that the booklet is "really only a variation of an old practice."[13] Which old practice? Diamant is not referring to a forgotten practice of the shtetl, or to one that has now been supplanted by something newer. The old practice, she claims, is the still ongoing practice of providing wedding guests with *bentschers* (*bentsch* is the Yiddish word for "bless"), commercially produced booklets containing the blessing of the grace after meals, the seven wedding blessings, and an assortment of Hebrew songs suitable for use at the *Shabbat* table. Typically, the *bentschers,* placed on the tables at the wedding reception, are printed with the name of the bride and groom on the cover, as well as the date of their wedding. At the end of the wedding meal, guests will consult them for the special grace and will take them home as useful souvenirs, adding them to an ever-growing collection. At home, they will take them out on *Shabbat* as the communal table grace is sung and they will perhaps remember "so and so's" lovely wedding (when couples divorce, their *bentschers* are sometimes withdrawn from the collection, lest they become conduits of bad luck). Why did Diamant compare the Jewish wedding booklet to the *bentscher* and not to the generic wedding program? Perhaps to assure a couple that what they are doing, in distributing a text, is linked to a venerable and familiar practice.

At the Nexus of Tradition and Innovation

As the wedding date approached, it appeared ever less likely that there would be time to find a solution.... Progress came only with Joel's wise suggestion that we stop talking and each write up our ideal ceremonies independently, from the reception ... through the breaking of the glass.[14]

The Jewish wedding booklet does something that neither the program nor the *bentscher* does. It is a new ritual object that has been described by folklore scholar Jody Shapiro as existing "at the nexus of innovation and tradition, dynamism, and conservatism."[15] What Shapiro is saying is that even when a wedding booklet appears to be presenting just the facts, it inevitably does more, preserving how the couple resolved what may have seemed to them like irreconcilable liturgical and ceremonial differences. And it does so with enough subtlety that the drama of change is downplayed.

Most wedding booklets employ various strategies to harmonize a couple's negotiations with each other and with Jewish tradition. Some will demonstrate the couple's success in moving toward resolution, others show how areas of contention were smoothed over, and others are frank in laying bare the struggle. In melding the radical quality of innovation with the security, familiarity, and weight of tradition, most booklets aim to leave communal feathers unruffled. This objective is illustrated most dramatically in the June 14, 1990, wedding booklet of Jacob Aryeh Davidson and Haviva Rena Krasner. It begins with this gentle and friendly introduction:

> *We would like to welcome you to our wedding. In order to make the event more meaningful, we have prepared a summary and explanation of the ceremony and the rituals leading up to it. We hope it is helpful to you in enhancing the occasion and making it more than just another celebration.*

The booklet promises enhancement, but what it will introduce, among other innovations, is a tremendously radical gesture for a young modern Orthodox couple: The bride has articulated and signed a "marital statement" (included in the booklet). In it, she makes the following vows: "I will love, cherish, honor, support, and maintain Jacob, as he has obligated himself in the *ketubah* to do for me. I will support his endeavors (within reason) and strive to make our marriage a true partnership of love, understanding, and friendship." The statement maintains that both bride and groom will provide moral and economic support for each other and will "share the household and familial duties so that together we can build a *bayit ne'eman b'Yisrael."* (Here they are using the formulaic language describing a couple's sturdy and faithful Jewish household, which serves to soften any overtly feminist tone.)

Booklet Writing as Spiritual Preparation

For many couples, the act of writing a booklet together constitutes a significant component of their spiritual preparation for the wedding. Tamara Cohen describes the booklet that she and her partner, Gwynn Kessler, composed for their 2004 wedding ceremony, explaining what the process of creating it was like (it fluctuated between exaltation and exasperation) and why they were willing to share it as part of an online exhibit of artifacts for the Jewish Women's Archive, one celebrating the spiritual accomplishments of Jewish feminism.

This booklet—like so many others from gay and lesbian and feminist weddings, "un-weddings," commitment ceremonies, *brit ahuvim,*[16] ceremonies of perpetual engagement, and otherwise named rituals held over the past three decades or so—is a document that attests to the evolving tradition of consecrating relationships largely unimagined by previous generations of Jews.

> *The booklet is a work in progress. At some point it became clear that the guests were arriving so we had to get to Kinko's copy center. My partner Gwynn and I spent the days before the hectic compilation of these Xeroxed sheets with my sister Ayelet, working through theological differences and questions, playing with liturgy, trying to find the right balance of tradition and innovation that would honor each of us and also somehow "work" as powerful liturgy for us and the community that would soon gather. I floated between moments of exaltation at what we were creating and moments of exasperation and tears at the difficulty of it all. We were taking a patriarchal heterosexual ritual that both infuriated me and enticed me with its familiar symbols and authenticating power, and trying to*

break it down into the tiny pieces of meaning at its core so we could rebuild it in a form that would have meaning for us. The resources we drew upon to create our ceremony included other booklets collected at the weddings and ceremonies of friends and friends of friends; Rachel Adler's chapter on brit ahuvim from her book Engendering Judaism; *material we downloaded from www.ritualwell.org; Gwynn's extensive knowledge of Rabbinic sources and keen critical approach informed by feminist and queer theory; my experience in creating Jewish feminist ritual honed over years of working with Ma'yan; and Ayelet's expertise as a Conservative rabbi serving Congregation Beth Simchat Torah, New York City's gay and lesbian synagogue.*

I humbly share this booklet ... as a document that I hope conveys the seriousness, the delight, and the power that can emerge when Jewish feminists engage with one another, with our tradition, and with our dreams of a freer future from a place of love, courage, and hope.[17]

The Booklet as Site of Negotiation

As guests entered the sanctuary in Deal, New Jersey, for the June 1996 wedding of Rabbi Dianne Esses and Lawrence Kohler, attendants handed out wedding booklets arrayed on a silver tray. The ceremony was slow in getting started, and the delay gave guests ample time to peruse the 14-page document. Dianne and Larry's close friends knew this would be a good read, and not merely because Dianne and Larry both write well.

If a quick read clarified the outline of the ceremony, a more careful read revealed how this couple, coming from such different places on the Jewish map, would bridge their different worlds. Alone, the bride presented a complicated amalgam of conflicting Jewish cultural identities. She was the only woman of Syrian Jewish origin ever to be ordained as a rabbi (a fact, she said, that would not make the Syrian Jewish community proud). She was also the only woman of Syrian origin ever to be ordained as a Conservative rabbi by the Jewish Theo-logical Seminary. With grandparents from Turkey and Syria, Dianne—born in Colombia—grew up in the midst of the Syrian Jews of Brooklyn and spent much time in Deal, New Jersey, the popular Syrian Jewish beach community.

What wedding ceremony could bridge Dianne's own identities? There were the traditional beliefs and practices of her Orthodox Syr-ian Jewish family and their friends—a community in which most women marry at 19 and do not go to college, let alone go to rabbini-cal school and postpone marriage until the age of 35. And there were the beliefs that Dianne had come to embrace in the midst of her friends, Upper West Side New York Jewish intellectuals, Conservative Jews committed to egalitarianism in Judaism and in family life. How could Dianne appease her family, concerned about what their Syrian guests would think, and still introduce the kinds of liberal egalitarian wedding innovations that were becoming de rigueur in her set?

And then there was the groom. His grandparents came to Amer-ica from the lands of Ashkenazic Jewry: Romania, Bohemia, and Lithuania. "Jewishly aware and educated," as Dianne described him, Larry was not himself an observant Jew. Could he, at least, feel com-fortable with the elaborate proceedings?

I was Dianne's colleague during the time that she, her fiancé, and their families busily worked through the details of this elaborate wed-ding for over 400 guests, a standard size in the Syrian community. I witnessed her fret about the many compromises and accommodations that needed to be made. I recall her joking that the only solution was to have two weddings: one Syrian and one Conservative.

This was not quite the solution they arrived at, but it came close. The very long ceremony included both Syrian and Ashkenazic offi-ciants and the wedding practices of both traditions. The "two-wed-ding solution" was ever more evident in the reception that followed. As their wedding booklet explained, "In the spirit of trying to include elements of both our heritages, we are having two bands." In one reception room, where tables were laden with Ashkenazic wedding foods, the Ashenazic Klezmatics played Eastern European Jewish wedding music. In the adjacent huge white tent, its tables laden with Syrian Jewish wedding foods, an Arab band played Syrian music familiar to the Syrian guests. The bridal party floated between the two rooms, guests trailing them.

I asked Dianne why she and Larry had created a wedding booklet. In part, she said, it was standard Jewish wedding etiquette. Everyone in their circle was handing out wedding booklets that welcomed the guests and explained Jewish wedding practices to those who would find them unfamiliar. But their own goal was to collaborate on creating a booklet that explained the Ashkenazic and Syrian wedding traditions they were drawing upon. In the writing, they had to negotiate differences of personal style as well. As Dianne explained, Larry was a journalist, accustomed to putting it all on the table. She, as a rebel among Syrian Jews, was used to obscuring her nonconventionality. Thus, for example, in the body of the wedding booklet, Dianne—in a nod to the Syrian guests—did not refer to herself as a rabbi.

If there were virtually two weddings, there were actually two wedding booklets: the "standard version" distributed at the ceremony and an even longer "uncensored version" given to the couple's dearest friends, who joined them for the entire *Shabbat* before the wedding.

In the uncensored booklet, the couple wrote, "In our case, the Jewish wedding tradition is meeting the worldview of a couple with a strong commitment to equality and mutuality in their relationship. And the questioning and challenging this has produced is, we believe, itself a product of Jewish tradition." The couple wanted to emphasize that these new innovations (which seemed radical at the time) were not disrespectful of Jewish tradition. In fact, their urge to wrestle and innovate was fueled by their desire to honor the Jewish traditions of personalization, debate, and adaptivity.

Interfaith Weddings

Many Jews who marry non-Jews want to have wedding ceremonies acknowledging their Jewish traditions. While many rabbis refuse to perform interfaith weddings, some rabbis are willing to officiate at the ceremonies of interfaith couples who pledge to keep Jewish homes and raise Jewish families. According to Rabbi Jamie Korngold of Boulder, Colorado, a rabbi who performs interfaith marriages for couples who have made this pledge, "The wedding can include most of the symbols that are commonly associated with a Jewish wedding such as huppah, kippot, blessing over the wine, *She-hecheyanu, Sheva Brachot,* and the breaking of the glass."[18] But alteration is required when it comes to the words a Jewish groom customarily recites as he places a ring on the bride's finger: *"Harei at mekudeshet li k'dat Moshe v'Yisrael"* (Behold, you are betrothed to me according to the law of Moses and Israel). For how can the non-Jewish groom, who is not a member of the people of Israel, be subject to its laws and customs? Thus, when Rabbi Kornghold officiates, she, like many others, substitutes this verse from Song of Songs: *"Ani le dodi v'dodi li,"* which translates as "I am my beloved's and my beloved is mine"—a phrase that can be spoken by both bride and groom. With the analogy of the "kosher style" restaurant in mind, is this a Jewish wedding or a "Jewish-style" wedding? Some will experience its Jewish authenticity on new terms, while others feel that while it may "count" as a civil wedding, it does not constitute a Jewish one.

The Commitment Ceremony Wedding Booklet: *Brit Ahava,* A Covenant of Love

The newest of Jewish wedding rituals being introduced and sculpted by wedding booklets is the commitment ceremony between same-sex couples. It reflects, in part, the increased participation of gay and lesbian Jews in synagogue and Jewish communal life, and with it, the greater willingness of liberal rabbis to officiate at the weddings (or civil unions, as they are called in certain states) of same-sex couples.

In 2000, at their annual convention, Reform rabbis passed a near-unanimous resolution affirming that the relationship of a Jewish, same-sex couple not only *could* be affirmed through an appropriate Jewish ritual, but also *should* be. Since the late 1980s, even before their denominations offered official sanction, both Reform and Reconstructionist rabbis were performing same-sex unions, patterning the services on the heterosexual model but not fully replicating it.

Conservative rabbis had been performing religious ceremonies for same-sex couples. In 2005, Conservative rabbis who wished to champion the religious rights of gay Jews created an organization called Keshet Rabbis: over 100 Conservative rabbis worldwide, including prominent leaders, signed on, affirming that "through our understanding of Jewish sources and Jewish values, we affirm that gay, lesbian, bisexual, and transgender Jews may fully participate in community life and achieve positions of professional and lay leadership."[19] The movement's Committee on Jewish Law and Standards met to reexamine its approach to homosexuality, and at their December 2006 meeting, it was established that Conservative rabbis could if they wished now officially perform commitment ceremonies and its seminaries could ordain gay rabbis.

A Public and Political Act

One of the most fully documented commitment ceremonies is the June 2002 Jewish wedding of Andrew Ingall and Dr. Neal Hoffman, which they called a "Covenant of Love: *Brit Ahava.*" Fully available on the Internet are the couple's deliberations, intimate reflections, ceremonial choices, and photographs. As much as this was a personal religious ritual for Andy and Neal and their families, it was, as they clearly acknowledge in their wedding booklet, a social and political act with consequences rippling out far beyond their inner circle of intimates.

Andy and Neal's wedding booklet not only introduces ritual innovations, as many others do, but it also reveals how the couple brought Jewish ethical sensibilities to the political process of advocating for legal recognition of same-sex unions. They announce that as part of their preparation for the ceremony, they "completed last wills and testaments and living wills, as well as power of attorney, health care proxies, and right to hospital visitation documents for each other" and in doing so, know that they are advocating for "the legal recognition of loving relationships" such as theirs. (Where civil marriage for gays and lesbians is legalized, couples are able to participate in family health insurance programs, visit their partners in hospitals or nursing homes as next-of-kin, and be recognized as legal heirs for inheritance.) They acknowledge that they stand on the shoulders of both the ancient Israelites who journeyed through an uncertain desert to a land of greater promise and the gay activists of the '50s and '60s. They explain, in the booklet, that they dedicate their ceremony

> *to the memory of our friend Sam Mintz Strauss, a gay man who came of age in the '50s and '60s. Back then, merely socializing with other gays and lesbians was grounds for harassment and arrest. It is on Sam's shoulders, and on the shoulders of so many other gay and lesbian people, that we stand today. We are thankful for the social and political progress that has given us the courage to create this public ceremony.*

Both sets of heirs—the ancient and the contemporary—come as role models for their own journeys together toward holiness. They are aware that in performing this ceremony and redefining whose union may count as a sacred union, they are becoming role models as well. And they are also allowing their guests to take an ethical stance, as they recognize and celebrate a relationship that would have, until recently, been relegated to the shadows.

One might think that the extensive body of materials documenting this wedding—newspaper articles, texts and images on a family Web site—was created by Andy Ingall, who as Assistant Curator for Media at The New York Jewish Museum would be well aware of the significance of such artifacts for an eventual historical recreation of a particular era of Jewish ritual life. In fact, it was Andy's late father, Michael Ingall, who lovingly and richly documented the entire wedding process (as he had done for many other family life-cycle events) for the sake of family history, adeptly assembling texts and images on his Web page, and posting it on the Internet.[20] Included in Michael Ingall's documentation are the blessings offered at the ceremony by friends who praised the couple for the way they renewed and reinvented the meaningful rituals of Judaism.

Particularly significant to us is the wedding booklet Michael posted, which is reproduced below.[21] It constitutes, not only for the wedding guests, but also for all who would read it, a vivid plan for how one might create and participate in a Jewish commitment ceremony. Because this ritual, of all the rituals I have documented in this volume, is so very new, I offer the complete text of the wedding booklet below, knowing that until the "New Jewish Commitment Ceremony" is published, it may serve as a temporary template.

Elaborate, exuberant, accessible documentation of the rituals of Jewish family life is an Ingall family custom that Michael Ingall passed on to his children. Andy's journalist sister Marjorie and her husband, Jonathan Steuer, already had an elaborate Web site created for their 1998 wedding.[22] The extensiveness offers us multiple vantages on Andy and Neal's commitment ceremony, for Marjorie described her version of her brother's wedding in her column in *The Forward* on February 21, 2003. Her narration captures an attitude toward innovation she had expressed earlier in reflections on her own wedding:

> *It's healthy, I think, to reexamine old institutions and futz with them rather than throw them out entirely. Working for change from within lets you feel connected; turning your back entirely sets you adrift.*[23]

For Marjorie Ingall, her brother's ceremony has broader implications, as it reflects how many Jews are remaking Jewish rituals to reflect their world and values, through a heartfelt process of examination. I imagine she was well aware that her matter-of-fact chronicle of a commitment ceremony, a narrative that put continuity and commitment in the foreground and innovation in the background, was likely to participate in making it just that: a matter of fact. Readers who may have considered a commitment ceremony of their own, but had never been to one, would by virtue of reading Marjorie's essay know pretty much what to do. They might intuit as well that this was a ceremony in which family members joyously and fully participated—it is impossible to detect any ambivalence about the capacity of Judaism to sanctify the relationship. The entire dramatis personae of the couple's familial and friendship circle participated,

not just as passive witnesses, but as fully engaged celebrants themselves, who sewed, wove, blessed, ate, and danced this very new Jewish wedding into existence.

Here is the text of Marjorie's article:

*It was a warm, sunny Sunday morning. Andy looked handsome
in a tan seersucker suit, a pink shirt and a navy, white, and
pink diagonally striped tie. Neal looked dashing in a blue seersucker suit, a blue shirt with a subtle pink-and-white window-
pane plaid, and a pink tie with tiny blue-and-white squares.
Josie [Marjorie's daughter] was delectable in a purple Liberty
print sundress with attached apron and appliquéd white and
lavender flowers. I wore a Björn. (When you have a fetching
baby, no one notices your outfit anyway.) Many guests sported
lavender kippot stamped on the inside with "I had a gay old
time at Andy and Neal's Brit Ahava."*

*The officiant was their friend Roderick Young, then the
assistant rabbi at Congregation Beth Simchat Torah, their (primarily gay) shul. Their friend Stephanie Caplan (see her work
at http://www.theketubah.com) made them a gorgeous, personalized, egalitarian ketubah. At the ketubah signing, my
mom, a professor at the Jewish Theological Seminary, gave a
derash, a brief lecture, on the week's Torah portion.*

*The huppah (wedding canopy) was amazing. Designed by
an artist friend, and sewn by my aunt, who is a quilter, it con-
sisted of three wide swaths of purple silk organza with seven
squares of nubby silk shantung—scarlet, gold, purple and
blue—sewn in the middle. The seven squares were decorated by
seven sets of friends or relatives to correspond loosely with the
traditional seven blessings recited at a wedding. I was assigned
the panel representing family. Josie helped me by chewing
thoughtfully on a spare (unused) brush.*

*Under the huppah, it was a fairly traditional Jewish wed-
ding. My husband, Jonathan, was Andy's ring bearer, and*

Neal's brother-in-law Jeff was his ring bearer. Andy and Neal placed rings on each other's forefingers (where tradition says a vein runs directly to the heart) and said in Hebrew and English, "With this ring you are consecrated to me according to the tradition of Israel" (a modification of the original, "according to the laws of Moses and Israel"). Seven sets of friends then gave their blessings based on the same seven themes depicted in the huppah. Both Andy and Neal broke glasses, wrapped in a silk scarf that had belonged to Neal's mother, who was killed many years ago by a drunk driver....

Since Andy and Neal are the last of their siblings to get married, they made all of us perform a mezinke, which is apparently a Yiddish dance congratulating parents on the marriage of their youngest daughter. (As Neal said, "Hey, what can we say?") Neal's little nieces and nephew made crowns out of beads, pipe cleaners, and tinsel to place on the parents' heads. Sadly, none of us actually knew how to do the dance, so we just flopped around like whitefish out there.... Elderly aunts and uncles waltzed.

... I'm a nontraditional traditionalist. My own wedding ... was an attempt to celebrate continuity and commitment, to turn a patriarchal (yet kookily beautiful) institution into something that didn't harsh my feminist mellow. Josie's baby naming was a similar opportunity to examine how to remake Jewish ritual into something that reflected my world and values. Andy and Neal did the same thing, beautifully, with their brit ahava.[24]

The wedding booklet Andy and Neal distributed was printed on lavender paper, folded in half, and held together with a black elastic string down the middle. In reading it, note that the presence of Judaism and the validity of Jewish ritual at this event is never described with ambivalence or anxiety. The celebrants take the presence of Judaism for granted on this holy occasion, and with that acknowledgment comes the presence of God, God's blessing in this new ritual, and God's blessing of their union. At the same time, the couple adds innovations in the form of an egalitarian *bentscher*, in which the name of God is rendered, alternatively, as male and female. Will the ancient practices of their people have meaning for them, even if some of the slight alternations or necessary adaptations—such as the dance performed for parents to help them celebrate marrying off their last daughter—are performed with a wink? This is never even a question.

The Wedding of

Andrew Ingall

and

Neal Hoffman

A Covenant of Love
Brit Ahava

Sunday, June 2, 2002
22 Sivan 5762

New York City

Huppa ceremony
at the Brotherhood Synagogue

Lunch and *klezmer* dance party
at Metronome Restaurant and Lounge

e are very happy that you can share our joy on this special day. Today, we stand under the *huppa* to proclaim our lifelong covenant of love with one another. Reflecting how much we value family and community, we invite you to participate as aydim, witnesses, and to help us fulfill the commandment of celebrating ... of making a simha.

This booklet helps explain today's ceremony and celebration, as well as other events of the weekend. Please bring it to the restaurant; it contains the *sheva brachot,* the Seven Blessings, which will be recited after the *birkat hamazon,* Grace after Meals.

Our ceremony incorporates rituals and customs from the traditional Jewish wedding, mostly Ashkenazi[c] (Eastern European). We have altered some elements to reflect our personal sensibilities and experiences. We call this ceremony a *brit ahava,* a covenant of love, to reflect our aspirations for an equal partnership. Like other Jewish families, we agree to share responsibility for the continuity and well-being of the community, by participating in *tikkun olam* (repairing the world). The Jewish wedding is considered to be a holy event. We view the commitment to partnership as one of many ways people can participate in this journey to holiness.

We thank Rabbi Roderick Young, Assistant Rabbi at Congregation Beth Simchat Torah (CBST), who has worked with Rabbi Sharon Kleinbaum to provide our synagogue and the larger community with spiritual leadership. We are honored to have Rabbi Young as *m'sader* (officiant) for our *brit ahava,* and to have had the benefit of his spiritual guidance over several months

in our journey to the *huppa* and to our partnership beyond the *huppa.*

We thank those of you who responded positively to our request to donate to Congregation Beth Simchat Torah, Jews for Racial and Economic Justice, Kolot, Mothers Against Drunk Driving, the National Cancer Institute Gift Fund, the New York Restoration Project, and the New Israel Fund.

We appreciate the family and friends who have advised us about so many aspects of this celebration and who have honored us with their participation. In particular, we thank Andy's parents, Michael and Carol Ingall; Neal's father, Martin Hoffman; Marty's partner, Elaine Kimmel; and Andy's grandmother Bess Spiro. They have provided guidance and support since the day we each told them we'd met our *beshert,* our soulmate. We are truly blessed to have been surrounded by so much love and wisdom all of our lives. Each of us is also blessed to have grown up with sisters—Andy's sister Marjorie Ingall, and Neal's sisters, Tracey Diamond and Barrie Stachel—who have continued to be our closest friends and confidantes. Our lives are intertwined with their lives and those of their families—our brothers-in-law Jonathan Steuer, Jeff Diamond, and Paul Stachel, and our nieces and nephews (from oldest to youngest), Amie Diamond, Samantha Stachel, Allison Diamond, Andrew Stachel, and Josephine Ingall. All are sources of comfort, joy, love, and strength.

For Neal, this is a bittersweet moment. He feels the presence and absence of his mother, Shirley Hoffman, every day, but especially today. Neal's mother, together with his father, helped create a world of love and stability

for her children. This brit ahava and celebration reflect the life Shirley led and the life she'd hoped for Neal.

Although this *brit ahava* is meaningful to us spiritually, socially, and emotionally, it has no legal status. Except for Vermont, Hawaii, and California (and a few nations of the European Union), states do not legally recognize domestic partnership, let alone gay marriage. Before this ceremony, we completed last wills and testaments and living wills, as well as powers of attorney, health care proxies, and right to hospital visitation documents for each other. We advocate for the legal recognition of loving relationships like ours. This ceremony is, for us, a public and political act. We dedicate it to the memory of our friend Sam Mintz Strauss, a gay man who came of age in the '50s and '60s. Back then, merely socializing with other gays and lesbians was grounds for harassment and arrest. It is on Sam's shoulders, and on the shoulders of so many other gay and lesbian people, that we stand today. We are thankful for the social and political progress that has given us the courage to create this public ceremony.

The Weekend's Events

Today's ceremony was preceded by several events, purposefully planned to lead us to the *huppa.*

On Friday afternoon before *Shabbat,* our friends Daniel Barash and Mark Jacobs, whose wedding last year inspired us to create our own, assisted us in a *mikva* ceremony. The *mikva* is a ritual bath used to mark life transitions and to separate the holy from the everyday.

According to writer Anita Diamant, "entering the *mikvah* is a private transforming moment." Although the ritual traditionally takes place in moving water, we dunked and splashed in the privacy of Marjorie and Jonathan's lap pool in the East Village.

Afterward we welcomed the *shabbat* with our immediate families, joined by Daniel and Mark, at Marjorie and Jonathan's home.

Together with several family members, we celebrated *shabbat* morning with our CBST community and its Liberal Minyan. Alongside Carol, Michael, Marty, and Elaine, we were called up to say the blessing before the Torah reading. The tradition of being called up on the shabbat before the huppa ceremony is known in Yiddish as *aufruf.*

On Saturday evening, we gathered at the Little Red School House in Greenwich Village to mark the end of *shabbat* and to welcome the new week. Our friend Rabbi Joel Alter led the *havdala* ceremony before an informal dessert reception. This event provided an opportunity for our loved ones to renew old ties and create new ones. Adding silliness and spectacle to the weekend's events, some family members and friends gave performances. Our friends Katherine Marx and Gwynneth Malin acted as *badkhanim* (wedding jesters). We called this evening of song and antics "That's Not Entertainment."

In preparation for the *brit ahava,* we have fasted from midnight Saturday night until after the *huppa* ceremony.

Signing the *Ketuba*

Prior to the *huppa* ceremony, Rabbi Young led a ceremony for the signing of the ketuba, the contract for our *brit ahava*. The *ketuba* was designed by our friend Stephanie Caplan. Stephanie used a motif she calls "Rothko 3" to depict abstractly three landscapes where we spend much of our time: urban, mountain, and desert. The text is a modification of the traditional *ketuba,* reflecting the principles of our *brit ahava*. Professor Carol Ingall gave a *drash,* a brief lecture, on the Torah portion of the week. Rabbi Young recited *el malay rachamim* in memory of Neal's mother. Our three sisters signed the *ketuba* as witnesses.

The *Huppa*

The *huppa* is a canopy representing the spiritual and physical home we will create together, a space open to family and friends. Designed by our friend Ellen Wertheim and sewn by Andy's Aunt Gilda Spinat, our *huppa* consists of three sections of organza silk. Seven additional silk pieces are sewn on the center panel in a pattern suggesting building blocks. The scarlet, purple, gold, and blue colors of our *huppa* are the ones once used to adorn the *aron hakodesh* (holy ark) built by the Israelites on their journey through the desert before reaching the land of Canaan.

From the *sheva brachot,* the seven blessings that are part of the traditional wedding ritual, we have distilled seven themes that are meaningful to us. Anita Diamant

points out that only two of the blessings specifically refer to the wedding, but "taken as a whole, the *sheva b'rachot* locate the couple under the *huppa* within the whole flow of Jewish history and theology." The following people artistically interpreted the themes on the seven silk panels:

- Tradition and Reinventing Ritual—Barrie Stachel, with Paul, Samantha, and Andrew
- Learning and Creativity—Ellen Wertheim
- Community—Tracey Diamond, with Amie and Allison
- Justice and Compassion—Susan Hicks
- Family—Marjorie Ingall, with Josie
- Love and Companionship—Renee Rivera and Jenny Worley
- Joy and Gladness—Chana Pollack and Irys Shenker

Ellen Wertheim incorporated an *aleph,* the first letter of the Hebrew alphabet, into her panel's depiction of learning and creativity to symbolize today's new beginning.

We begin the day by singing *hinei ma tov,* led by Rabbi Ayelet Cohen, Tamara Cohen, and Miya Rotstein, acknowledging the simple goodness of having gathered together today.

> *Hinei ma tov umah na'im shevet ahim gam yahad!*

> *Hinei ma tov umah na'im shevet ahim gam yahad!*

> *Behold, how fine and how pleasant when families and friends dwell together! (Psalm 133:1–2)*

Procession

Margot Leverett, clarinet
Music: Doina

Huppa Bearers

Our friends Liz Galst, Aaron Knappstein, Sara Levin, and Aviva Weintraub created a universe for us in which we orbited loosely around each other for a long time. Through them, we became increasingly aware of each other until at last we were ready to see each other more clearly and open our hearts to one another. By holding up the *huppa* and standing with us on the bima, our friends represent that universe.

M'sader
Rabbi Roderick Young

Family Members
Music: *Firen di Mekhutonim Aheym*/Driving the in-laws home

Bess Spiro, escorted by Andy's aunt Nancy Hirschtritt
Martin Hoffman and Elaine Kimmel
Michael and Carol Ingall
Amie Diamond, Allison Diamond, and Haley Goldblatt
Barrie Stachel, Jeff and Tracey Diamond
Marjorie Ingall, Jonathan Steuer, and Josie Ingall

Re'im Ahuvim, Loving Companions
Andrew and Neal
Music: *Lustige Hasidim*/Happy Hasidim

Circling

Before entering the *huppa*, we will each circle the other three times and then join hands to create a seventh circle. The circling connotes protection and uses the mystical number seven, which represents the seven days of Creation. For us, it also represents the journeys that have led us to this moment and the lifetime journey that we begin today.

At this point, we ask that no further photographs be taken until the end of the ceremony.

Mi adir al hakol
Splendor is Upon Everything

Rabbi Young will offer an invocation, then bless the first cup of wine. It will be shared with all those around the huppa. We are using Andy's silver *Kiddush* cups, given to him at his *bar mitzva*. Rabbi Young will also recite an adaptation of the traditional *birkat erusin,* the betrothal blessings. These blessings were once recited a full year before the actual wedding, but ever since the eleventh century, the Jewish wedding has combined these two previously distinct rituals.

Kinyan Acquiring a Partnership

Following ancient tradition, we will each place a ring for the other into a communal pouch as tokens of partnership. We will then lift the pouch together and recite the blessing one says upon seeing a rainbow. This expresses our hope that a trustworthy covenant has been made. Our brothers-in-law Jonathan Steuer and Jeff Diamond will act as ring bearers.

Baruch ata adonay, eloheynu melech ha'olam, zocher habrit vene'eman bivrito vekayam bema'-maro.

Blessed are you, Eternal One, who remembers the covenant, remains faithful to it, and fulfills its word.

We will then take the rings from the pouch, place them on each other's hands, and recite an adaptation of the traditional vow:

Haray ata m'kudash li b'taba'at zo k'misoret yisrael.

With this ring, you are consecrated to me according to the traditions of the people Israel.

We will also recite the verse associated with donning tefillin, the small leather boxes that one straps to the forehead and arm during weekday morning prayers:

V'erastich li l'olam. V'erastich li b'tzedek uv'mishpat uv'chesed v'rachamim. V'erastich li b'emuna.

I will espouse you forever. I will espouse you with righteousness and justice and loving kindness and compassion. I will espouse you in faithfulness.

We will each place a ring on the other's right index finger, which is considered to be a direct route to the heart. We will then move the rings to the fourth finger of our left hands.

Rabbi Young will read aloud the ketuba that we signed before coming to the huppa. Then he will deliver a *drash*.

Sheva brachot

Rabbi Young will recite the *sheva brachot,* the traditional seven blessings that mark the nissuin. As in other parts of today's ceremony, the blessings have been slightly altered. The sixth and seventh blessings refer to *re'im ahuvim,* loving companions.

Adapting a Sephardic tradition, Neal's Aunt Arlene Russo and Andy's Aunt Belleruth Naparstek will wrap us in a *tallis* prior to Rabbi Young's recitation. The *tallis* (prayer shawl) represents a huppa within a huppa. Aunt Arlene and Aunt Belleruth represent all of our aunts and uncles, who have been sources of love and support. Their participation in this part of the ceremony also serves as our acknowledgement of the roles that so many gays and lesbians play as aunts and uncles, providing love and support to children of friends and family.

The first of the seven blessings is the blessing over the wine. In contrast to the first cup of wine, shared by many, only the two of us will drink from the second cup. We will use a kiddush cup purchased in the old Jewish ghetto in Venice and given as a gift many years ago by Neal's sister Tracey.

The following friends will offer blessings based on the same seven themes depicted in the *huppa:*

- Tradition and Reinventing Ritual—Natan Meir
- Learning and Creativity—Joanne Jacobson
- Community—Yehuda Hyman
- Justice and Compassion—Marilyn Neimark and Alisa Solomon
- Family—Colleen Kelly and Dan Jones
- Love and Companionship—Nina Browne and Carl Biers
- Joy and Gladness—Stephanie Singer

Breaking the glass

Like many other parts of a wedding ceremony, the breaking of the glass is a well-known custom without real religious significance. It is meant to mark the transition from the solemn, formal ceremony to the joyous celebration to follow. We will each break a glass to remind ourselves of our shared responsibility to participate in *tikkun olam,* repairing the world. We bought colored glass from the Chelsea flea market and have wrapped it in a silk scarf that belonged to Neal's mother.

Yichud (Togetherness)

After the ceremony, the couple traditionally spends some time alone. *Yichud* is considered to be the final part of Nissuin. We will depart by ourselves for the Metronome, where we will break our fast together.

After the Ceremony

Take some time to enjoy the synagogue and its anterior courtyard. Stroll around Gramercy Park, smell the flowers, and make your way to the Metronome. It's on Broadway and East 21st Street, a leisurely eight-minute walk from the synagogue. The celebration will start at 1 PM. Before entering the Metronome, look north (right) to view the splendor of two of New York City's architectural jewels, the Empire State Building and the Flatiron Building.

The celebration at the Metronome will include:
- An hour of cocktails, hors d'oeuvres, and refreshments
- Frenzied *Klezmer* dancing accompanied by Margot Leverett and her ensemble, along with any shtick or frivolity you'd like to offer
- A tasty lunch, preceded by our fathers reciting the *motzi,* the blessing over the bread
- More *klezmer* dancing. As we are the last of their children to couple, we will show tribute to our parents with a song and dance called the *mezinka,* which in Yiddish means the youngest daughter. (What can we say?!) The wreaths to be placed on their heads were made by Amie, Allison, Samantha and Andrew.
- Dessert
- Birkat *hamazon,* led by Rabbi Oren Postrel
- The repetition of the *sheva brachot* chanted by Andy's Great Uncle Sid Gottler....[25]

NOTES:

1. Wedding booklet of Jacob Aryeh Davidson and Haviva Rena Krasner, June 14, 1990.

2. Wedding booklet of Dianne O. Esses and Lawrence N. Cohler, June 23, 1996.

3. Wedding booklet of Stephanie Nussbaum and Michael Kress, July 1, 2001.

4. Ibid.

5. Anita Diamant, *The New Jewish Wedding* (New York: Schocken Books, 1985), 15.

6. Ibid., 15.

7. Ibid., 19.

8. Anita Diamant, *The New Jewish Wedding* (New York: Simon and Schuster, 2001), 17.

9. Ibid.

10. The booklets have become so commonplace at Jewish weddings that when my daughter chose not to prepare one for her 2006 wedding and let the ritual speak for itself, some guests remarked that it was an innovative gesture.

11. Chaia Beckerman, "*Kiddushin* and *Kesharin:* Toward an Egalitarian Wedding Ceremony," *Kerem* (1997), 90.

12. Diamant, New Jewish Wedding, 66. Many would agree that when Jewish ritual is burdened by too much explanation, it feels less genuinely Jewish—the grace of implicit understanding is gone. I do question the use of the word "Protestantism" to describe remedial Judaism, as if the use of English words in a once all-Hebrew service signaled a leap outside the faith.

13. Diamant, 67.

14. Beckerman, "*Kiddushin* and *Kesharin.*"

15. Personal communication, July 14, 1996.

16. The *brit ahuvim* (lovers' covenant) is a new wedding ritual formulated by Jewish feminist theologian Rachel Adler in her book *Engendering Judaism: An Inclusive Theology and Ethics* (Philadelphia: The Jewish Publication Society, 1998). It replaces the traditional property-based model of marriage, in which a man acquires a woman, with a covenantal model, in which both members of the couple enter into a partnership as loving companions. Based on a talmudic practice of forming a business partnership, the couple makes a verbal and written commitment (called a *shtar*) to the partnership. As a symbolic gesture of partnership acquisition, each puts an object (such as a ring) into a pouch, and they lift it together. They say, "Blessed are You Source of Life who remembers Your covenant and is faith-

ful to Your covenant and keeps Your word." In Diamant's second edition, the *brit ahuvim* is presented as a choice especially suitable for same-sex couples.

17. Statement by Tamara Cohen, part of online exhibit called Jewish Women and the Feminist Revolution, Jewish Women's Archive, at http://www.jwa.org/feminism/_html/JWA100.htm.

18. See the Adventure Rabbi site at <http://www.adventurerabbi.com/rabbi/weddings.htm.

19. See the Keshet Rabbis site at http://www.keshetrabbis.org.

20. See *"Brit Ahava*—Andy & Neal" at http://www.farklempt.com/BRIT.AHAVA.

21. Reproduced with the permission of Dr. Hoffman and Mr. Ingall.

22. See the Snarly/Cheese Wedding Pages at <http://www.snarly.com/wedding.

23. See the Snarly/Cheese Wedding Pages—"why are they marrying?" at http://www.snarly.com/wedding/couple/whymarry.html. This essay appeared in *Ms.* magazine in 1997. It is worth mentioning that the mother of both Marjorie and Andrew is Carol K. Ingall, author of *Transmission and Transformation: A Jewish Perspective on Moral Education* and professor of Jewish erducation at The Jewish Theological Seminary.

24. Marjorie Ingall, *The Forward*, February 21, 2003. Published with author's permission.

25. From "The Program Book Text," at http://www.farklempt.com/BRIT.AHAVA/index18.html.

EPILOGUE

I follow the instructions I have been sent in the mail to prepare for a retreat held by the Institute for Jewish Spirituality. It is for rabbis and cantors of various denominations who already have begun a training program in contemplative practices; some Jewish scholars like me have been invited too. Reading the packing list reminds me of getting ready for Jewish summer camp.

The insect repellant, suntan lotion, a hat, and sunglasses are the same. Now, I am also invited to bring along a tallit and tefillin ("if you use them"). I smile, for at camp, tallit and tefillin were obligatory only for boys of bar mitzvah age. We girls were assigned "sanitary items." Now we are all told to pack something neither boys nor girls needed for camp: "loose comfortable clothing, easy for sitting in meditation, and also for yoga."

I read on. We will study Hasidic texts. The study will affirm that Jews have been engaging in contemplative practice for hundreds of years. I gather this affirmation will serve to justify the Jewish authenticity of a practice that might otherwise appear distinctly derivative of eastern religions. During our week together, with our teachers Rabbis Rachel Cowan, Sheila Peltz Weinberg, and Jonathan Slater, "we will *daven*, do yoga, eat, and share evening programs together. All of this will take place in the context of a traditional IJS program day: silent practice from the end of the evening program through lunch, prayer, meditation, yoga, text study, contemplative conversation, core groups."

I smile: a *traditional* program? Surely this text was written with a twinkle of the eye. Meditation, yoga, and silence (except during the *Amidah*, often called "the Silent Devotion") are hardly traditional, even for the clergy who are gathered here. While there have been earlier efforts to return contemplative practice to Judaism,[1] this institute is but a few years old.

I arrive at the retreat held at the Trinity Conference Center along the Housatonic River in Connecticut, and another letter awaits us. This one says our week together has a special "intention" (a translation of the Jewish practice of having a *kavanah* in mind—starting out an activity, such as a prayer or a commanded deed, with a stated sacred purpose). It is the "desire to settle in to silence, to openness, to awareness." When I meet the rabbis and cantors, some attending their third retreat, I can tell they are all at ease with the program. If they once asked, "Can we, as Jews, do this?" they no longer do so. Now they ask, "How can we do this more deeply and more often?"[2]

When we begin our practice of yoga with Rabbi Peltz Weinberg, we chant "*Hineni*" (Here I am—as Moses answered to God, when called) and when we end, we chant "Shalom." I notice that the rabbis and cantors standing on their yoga mats evince a familiarity and reverence for the practice that can justifiably be called "traditional." We are instructed to enter into the tree pose: hands overhead, palms together; right foot lifted up, balancing on the calf or, for the limber, just above the knee. Standing before us on one foot, Rabbi Weinberg jokes gently: "This is the Rabbinic yoga pose."

She alludes, we know, to the man who asked Rabbi Shammai, and then Rabbi Hillel, to reveal all of Judaism while he stood impatiently on one foot. It is a challenge only Hillel chose to meet, and he did so by teaching a Torah of loving kindness ("What is hateful to you, do not do to another. That is the whole Torah. The rest is commentary. Now go study"). In Hillel's words, I also hear an unspoken nod toward the Buddhist practice of *metta* meditation, cultivating love and compassion for all beings and for the environment. In *metta* meditation, one wishes—for oneself and others—happiness, freedom from sorrow, peace, safety, and security. Our teacher does not use the word *metta*; it is the familiar Hebrew word *hesed* that she uses.

On our last day together, Cantor Lorel Zar-Kessler of Massachusetts leads us in morning prayers in a tiny stone chapel off the main retreat house; the signs of Episcopalian Christianity have been draped over with either maroon tablecloths or blue napkins. Pinned onto her short silvery hair, Lorel wears a crocheted *kippah:* in the center is a pink flower, and it radiates into circles of yellow, lime green, deep blue, and purple. She wears a tallit and tefillin too, as do all of the men, but most of the women pray only with tallit, myself included. We use a loose-leaf prayer book that is labeled "Experimental." As experiments go, it is mild: the central parts of the morning service have been copied from Conservative, Reform, and Reconstructionist prayer books, leaving us free to choose among pages that are familiar or challenging.

We are roused to begin by singing, "Awaken, arise to the wholeness of your being ... *Hitoriri, ki va orech kumi ori*," chanting it again and again. These are words taken from the *Shabbat* evening service, put to music by Hannah Tiferet Siegel, who has composed many of the new prayer melodies of Renewal Judaism. Cantor Zar-Kessler suggests a theme for this morning's prayers: "Searching for our good points, as we awaken from sleep like lions." She relates that in her own prayer, she has been inspired by having gone to gospel camp, and, in the spirit of the morning blessings of gratitude, she shares a song that we catch onto right away: "I still got joy after all the things I've been through." She invites us to improvise with our own words, and the rabbis and cantors do so with gusto: "I still got love," someone shouts; "I still got tomatoes," the cantor adds.

Preparing us to recite the *Shema*, Cantor Zar-Kessler offers this *kavanah:* "As we gather together our tzitzit, we gather together the scattered parts of our being in our search for what unites our own soul and the souls of the world." She holds her tzitzit to her heart, and we are invited to repeat the verses of a chant by Cantor Jeff Klepper that is clearly familiar to many in the group:

Open up our eyes, teach us how to live,
Fill our hearts with joy and all the love You have to give.
Gather us in peace as you lead us to your name
And we will all know that You are one.

When it is time to pray the *Shema,* she tells us to sing it not once, but several times, as a group. Of those times, we are to sing aloud only once: for the rest we are to listen, and to hear ourselves being summoned by God and by our people: "Hear O Israel!"

This service—quite moving to me—may sound to most curious, even revolutionary, or simply misguided. Singing a *Shabbat* evening prayer in a weekday morning service. Offering a theme for the service. Preceding prayers with intentions. Jews in tallit and tefillin singing gospel music. The *Shema,* sung over and over again.

What is curious to me is that nothing in this prayer service is new to me. In the last 15 years, I have been to many services like this. I have encountered each practice several times before—I know variations, have my favorites, and apparently have evolved my own criteria for judging how well the service is being led.

This is what I now recognize as a face of Jewish tradition. All these new practices have acquired the aura of the customary: they are for me and others *minhag.* I think about the once-new liturgies and ritual objects that I have saved at home, and picture how they have become worn with use. They are beginning to look venerable in their datedness.

There are Jewish ritual innovations that will still shock me. These are the innovations on the verge of being created.

An Overview of New Ritual Practices

Life Cycle/Rites of Passage

Simchat ha-bat: a naming ceremony for girls
Providing a "Miriam's chair" at a *simchat ha-bat*
Naming ceremonies for baby boys that omit circumcision
Adoption rituals
Rituals for the beginning of menstruation

"Car mitzvah:" presenting teenagers who have gotten their drivers
    licenses with prayers of protection and a special key chain
    inscribed with the "Traveler's Prayer"
Internet dating
L'chaim party for an engagement
Making a *huppah* at a bridal shower
Interfaith and egalitarian *ketubot*
Prenuptial agreements signed at weddings protecting women in the
    case of divorce
Prayers said for *agunot*, women whose husbands refuse to grant
    them a *get*, a decree of divorce
Commitment and wedding ceremonies for gay couples
Divorce rituals
Pregnancy rituals
Infertility rituals
Miscarriage and abortion rituals
Rituals for mourning a stillbirth
Nursing and weaning rituals
Adult bat/bar mitzvah
Ceremony for taking on a Hebrew name as an adult
Hanukkat ha-bayit: moving to a new house
Leaving-for-college rituals
Coming-of-age ceremonies (40th, 50th, 60th, 70th, and 80th birthdays)
Menopause rituals
Simchat hokhmah/eldering
Retiring ceremonies
New yahrzeit practices/memorial Web sites

Holy Days

Sending interfaith and comic Jewish holiday greeting cards
Rosh Hodesh groups
Shabbat practices: communal ritual baths, *Shabbat* angel cards
Spiritual preparations for Rosh Hashanah and Yom Kippur
Holding a Rosh Hashanah seder
Ushpizin ceremonies on Sukkot honoring great Jewish women
Spending Christmas in Jewish ways

Tu b'Shevat seder

Sending community-wide *mishloach manot* (Purim baskets) as a
    fund-raiser

A feminist Ta'anit Ester (fast before Purim)

"Unmasking Esther," a woman's Purim observance

Esther/Vashti flags

Homemade, feminist, and social-action *haggadot*

Holding a communal *tikkun* (all-night study) for Shavuot

Yom ha-Atzmaut at the JCC

Communal Holocaust memorial days

Mitzvah days

Spiritual Practices

Going on a Jewish retreat

Jewish meditation practices

Torah Yoga

Aleph-Bet Yoga

Group *aliyot*

The one-way *mechitzah* in Orthodox settings

Women's *tefillah* groups for Orthodox women

Virtual prayer, cyber Torah study

Healing services

Healing practices for patients and caregivers

Wearing healing amulets

Ceremonies for healing from abuse

Ritual displays of Jewish identity: wearing jewelry of Jewish
    charitable organizations (such as Lion of Judah jewelry)

Communal pieties: communal "mitzvah days," solidarity rallies,
    prayer vigils, Super Sundays, missions to Israel

Attending a Jewish film festival

Keeping or reading a Jewish blog

Collecting and preserving Yiddish books

Taking home videos of Jewish ritual events and watching them

Composing new Jewish music

Creating Jewish performance art

Creating a scrapbook of Jewish family life

Researching and documenting genealogy
Applying Jewish ethical principles to agriculture, ecology, and
    current pressing issues in social justice

NOTES:

1. Texts introducing Jewish seekers to Jewish meditative traditions were available long before programs, such as those funded by the Cummings Foundation, were created to make those traditions available to clergy and laypeople. Three of the earliest contemporary books on Jewish meditation, apparently responses to the many young Jews who were seeking outside of Judaism for spirituality and meaning, were written by the prolific Orthodox rabbi and physicist Aryeh Kaplan before his death in 1983: *Meditation and the Bible* (York Beach: Weiser, 1978); *Meditation and Kabbalah* (York Beach, ME: Weiser, 1982); and *Jewish Meditation: A Practical Guide* (New York: Schocken, 1995), the most detailed in instruction, which first came out posthumously in 1985. In the last book, Kaplan offered Kabbalah-based instructions in meditation, candle meditation, contemplation, and visualization.

2. We are sent home with two CDs—one by Rabbi Peltz Weinberg called *Meditations for Jewish Spiritual Practice* and another by Rabbi Myriam Klotz for Jewish Yoga.

RECORD,
TAKE IT DOWN,
AND COLLECT

Perhaps in the course of your reading, you have begun already to observe and assess Jewish ritual innovations. Should you choose to do so more intensively, I offer these methodological suggestions. This open-ended approach to collecting evidence of new ritual, inspired by the Yiddish writer Shlomo Ansky, characterizes my own research process and might inspire yours.

Let Ansky Inspire You

Between 1911 and 1915, Ansky (best known for his play *The Dybbuk*) led ethnographic expeditions to the Eastern European shtetls to preserve and document the artifacts, stories, songs, clothing, and even healing practices of Jewish life. He feared they would be forgotten, the inevitable consequence of a growing abandonment of a traditional Jewish way of life, or be destroyed, as a consequence of the devastations of war. He gathered an entourage that included the writer Y. L. Peretz, a composer, an ethnomusicologist, a painter, and a photographer. Abraham Rechtsman, one of the assembled, recalled:

> *Everywhere we came we collected the historical treasures we found: we noted down tales, legends, sayings, spells, remedies and histories told to us by men and women; we documented stories about demons, dybbuks ... we recorded old melodies— nigunim—, as well as prayers and folksongs; we photographed old synagogues, historical places, tombstones, shtiblech of tzadikim [the prayer houses of revered, holy men] ...; and we collected or bought Jewish antiques, documents, pinkassim [record books], religious articles, jewelry, costumes.*[1]

On January 1, 1915, Ansky and Peretz wrote an open letter to the readers of the Warsaw Yiddish daily, entreating Jews everywhere to follow their lead and preserve Jewish life. Their plea, so painfully prescient, would anticipate the even more horrible era to follow:

> *Record, take it down, and collect. See to it that nothing is lost or forgotten ... record everything, knowing thereby that you are collecting necessary material for the construction of Jewish history during this horribly important and terribly vital moment ... whatever can be recorded should be recorded, and whatever can be photographed should be photographed.*

Collecting in Ansky's Day, and in Our Own

There are important differences between Ansky's collecting and my own. There is the clear matter of rationale. Ansky collected and admonished others to do likewise because he saw strong evidence that a way of life (though one he no longer embraced, as we shall see) would soon be lost. Jewish life that had flourished in the Pale of Settlement and in Galicia was indeed as vulnerable as Ansky believed it was and even more so; the barbaric massacres he witnessed called for emergency measures.

By blessed contrast, American Judaism is not on the verge of being lost, though some sound the alarm. I resist embracing the persistent popular anxiety that erupts, one that is possibly fanned for its salubrious effects on fund-raising. It holds that Jewish ways of life, practices, beliefs, study, and memory are more vulnerable in our hands than in those of our ancestors. Perhaps I delude myself, but I see no evidence that American Jewry stands on the precipice of annihilation. When we are privileged to know power, influence, and affluence, prudence becomes us more than anxiety.

I collect evidence of Jewish innovation because I am inspired by the plethora of new and emerging spiritual practices, rituals, liturgies, and ritual objects that expand the possibilities for contemporary sacred Jewish experience. I collect because I know objects will teach me to discover practices that I cannot yet see. I have collected in the spirit of one amassing a collection of contemporary paintings: not merely to possess but to contemplate. Unlike Ansky, I am privileged to collect at a pace that is at times slow and deliberate, and at other times, spontaneous and exuberant.

ETHNOGRAPHIC EXPEDITION

My ethnographic expedition took place at my synagogue, my JCC, one daughter's Jewish day school, the other's college Hillel, my grocery store, at friends' homes. It took place in my kitchen, my living room, my jewelry box. Some of my collecting was done without ever leaving home, and was based on close readings of texts that came my way, all providing evidence pointing to new practices being generated.

My research began when cyberspace was not as cozy to us as our own kitchens, and before we were relying on the Internet to access religious information and even have spiritual experiences. Now nearly all my access to new Jewish rituals, texts, and objects comes by way of the Internet, and the materials I can now gather are dazzling. But in the study of Jewish ritual innovation, having tangible artifacts in hand matters, and for that reason, I am glad that this study bridges the years before and after computers. Holding artifacts of Jewish ritual innovation in hand, layers of meaning within them reveal themselves. You can feel the difference between the handwritten and hand-illustrated pages, the glossy Xeroxed sheet, the fibrous newspaper clipping, the mimeographed page, and the "cut and paste" document that was cut with scissors and pasted with Scotch tape or Elmer's glue. You can touch the objects, shake or wave them, try them on and wear them as Purim costumes (I have done this often) or bat mitzvah finery; you can almost smell them (wine stains on new wedding booklets) or hear their bells ring (the Esther-Vashti flags).

When I could interact with the people making or using the artifacts, I could get even closer to comprehending the practices that were catalyzed, the emotions felt, and the webs of community and connection spun out and maintained. When I hold a carefully typed up and collated ceremony for acknowledging a couple's infertility that they have shared with me, I can remember how the couple stayed up nights compiling just the right texts and constructing their ritual, and I can recapture the weightiness of standing with them in their living room on the day of the ceremony.

The unwieldy collection of artifacts I have gathered, however precious to me, is not costly—I have not invited Lloyd's of London for an appraisal. The word "tchotchke" would come to mind before "Judaica."[2] Grassroots, homemade, and mass-produced artifacts made of cloth, paper, and plastic are the objects many people own, use, or encounter, and they are the ones that help me to understand individual practice—the everyday, improvised, complex, and creative, make-do lived religious practices of laypeople. Had finances allowed, however, I'd have gladly reached beyond knickknack drawers, kitchen cabinets, kosher sections of the supermarket, synagogue gifts shops, and the "shuks" of Hadassah conventions and Jewish Renewal retreats, and collected items of a higher register: one-of-a-kind stitched women's *tallitot,* artist Tobi Kahn's wooden ritual objects, hand-beaded women's *kippot,* new illuminated *ketubot* ... Of such elegant items, I have only pictures in museum and Judaica store catalogs.

Unlike Ansky, I have collected not to rescue, but to better understand this most vibrant Judaism that American Jews are innovating.

Beyond synagogue and home, innovation is taking place in multiple venues like Jewish community centers, Jewish schools, summer camps, memorial sites, and parades. In the public sphere, it happens in colleges, public libraries, museums, and film festivals. In the commercial arena, venues include the grocery store and the mall, and in the social service sphere, the soup kitchen, the hospital, and housing developments.

Like Ansky, I believe that artifacts can teach us both what we need to discover and what they can lead us to discern. They suggest how Jewish ritual innovation in America comes as a response to internal needs, external pressures, and emergencies. They demonstrate that when new rituals emerge in an environment that is both nostalgic for tradition and suspicious of it, they will reflect the push and pull between yearning for ethnic cohesion and acculturation. They show that the new rituals reflect the tension between institutionalized, text-based Judaism and the Judaism actually practiced by the whole range of people who constitute a folk.

Unlike Ansky, I do not imagine that in generations to come, Jews seeking sources of Judaism that feel more genuine than their own will find our contemporary rituals for baby girl naming ceremonies any more enlightening or relevant to their lives than we find the circumcision liturgies entrenched in prayer books. I do believe that when we scrutinize the new rituals and ritual objects of our era, they will reveal how we have embraced enduring Jewish sensibilities in ways that resonate with our lives.[3] Just as ritual innovators turn back to practices of the past for inspiration and anchoring, perhaps our descendents will hark back to the "ancient practices" of going on a Birthright Israel[4] trip or attending a Rosh Hodesh: It's a Girl Thing![5] group. Mine is not an ethnography of salvage, but one linked, in anthropologist Harvey Goldberg's terms, "to a sense of advocacy and empowerment."[6] I think we can take pride in our spiritual artistry as we engage with Jewish tradition and interpret it for our lives. Given my own experiences in ritual innovation, I would say that the better one understands how ritual is innovated, the better one is able to create ritual objects, sacred spaces, ceremonies, and liturgies that will forge paths to greater holiness. There is no way I can anticipate what meanings Jews will derive from my collection in 100 years, but I do trust that just as Ansky's collection (as well as his collecting!) inspires me, collections such as mine may be valuable resources.

Another distinction between Ansky's collecting and mine lies in matters of place and stance. Ansky left his own cosmopolitan milieu and journeyed to be with village people who practiced a Judaism unlike his own. Because *The Dybbuk* portrays a traditional form of Judaism, one might assume that Ansky was a pious yeshivah boy with a flair for playwriting and an avocation for ethnography. This is not so: by 17, according to Joachim Neugroschel, Ansky was "running a commune on the edge of Vitebsk for boys like him who had fled the rigidity of a yeshivah education."[7] After a period of promoting socialism, he returned to St. Petersburg where he would embrace Jewish culture and Yiddish writing; he became an activist, engaging in relief efforts on behalf of the Jews in the Pale. The world he witnessed was, in his estimation, neither self-conscious nor tainted by an admixture of new ideas and cultural borrowings. It could be said that Ansky's ethnographic work emerged out of a romanticized understanding of anthropology[8] that was characteristic of his time. It saw as its mission salvaging elements of an endangered culture, typically one more exotic and more cohesive than one's own, before it disappeared. Ansky and his colleagues believed they were encountering a near-mythic world in which time did not move: customs and tradition were passed on, without change, from one generation to another. They believed that studies of folk people and folklore (in contrast to study of sacred texts or the scholarship of the elite) might preserve what Goldberg calls "features of the 'spirit' of the 'folk' that had value for future Jewish existence."[9] They hoped that the essence of these Jewish folkways, locked and preserved within artifacts and stories, could have the power to reinvigorate Judaism when released in less tumultuous times.

Record, Take it Down, and Collect

I read Ansky's directive so many years later, but still I took it to heart, adapting it to my purposes. In New Jersey, New York, Virginia, and the many other places across America I have traveled among Jews, I vowed to "record, take it down, and collect. See to it that nothing is lost or forgotten."

I would encourage you to follow Ansky's instruction, turning your gaze on your home, your hometown, and the Jewish communities you visit. One need not be trained as an ethnographer to do this. Your research will reveal many of the innovations I have described in this volume, and it will reveal new and emerging practices as well.

Keeping an Open Mind

To begin collecting evidence of Jewish ritual innovation, imagine knowing less about American Judaism than you actually do. Obviously I am not suggesting that you feign total ignorance—the goal is to look with a fresh eye, untainted by past expectations and free of judgment. Unlike Ansky, we are not looking for a familiar Judaism on the verge of being lost—we are looking at a Judaism on the cusp of being innovated. That requires that we not jump to conclusions (as a person knowledgeable in Judaism might) or come with preconceptions about what does and does not count as being "genuinely" Jewish. Often, my Jewish students with training or life experience in Judaism will complain—and rightfully so—that their classmates who know less can have an advantage when it comes to studying innovated Jewish practices in the field.

Consider this: learned Jews might scan a Jewish home and "know" that the most "important" Jewish items are the conventional ones: *mezuzot*, *Shabbat* candlesticks, prayer books, and a Bible. Finding items that "count," so to speak, they may not look further. They might miss the calendar posted on the refrigerator indicating that the residents are going to a fund-raising dinner for a new liberal *mikveh* their community is building, or to a prayer vigil outside the Israeli consulate. Less learned Jews, or those feigning ignorance, might go into a different home and see a fireplace mantle lined with December holiday greeting cards. Some are for Hanukkah, but others are for Christmas, and still others would be the comic interfaith Christmas-Hanukkah cards becoming increasingly popular. They might also see a Christmas tree decorated with Stars of David and menorah ornaments, another trend. They would not see the cards and decorations as evidence disqualifying the space as a Jewish home. Instead, they might see the cards and decorations as evidence of a family that is trying to articulate its Jewish spiritual identity between faith traditions.

You might be inspired too by the spirit that Ari Goldman, an Orthodox Jew and former religion writer for *The New York Times,* modeled in his book, *Being Jewish,* when he looked respectfully at ways of being Jewish that could be considered idiosyncratic. Being Jewish in nonconventional ways has long been degraded and called "a religious free-for-all that allows people to pick and choose Judaism."[10] Goldman chose to view the "Smorgasbord Judaism" (some call it "pick-and-choose Judaism") that most American Jews actually live in a favorable light. He portrayed Jews surveying a huge "table" of Jewish practices, teachings, memories, texts, art, and relationships, and from it selecting the ingredients necessary to create a Judaism that made sense for themselves. According to Goldman, a Judaism that is picked and chosen is enriching, spiritually and culturally, because it has the capacity to connect the individual Jew to all Jews in the world, those living now, and those who lived in the past and will live in the future. The same smorgasbord allows a Jew to make connections on the "horizontal" interpersonal plane and to connect 'vertically" with God. To those who worry that this approach to Judaism can lead to extinction, Goldman counters that "feel good" Judaism is okay: "Being Jewish *is* about feeling good. It *is* about finding meaning." Goldman proposes that one need not be observant according to *halakhah,* or according to denominational conventions, to consider oneself a religious Jew. What if we took all the new practices that American Jews actually perform seriously, placing them in the context of "what the tradition demands"?

That would include, Goldman observes, the person who keeps three sets of dishes—for meat, milk, and Chinese. It includes the woman from Tucson who takes pains to order expensive, carefully supervised *shmurah matzah* for Passover and then tops them with non-kosher foods; the Jewish Federation executive from L.A. who drives on *Shabbat,* but not on freeways; and the Orthodox college student who opens his condom packet early on Friday so he won't tear and break *Shabbat* when he sleeps with his girlfriend that night. In all these ways, and in messy ways of our own that we may be reluctant to confess, American Jews are engaging in distinctly Jewish "efforts to reach for the holy." Those who transmit pride and internationality in Jewish practices, however quirky and personalized, pass that down;

those who transmit ambivalence, alienation, hatred, or ignorance about Jewish ritual pass that on.

Just as I train my students to be attentive to the many new Jewish practices taking place just outside a narrow and conventional range of vision,[11] I needed to train myself. Previously I tended to notice mostly those new Jewish practices that involved people coming together to mark or address something with liturgical words and symbolic action. Now I define new Jewish practices more broadly as ways people repeatedly experience and express their Judaism meaningfully, or ways people intensify[12] their experiences in Jewish ways, giving them meaning. Doing so, I began to notice many new practices. I observed people improvising upon familiar rituals and saw that through their gestures of private appropriation, they were making the group's rituals more meaningful to themselves.

Everywhere, then, you will look for signs that Jews live, worship, recreate, or study here. Seek signs—even ones that surprise you—that Jews are expressing themselves in Jewish ways.

See what clues—true and false—the placement of objects gives you. Sometimes placement indicates greater or lesser importance, but it is hard to know that for sure without asking your "informants" for more information. I encourage you to do that. For instance, I display a Hanukkah menorah prominently on my living-room shelf and keep all my *Shabbat* implements—candleholders, candles, challah board and cover, and *Shabbat* angel cards—in a closed cabinet in my dining room. Unless you asked me, you might think the menorah is in some way more holy or precious to me. In fact, it is the *Shabbat* items that are most dear, as they are used each week: they are stored for my convenience and to protect them from dust.

Try to distinguish between objects that are explicitly and implicitly Jewish. See if you can determine how the holiness of the object might be measured by traditional means, and how it might be experienced more idiosyncratically. Especially memorable in my own ethnographic journey was the Morristown, New Jersey, home of Susan Adler, where, in her kitchen alone, I found piles of magazines: *Sh'ma*, *Moment*, *Tikkun*, *Hadassah*, and a *Bon Appetit*, dog-eared on pages featuring latkes and flourless Passover tortes.[13] This suggested to me that Jewish ritual "text" study was no longer really limited to the canonized texts, and that the place of study had extended beyond yeshivot and synagogues and into the home. (Does the study of Jewish recipes "count" as Jewish study? Given that Leviticus contains "recipes" for the grain offerings of the priests, I could contend that recipes have an illustrious place in Jewish text.) On Adler's wall, there were prints of an old synagogue in Prague, with images of Jewish people floating, a cross between Kabbalah and Chagall. These were souvenirs from "roots" trips: "Having them reminds me where I was, gives me a good-luck charm," she said. "I like the mystical piece of it." On one wall was a framed needle point of the word *shalom* made 25 years ago, a framed photograph of Susan as chair of the UJA Women's division, *bubbe* and *zayde* dolls, over a dozen Jewish cookbooks, a refrigerator covered with bar and bat mitzvah invitations and photographs of a nephew's recent bar mitzvah, a synagogue calendar and directory, and *tzedakah* boxes. Such images and objects spoke to my informant as creators of Jewish identity for herself and her family—they were not just décor.

There was a tray of silver *Kiddush* cups that stayed out always: some were conventional, but others were "reclaimed": "I buy *Kiddush* cups at antique shops," Susan told me. "I take them away. I rescue them. I don't want anyone who doesn't know what they are to have them." These reclaimings too suggested rituals of redemption, perhaps inspired by her community's emphatic embrace of Jews coming from the former Soviet Union.

You will discover, as I did, how to locate new Jewish practices by examining the texts and ritual objects the practices are generating. For instance, in my mail I found invitations to seminars on Jewish meditation; newsletters from the National Center for Jewish Healing that provided healing blessings for patients and doctors as well as healing practices for many of the Jewish holidays; and advertisements for personalized Rosh Hashanah cards I could order from three different organizations. In my wicker baskets at home where I keep miscellaneous objects, I found bar and bat mitzvah souvenirs, women's *kippot*, Passover/Easter and Hanukkah/Christmas cards, Hanukkah novelties and decorations, an advertisement for a Passover "plague" kit, and healing amulets my daughters had made. Behind these texts and objects lay new practices particular to this generation, ways of being Jewish that are ethical, creative, vibrant, and celebratory.

Ask

Above all, ask questions. Ask people to tell you what the Jewish objects in their lives mean to them. Assure them that you do not need to hear the "official" story of an object's meaning or traditional use, one that a rabbi might know. Hear their own story, especially the story of how the objects came into their lives and learn how they actually use them or reflect upon them. Ask about their memories of new practices, and encourage them to reflect upon how their reactions have changed over time. Undoubtedly, you will hear more stories, reflections, and memories than you counted on—again, as Ansky adjured, "Record!"

Formulating Your Own Categories

As you gather your findings, you will find yourself developing meaningful categories in which to place them. (Now you can "reclaim" the knowledge of Judaism you relinquished in your collecting phase!) For instance, you might organize your findings by generations: "things that were also in my grandparents' or parents' houses," "things I had growing up," and "things that feel practically brand-new." Or you might organize them by their use within life-cycle rituals, holidays, and daily spiritual practices carried out in public and private, within one's own home and within Jewish institutions.

Altogether, my Ansky-inspired collecting has provided the basis for reflections on new constructions of Judaism, even for practical reflections on how we might continue to participate, with greater consciousness, in the process of shaping and experiencing new traditions. I trust you will find your collecting similarly inspirational.

NOTES:

1. Mariella Beukers and Renee Waale, *Tracing AnSky, Jewish Collections from the State Ethnographic Museum in St. Petersburg* (Zwolle, Netherlands: Waanders Uitgeverij, 1992), 13. The material evidence they collected was sent to the Jewish collection of the State Ethnographic Museum in St. Petersburg; in recent years, it was made available in a traveling exhibition in the United States.

2. Far be it from me to make light of the potent *tchotchke*. In 2004, the Jewish Museum of Maryland created an enchanting exhibit called "Tchotchkes!" treating them as treasures that "hold important memories, carry substantial meanings, and mark our homes as Jewish and American" (exhibition catalog).

3. See Vanessa Ochs, "Ten Jewish Sensibilities," *Sh'ma* (December 2003).

4. A consortium of philanthropists founded Birthright Israel in 1999. Its goal is to give every diaspora Jew a free 10-day visit to Israel. Thus far, thousands of young people have gone to Israel with this program.

5. Rosh Hodesh: It's a Girl Thing! is a national program of informal education for adolescent Jewish girls that draws upon the tradition of Rosh Hodesh celebrations and promotes Jewish identity, leadership, and a positive sense of self. Group leaders are trained and given sourcebooks for the monthly meetings held in their communities. See http://www.roshhodesh.org.

6. Harvey Goldberg, "Survey," in *Modern Judaism: An Oxford Guide*, ed. Nicholas De Lange and Miri Freud-Kandel (Oxford: Oxford University Press, 2004), 199.

7. S. Ansky, *The Enemy at His Pleasure*, ed. and trans. Joachim Neugroschel (New York: Metropolitan Books, 2003), xi.

8. Goldberg, "Survey," 197.

9. Ibid.

10. Ari Goldman, *Being Jewish* (New York: Simon & Schuster, 2000).

11. David Kraemer, of the Jewish Theological Seminary, has called these "emerging Jewish practices."

12. A strategy for expanding the definition of what constitutes sacred experience, developed by my teacher Rabbi Yitz Greenberg, is part of a broadening system he calls "holy secularity."

13. Vanessa L. Ochs, "What Makes a Jewish Home Jewish?" *Crosscurrents* (Winter 1999/2000): 491–510.

INDEX

A

actions, used in rituals, 6
agency
    for creating rituals, 40–41,
      89, 159–161, 217,
      218–219
    of material objects, 97–98,
      167–168, 182
    of new Jewish objects,
      108–109
agents of change, 159–160, 217,
    220
amcha, 147, 148
amulets, 144
angel cards, 16
Ansky, Shlomo, 259–264
anthropology, 30–34, 90–91,
    264
Ayinroah, 121–122

B

badkhanim, 239
bedeken, 62, 63, 216
bentschers, 222
birkat erusin, 243
birth
    as metaphor for redemption,
      175
    baby girls, 2, 21–24, 147–148
      (*see also* simchat bat)
    of beautiful children, 142
blessings, 142
bread, on *seder* plate, 79
brit ahava, 228–229, 236

C

car mezuzah, 87–88
catalog Judaism, 39–43
circumcision, 131–133

college campuses, 123–128
commitment ceremonies, 44–45,
    146, 228–229, 231. *see also*
    same-sex weddings
continuity of Judaism, 113–115,
    266

D
daf yomi, 120
democracy, as source of new
    rituals, 40
dreams, 142–143

E
"e-o" song, 70–78
ethnographic expeditions, 34, 67,
    259, 261–262, 264, 267–268
explicitly Jewish objects, 102–106

F
feminism
    approach to Judaism, 46–47
    liturgy of, 19, 49
    and Passover, 48

G
genizah, 187
gezerot, 145
guardians of continuity, 159–160
Guidebooks to new ritual, 53

H
haggadot, 11–12
halakhah, 7
haredim, and innovation,
    120–121. *see also* Miriam's
    Tambourine
havurot, 24–25
healing, 89
healing service, 8–11
hifsikan, 145

Holocaust Torah. *see also* Torah
    definition, 188
    halachah for, 194–195
    narrative, 192–194, 196–198,
        199
    problematic aspects of, 188
    reconsecration of, 200–205,
        205
    restoration of, 199
Holy Days, 255–256
housewarmings, 3
huppot, 62, 140–141, 222,
    232–233, 240–241
Hurricane Katrina, 129–131,
    189–190

I
implicitly Jewish objects,
    106–108
innovation. *see also* new rituals
    artistic, 157–158
    collecting evidence of,
        261–264
    on college campuses, 15,
        123–128
    and *haredim,* 120–121
    naturalization of, 115–117,
        151, 157
    non-Jewish sources of,
        140–144
    not disrupting continuity,
        113–115, 266
    official sanction for, 145–147
    and Orthodoxy, 119–120,
        150–155
    pace of, 128–131
    rabbinical justification of,
        143–145, 148
    and Reform Judaism, 119
Institute for Jewish Spirituality,
    251–252

interfaith couples, 123, 149
interfaith weddings, 227–228
Internet, 55, 120–121, 128, 261
invented tradition, 141

J

Jewish Catalogs, 39–43
Jewish feminist rituals, 47–48
Jewish feminist sourcebooks, 46
Jewish homes, 96–97, 106–107,
    125, 265
Jews in the Woods, 69–74

K

kavanah, 27
ketubah artists, 44–45
ketubot, 43–45, 221, 223–224,
    232, 240
kinyan, 216, 243–245
klei kodesh, 98

L

Life Cycle/Rites of Passage,
    254–255
Lubavitcher Hasidim
    behavior upon death of
        Rebbe, 177–178
    reconciliation after death of
        Rebbe, 179–185
    spirit of during Passover
        1994, 168–176
    use of Internet, 120–121
Lubavitcher Rebbe
    as messiah, 168–176
    attitude toward after death,
        179–183
    death of, 177–179

M

matchmaking, 122–123
material culture, definition, 90–92

material objects. *see also* sacred
    objects
    as indicators of observance,
        96
    creating rituals, 89–90,
        108–109
    explicitly Jewish, 102–106
    implicitly Jewish, 106–108
    importance in rituals, 93–95
    in Jewish homes, 96–97
    purchasing, 100
    reading, 92–93, 203–205,
        261–262, 263
    spirituality of, 97–98, 175,
        176, 181, 185
    sustaining community mem-
        ory, 189, 190–191, 203–205
    traditional Jewish classifica-
        tion of, 98–101
matzot, 32, 95
Messiah, signs of arrival, 168–169
metta meditation, 253
mezuzah
    as necklace, 104–105
    for cars, 87–88
    conventional, 4, 104
    interactive, 4–5, 65–66
    personal meanings of, 106
Mi Shebeirach, 8
midrash, 145, 169–170
minhag America, 34–35
mipnei darkhei shalom, 145
mipnei tikkun olam, 145
Miriam's Cup
    description, 170–171
    museum exhibits of, 171
Miriam's Tambourine. *see also*
    tambourines
    narrative of, 171, 174–176,
        182–184
    origins of, 171

mitzvah days, 210–211
mitzvah projects, 209–210

N
narratives
    as chronology of new ritual,
        69–78, 208
    as educational essays, 61–63
    as personal chronicles,
        59–60, 232–233, 269
    as rituals, 79
    characteristics of, 57–59
    creation and form of, 65–67,
        108
    evolution of, 82
    of explicitly Jewish objects,
        103–104
    limitations of, 78–79
    Miriam's Tambourine, 171,
        174–176, 182–184
    in newspapers, 60–61
    political aspects of, 83
    Talmudic, 67–69
    in wedding booklets,
        222–225, 230, 231,
        232–233
National Center for Jewish Heal-
    ing, 8, 268
new Jewish objects, 108–109
New Jewish Wedding (book),
    218–219, 221–222
new rituals. *see also* Holocaust
    Torah; innovation; Miriam's
    Tambourine
    acceptance of, 28, 30, 34–35,
        54, 62–63, 66, 109,
        117–118, 141, 156–157,
        158–159, 194–195, 219,
        220, 266
    as response to crises, 69,
        173, 204

authenticity of, 28–30,
    156–157
biblical source of, 64–65
categorizing, 269
chronologies of, 69–78, 171,
    173–175
definition, 267
detecting, 265–269
endurance of, 28–30,
    115–117, 159–161, 207,
    254, 263
feminism as source of,
    47–52
general public as source of,
    40–42, 65, 80, 147–150,
    155, 194, 217
guidebooks for, 52
innovation of, 31–34, 82
leaders as source of, 66–69,
    148
listing of, 254–257
objects creating, 89–90
politics as motivation for,
    22–24, 51–52, 229–230
precedent for, 69
resistance to, 14, 18, 58–59,
    65–67, 117, 150–155,
    194–195, 200–202
steps of development,
    88–89
Talmudic, 142–145
Web sites for, 55
nostalgia, as source of rituals,
    31–32

O
objects, used in rituals, 6
observance, perceptions of
    correct form, 13–15, 100–101,
    104
office dedications, 3–5

old rituals, rejecting, 12, 40, 62–63
open access, as source of new
    rituals, 40
orange, on seder plate, 79–81
Orthodoxy, incorporating new
    rituals, 7, 62–63, 119–120,
    150–153, 223–224

P
Passover
    alternative form in Talmud,
        67–68
    and feminism, 48
    material objects of, 95
philanthropy, 209–211
prayer shawls. *see tallitot*

Q
quilting-bee, 141

R
recording Jewish life, 260–264,
    265
red threads, 9–11
Reform Jews, and traditional
    observance, 119
religions, transformation of,
    139–140
Renewal Judaism, 253
reshut, 100
ritual committees, 146–147
ritual facilitators, 131
ritual toolbox, 5–7, 198–199
rituals. *see also* new rituals
    characteristics of, 48–52
    historical background of,
        63–64
    meaning *vs.* origin, 79–81,
        140
    purpose of, 30–31, 134, 156,
        161–162

scholarly approaches to,
    33–34
Rosh Hashanah, 68–69
Rosh Hodesh, 1, 49, 115,
    116–117. *see also* women's
    tefillah groups

S
sacred objects. *see also* material
    objects
    desecration of, 187
    rescuing, 189–190
same-sex weddings, 54, 146. *see
    also* commitment ceremonies
seders
    chocolate, 125–127
    at colleges, 123–128
    ecological, 127–128
    feminist, 48
    Greek, 127
    Internet-based, 119
    matzot at, 95
    orange, origin of, 79–81
    personalizing, 60–61
    in restaurants, 114
September 11th, 128–129
Shabbat
    angel cards, 16
    blowing shofar on, 68–69
    material objects of, 94
Shema, 26–28, 253–254
sheva brachot, 240–241, 245–246
simchat bat, 23. *see also* birth
Spiritual Practices, 256–257

T
takkanot, 145
tallitot
    attitudes towards women
        wearing, 18
    inauguration for using, 19

tallitot, continued
    selecting, 20–21
    styles for women, 20
Talmudic narratives, 67–69
tambourines, 167–168
    feminist, 51, 52, 174–175,
        180, 183
    at Red Sea, 171, 176, 177
tashmishei kedushah, 98–99
tashmishei mitzvah, 99
tattoos, 118
texts, used in rituals, 5–6
time, facilitating acceptance of
    new rituals, 157
Torah. *see also* Holocaust Torah
    as source of rituals, 31
    purchasing, 192–193
    rescuing, 189–190
Torah Yoga, 16–17, 252
traveler's prayer, 88

W
wedding booklets
    as negotiation tool, 225–227
    as spiritual preparation,
        224–225
    contents of, 222, 223–224,
        227, 233–234
    definition, 219–220, 221
    example, 235–247

    legitimizing new practices,
        220
    narratives in, 222–225, 230,
        231, 232–233
weddings
    breaking the glass, 33,
        220–221, 233, 246
    circling, bride and groom,
        62–63, 220–221, 222, 243
    couples' decisions, 215–218
    for homosexuals, 228–229
    innovations of, 218–219
    interfaith, 227–228
    modifications among Ortho-
        dox, 62–63, 223–224
wigs, 148–149
women
    bringing redemption,
        169–184
    participation in Orthodox
        ritual, 150–153
women's tefillah groups, 8-11,
    49-50, 120, 151-153, 173.
    see also Rosh Hodesh

Y
yichud, 216–217, 246
Yoga, and Torah study, 16–17,
    252